The
Review of
Contemporary
Fiction

ISSN: 0276-0045

Editor

JOHN O'BRIEN

Senior Editor

STEVEN MOORE

Associate Editors

JACK BYRNE
BROOKE HORVATH

Contributing Editors

DOMINIC DI BERNARDI
LOWELL DUNLAP
IRVING MALIN
JOHN TAYLOR

Guest Editors

SUSAN BERNOFSKY AND
TOM WHALEN

Typesetter & Designer

SHIRLEY GEEVER

Acknowledgment is made to the Swiss Cultural Association Pro Helvetia, whose grant support made this volume possible.

Copyright © 1992 *The Review of Contemporary Fiction*. No part of this periodical may be reproduced without the permission of the publisher. Address all correspondence to: *The Review of Contemporary Fiction*, 236 S. Washington, Naperville, IL 60540 USA. *The Review of Contemporary Fiction* is a member of CLMP.

SUBSCRIPTIONS. Send orders to *Review of Contemporary Fiction*, 236 S. Washington, Naperville, IL 60540 USA.

Single volume (three issues):
Individuals: $17.00; foreign, add $3.50;
Institutions: $24.00; foreign, add $3.50.

DISTRIBUTION. Bookstores should send orders to:

Inland Book Company, 140 Commerce St., East Haven, CT 06512.

Bernard De Boer, 113 E. Centre St., Nutley, NJ 07110 (national distributor).

Small Press Distribution, 1814 San Pablo Ave., Berkeley, CA 94702.

Cover: Walser in the Biel years, probably taken on a visit to his sister in Bellelay in 1915.

Indexed in *American Humanities Index, International Bibliography of Periodical Literature, International Bibliography of Book Reviews, MLA, Book Review Index.* Abstracted in *Abstracts of English Studies.*

The Review of Contemporary Fiction is also available in 16mm microfilm, 35mm microfilm, and 105mm microfiche from University Microfilms International, 300 North Zeeb Road, Ann Arbor, MI 48106-1346.

This issue is partially supported by grants from the Illinois Arts Council, a state agency, and the National Endowment for the Arts, a federal agency.

The Review of Contemporary Fiction

Future issues devoted to: José Donoso, Angela Carter, Severo Sarduy, Philip Roth, Juan Carlos Onetti, Jacques Roubaud, Tadeusz Konwicki, Danilo Kiš, Ed Sanders, Georges Perec, Jerome Charyn, Guillermo Cabrera Infante, Paul Auster, Jean Echenoz, Samuel R. Delany, Christoph Hein, Maurice Blanchot, Edmond Jabès, José Lezama Lima, Alasdair Gray, Gil Orlovitz, Steven Millhauser, George Garrett, Susan Daitch, Felipe Alfau, Georges Bataille, Robert Creeley, Rikki Ducornet, William Vollmann, and David Foster Wallace. Special fiction issues will feature translations from Italian, Japanese, Spanish, Flemish, Czech, and Arabic.

The *Review* welcomes inquiries from qualified individuals interested in guest-editing issues on any of the following: Harry Mulisch, Raymond Queneau, David Antin, Stanley Crawford, Edmund White, Josef Skvorecky, Brigid Brophy, and Mario Vargas Llosa.

Back Issues

Back issues are still available for the following numbers of the *Review of Contemporary Fiction* ($8 each unless otherwise noted):

PAUL METCALF / HUBERT SELBY, JR. ($15)
DOUGLAS WOOLF / WALLACE MARKFIELD
WILLIAM GADDIS / NICHOLAS MOSLEY
PAUL BOWLES / COLEMAN DOWELL
WILLIAM EASTLAKE / AIDAN HIGGINS
WILLIAM S. BURROUGHS ($15)
JUAN GOYTISOLO / ISHMAEL REED
CAMILO JOSÉ CELA
CLAUDE SIMON ($15)
B.S. JOHNSON / JEAN RHYS

LUISA VALENZUELA
CHANDLER BROSSARD
SAMUEL BECKETT
HARRY MATHEWS
ARNO SCHMIDT
CLAUDE OLLIER / CARLOS FUENTES
JOSEPH MCELROY
JOHN BARTH / DAVID MARKSON
ALEXANDER THEROUX / PAUL WEST
DONALD BARTHELME / TOBY OLSON
WILLIAM H. GASS / MANUEL PUIG

KATHY ACKER / CHRISTINE BROOKE-ROSE / MARGUERITE YOUNG

SPECIAL FICTION ISSUE: Fiction by Pinget, Bowles, Mathews, Markfield, Rower, Ríos, Tindall, Sorrentino, Goytisolo, McGonigle, Dukore, Dowell, McManus, Mosley, and Acker

NOVELIST AS CRITIC: Essays by Garrett, Barth, Sorrentino, Wallace, Ollier, Brooke-Rose, Creeley, Mathews, Kelly, Abbott, West, McCourt, McGonigle, and McCarthy

NEW FRENCH FICTION: Fiction by Grainville, Roubaud, Boulanger, Rezvani, LeClézio, Chawaf, Cerf, Cholodenko, Modiano, Roche, Navarre, Savitzkaya, Bénézet, Sallenave, Ernaux, Hyvrard, and Vautrin; forum on book reviewing in America

GROVE PRESS NUMBER: Contributions by Allen, Beckett, Corso, Ferlinghetti, Jordan, McClure, Rechy, Rosset, Selby, Sorrentino, and others

Send payment (plus $1.00 postage for one copy; $1.50 for two or more) to:

Review of Contemporary Fiction, 236 S. Washington, Naperville, IL 60540

Acknowledgments

The guest editors would like to thank the following for their assistance with this volume:

Pro Helvetia, the Swiss Cultural Association, for their generous support in the way of research and publication grants that made this work possible;

Dr. Elio Fröhlich and the Carl Seelig-Stiftung for permission to publish work by Robert Walser and photographs;

Dr. Werner Morlang and Bernhard Echte of the Robert Walser-Archiv for their advice, suggestions, and generosity once again;

Fritz Senn of the Zurich James Joyce Foundation for his time, space, insight, and computers;

Suhrkamp Verlag Frankfurt am Main/Zürich for Walser texts and letters © 1979, 1985, 1990;

Suhrkamp Verlag Frankfurt am Main for the essays by Martin Walser, Hermann Hesse, and Adolf Muschg, and Bernhard Echte's "Robert Walser's *Räuber* Novel," © 1978, 1985;

Ex Libris Zürich for Peter Bichsel's essay, © 1983;

Northeastern University Press, Boston, for Christopher Middleton's "Translation as a Species of Mime," © 1989 by Rosanna Warren. From *The Act of Translation: Voices from the Field,* edited by Rosanna Warren.

Many people contribute to a project such as this one, and, named and unnamed, we thank them all for their support.

Contents

Introduction

Susan Bernofsky and Tom Whalen

NEARLY THIRTY-FIVE YEARS have passed since Robert Walser's first appearance in English in 1957, a period roughly equal in length to his entire literary career, but still he remains in England and America what Peter Bichsel describes him as having been in Berlin in his early years as a writer: an insider's secret, ardently admired by a limited few. That the *Review of Contemporary Fiction* should devote an issue to this "secret" is in itself unusual; a writer who stopped writing in 1933 and died in 1956 can no longer, strictly speaking, be called contemporary. But Walser's work and his artistic innovativeness are as striking today as they were during his lifetime. He displeased his public by abandoning the ideology and narrative strictures of much late nineteenth- and early twentieth-century fiction; today he seems more truly contemporary than many contemporary authors. Even the reader familiar with the work of, say, Kafka, Nabokov, Beckett, and Donald Barthelme will not necessarily be prepared for the shocks of Walser's self-reflexivity, his synapse-quick associations, his unfathomable irony.

The older of this editing and translating team, Tom Whalen, first encountered Walser's work in the Dell paperback *Great German Short Stories*. The "story" was "A Village Tale," translated by Christopher Middleton (*Selected Stories,* 167-68).* The piece was dazzling, delightful. And confusing. How had Walser done it? What was his method? How did this odd little fiction work? Why didn't it fly apart? What kept it in motion? What legerdemain gave it life? It resembled a Tinguely machine, a Klee, a song by Satie. No naive artist was ever this complex.

"A Village Tale" ("Dorfgeschichte") uses typical elements from the *Dorfgeschichte* genre: a potato famine, a parson "elucidating for his young protégés the planetary system," a young girl's suicide, a bailiff who paints in his spare time, and a love/murder incident in which a man shoots his rival "with authentic popular wrath." "Never," Walser writes, "in all my years as a writer have I written a tale in which a person, struck by a bullet, falls down. This is the first time in my work that a person has croaked." A statement whose obvious inauthenticity is authenticity itself. Walser's aesthetic of affirming the artifice of art is stated clearly in the story's last paragraph.

---

*See the bibliography at the end of this issue for publication details.

"A stork flew through the azure air high over the village drama, bearing in its beak a baby. Wafted by a slight wind, the leaves whispered. Like an etching it all looked, anything but natural." "The Elephant" (*Masquerade and Other Stories,* 132-33) ends with something comparable to that fairy-tale stork, with Cupid drawing the curtain on a couple attempting their first kiss—a self-reflexive gesture, this drawing of the curtain, which also appears in *The Blacksmith,* a film by Buster Keaton, another spirit akin to Walser.

Walser's naïveté was, of course, one of his many masks. "Although I may cut a most carefree figure," he wrote in "The Walk" (*Selected Stories,* 54-104), "I am highly serious and conscientious, and though I seem to be no more than delicate and dreamy, I am a solid technician!" He was as voracious a reader as he was prolific a writer. Balzac, Baudelaire, Brentano, Büchner, Cervantes, Chekhov, Dickens, Dostoyevski, Eichendorff, Flaubert, Goethe, Gotthelf, Hölderlin, Hamsun, Jean Paul, Keller, Kleist, Lenau, Lenz, Maupassant, Molière, Nietzsche, Poe, Raabe, Rimbaud, Rousseau, Schiller, Shakespeare, Stendhal, Stifter, Sue, Tieck, Tolstoy, Verlaine—all these and many more he read and commented on in his books. Just as he utilized historical events (see Tamara S. Evans's essay included here on Walser's "new historical" approach to a famous battle in Switzerland), historical and contemporary personages (Jesus, Napoleon, Hofmannsthal, Lenin), painters (Beardsley, Cézanne, Cranach, Klinger, Michelangelo, Rembrandt, Rubens, Titian, Van Gogh, Watteau), and musicians (Berlioz, Caruso, Mozart, Verdi, and Wagner).

But Walser was no elitist. Like some of the visual artists of his time, he could incorporate the most mundane material into his work. These "found objects" might include what he encountered on his walks, his visits to theaters, pubs, markets, or even the plots of films or *Bahnofhallenbüchlein* (as he referred to the penny dreadfuls he found in train-station kiosks), much as Satie incorporated cabaret songs into his music. One thinks, too, of the source material for Shakespeare's plays, or Cervantes and the popular romance, or the more contemporary examples of Nabokov's parodies or the fiction of Donald Barthelme in which one can find the language of advertising jangling beside the prose of Kleist. Walser's use of popular literature was equally fruitful and various.

"The complete rejection of literature as an institution" is how Michael Hamburger describes one of the goals of writers like Walser and Kafka. For such a writer, hierarchies matter little or not at all. Everything around him, it seems, offered Walser access to the bridge linking the truth of the self to the truth of the world. Especially in the writing from his Berne years we see him tinkering inside the very mechanisms of fiction, where he could "tailor, cobble, weld, plane, knock, hammer, or nail together lines," as he put it in "Eine Art Erzählung" (*Selected Stories,* xi), and return from his work with a new machine all shimmery and odd with curious perspectives offered and riddled about with bits and pieces of things we've often seen before if in a less illuminating light.

For those not familiar with Walser, perhaps the following little ramble through biographical terrain will provide a context for the material in this issue.

Born on 15 April 1878 in the Swiss city of Biel, Walser attended school only until the age of fourteen, after which he completed a bank clerk's apprenticeship. He lived briefly in Stuttgart, where he tried and failed to break into acting, then moved to Zurich, which was to remain his home for almost nine years. Here he worked in an insurance agency as well as in banks, and here began the life-rhythm he was to maintain for many years: as soon as he had saved up enough money, he would quit his job to devote himself full-time to writing. He accumulated seventeen addresses between 1896 and 1905, all of them furnished rooms, many of them garrets. When he found himself penniless, he copied addresses for day wages at an office for the unemployed.

In 1898 Walser was "discovered" by Josef Viktor Widmann, editor of the Berne newspaper *Der Bund,* who printed a selection of the twenty-year-old's poems (but not, however, the author's name; cf. the letter to his sister Lisa printed below). Walser's poems and prose pieces then began to appear in newspapers and magazines in Switzerland and Germany. In 1904, Insel Verlag published his first book, *Fritz Kochers Aufsätze,* a collection of prose pieces masquerading as the essays of a sensitive young schoolboy. When, a few months after its publication, Walser wrote to the publisher to request an additional honorarium he had been promised if the book's production costs were met, he was informed that of the edition of 1300 a mere forty-seven copies had been sold.

Meanwhile, Walser's brother Karl, one year his senior, was making a name for himself in Berlin as an illustrator and stage designer. In addition to books by Cervantes, Kleist, E.T.A. Hoffmann, and Hesse, he illustrated *Fritz Kochers Aufsätze* and a number of his brother's later works. In 1905, Robert joined him in Berlin to share his apartment studio. While Karl was off painting frescoes in villas belonging to the likes of Walther Rathenau, publisher Samuel Fischer, and art dealer Paul Cassirer, or working late at the theater, the apartment became the writer's private study ("At three or four in the morning he would come home, and there I'd be sitting, enraptured by all the thoughts, all the beautiful pictures going through my head" [*Geschwister Tanner*]).

The Walser brothers were notorious for their pranks in the artistic circles in which Karl mixed, a society of actors, painters, and writers. On one evening, for example, an inebriated Karl offended the delicate Frank Wedekind by challenging him to a round of *Hoselupfe,* a sort of Swiss wrestling in which each participant seizes his opponent's belt and tries to throw him to the ground. The brothers later encountered Wedekind at a café to which he'd fled. When one brother called Wedekind a *Schafskopf* (i.e., sheephead or blockhead), he fled again, only to be caught in the revolving doors and whirled back into the café for another vociferous "*Schafskopf!*"

Robert may have been more tolerated than accepted by his brother's friends (one dinner invitation encouraged Karl to bring his brother along "provided he's not all that hungry"). This tall, perhaps gangly but definitely robust young Swiss strolled about the foppish *Weltstadt* of Berlin in ragged clothes, and was known for occasionally eccentric behavior. He scandalized acquaintances by enrolling in a school for servants, after which he spent the winter of 1905 as a butler at Dambrau Castle in Upper Silesia. (In a letter to his publisher, he requested that no envelopes bearing official letterhead be sent to him; how unseemly it would have been for epistles from Insel Verlag to be delivered not to the master but to the servants' quarters!) He later documented these experiences in the long story "Tobold (II)" (1916) and elsewhere; but first, in 1908, he transformed the servants' school into the setting for *Jakob von Gunten,* perhaps his most perfect novel. Martin Walser, in a 1990 lecture in Zurich, called it "the most radical book I know."

Walser's Jakob is a pupil at the Benjamenta Institute, where "the educators and teachers are asleep, or they are dead, or seemingly dead, or they are fossilized, no matter, in any case we get nothing from them." What sort of school is this? It has only one class: "How should a boy behave?" The only staff are the principal ("a giant") and his sister, the mysterious, sad, beautiful Lisa Benjamenta. Even Jakob, since his arrival there, has "contrived to become a mystery to myself" (23). The novel, despite its realistic basis, is bathed in unreality. Jakob is a dreamer, a sort of King Midas who turns everything he touches into riddles. He has suspected from the outset that some secret lies buried at the heart of the school, and later Fräulein Benjamenta leads him down into the "Inner Chambers," a tour through "the vaults of poverty and deprivation," then a sort of bright nocturnal landscape she identifies as "freedom" ("it's something very wintry, and cannot be borne for long"), a "proper pillowy boudoir," and a "gluey and most unpleasant river of doubt" (101-02). *Jakob* is faithful not to external reality, but to an internal, truer one. If Walser had up to this point written primarily stories of wanderers in landscapes in the external world, in Jakob he created an inner wanderer, a *Wanderbursche* of the soul. Jakob is always infatuated, and the novel is one of extremes. Nowhere does Walser's smallness theme come more radically into play than in Jakob's aspiration to become a "charming utterly spherical zero."

It was during this time that Kafka began to read Walser (he gave *Jakob* as a birthday present to Max Brod). According to Brod, Kafka would search out Walser pieces in the feuilleton sections of newspapers and read them aloud to his friends. One can find Walser touches in Kafka's first book,

Meditation, as did Musil when he noted Kafka's work seemed too much "like a special case of the Walser type." In the following sentence from a 1908 letter, Kafka strikes a surprisingly Walseresque tone: "The world's a sad place, but still it's a bit flushed with sadness and is animated sadness so very far from happiness?" (*Letters to Friends, Family and Editors* [New York: Schocken, 1977], 41). Additional interesting parallel lines of development between these two authors are discussed in Christopher Middleton's "The Picture of Nobody" and George Avery's study of Walser, *Inquiry and Testament* (250-59).

Of Walser's earlier novels, the first was *Geschwister Tanner* (The Tanner Siblings, published in 1907), a highly autobiographical and realistic novel for Walser, full of snow, melancholy, and the long, mannered speeches that were to become one of his trademarks. He wrote it in a matter of a few weeks, his only companion Karl's cat, Muschi (who, he remarked in a later text, was eventually given away to a bakery, whose owners, when she proved a poor mouser, sent her to the Zoological Gardens to be fed to snakes). The poet Christian Morgenstern, then a reader at Cassirer Verlag, spoke up in Walser's behalf and brought about the book's publication.

All this time Walser had been energetically turning out prose pieces (many inspired by the theater, some published under the pseudonym Kutsch) that appeared in numerous publications, including such important journals of the time as *Kunst und Künstler, Die Schaubühne, Die Neue Rundschau, Simplicissimus,* and *Der Neue Merkur.* For a brief period he was employed as secretary at the Berliner Sezession, an avant-garde gallery that promoted Impressionist work, but seems, by his own account, to have been poorly suited to the post. A "business letter" he wrote to Rathenau on 15 May 1907 inquires whether the latter "would be so good as to let us know when it would be possible for you to drop by so as to purchase something from us. Won't you please do this? We hope you won't be angry with us for reminding you of your promise to buy an E. R. Weiss. We've already taken the Sezession's percentage into account, i.e., the profit has already been used up (drunk). Isn't this fabulous weather we're having?"

In 1906, after *Geschwister Tanner,* Walser wrote a novel entitled *Der Gehülfe* (The Assistant) whose manuscript was lost. We know only that the novel's protagonist travels to Asia as the assistant to a "mad scholar," "the devil in a summer coat," on a scientific expedition, and that Christian Morgenstern, who read the manuscript for Cassirer Verlag, praised it highly. A second novel with this title was composed by Walser in six weeks in 1907, on the occasion of a contest announced by Verlag Scherl. When his manuscript was returned without comment, he appeared in person at the publisher's offices to demand an explanation; upon being told it had been inappropriate of him to include with the manuscript a demand for an eight thousand mark honorarium, Walser reportedly shouted, "You idiots know nothing about literature," and stormed out. Published in 1908 by Bruno

Cassirer, *Der Gehülfe* is a master-and-servant tale of an inventor's assistant who enjoys a pampered existence in the home of his employer but is never paid, who finds himself in a position of uncomfortable intimacy within a household being destroyed by bankruptcy and failure. A brief essay on the novel by Hermann Hesse, who wrote six articles on Walser's work, is included here.

Walser moved out of his brother's apartment in 1908, moved back in with his brother and sister-in-law in 1910, out in 1912. Besides the three novels, the Berlin years saw the publication of a book of poems, *Gedichte* (1909), and two volumes of stories, *Aufsätze* (1913) and *Geschichten* (1914). By his own report he wrote and destroyed an additional three novels during this period, including the early *Gehülfe*. His attempts to interest publishers in other book projects failed. Except for a two-year interlude in which a "noble-hearted, wealthy lady" supported him (and possibly wanted to marry him), his financial situation worsened steadily, despite his numerous publications in periodicals. In 1913, feeling he had suffered a great defeat, he returned to Biel.

After brief stays with his sister Lisa, now a teacher in Bellelay, and his aged father, who died less than a year afterward (his mother had died when he was sixteen), Walser settled in a garret in Biel's Hotel zum Blauen Kreuz, his home for seven years. Here the "Prosastückligeschäft" (prose piece business) seems to have quickly picked up, with a number of book as well as magazine and newspaper publications (1914: *Kleine Dichtungen;* 1917: *Prosastücke, Der Spaziergang, Kleine Prosa;* 1918: *Poetenleben;* 1919: *Seeland, Komödie*). Still, his finances were little improved. Walser saved where he could (for instance by not having his room heated in winter) and was insistent in demanding the prompt payment of honoraria by his publishers. In a letter to Rascher Verlag, the publisher of *Seeland,* he wrote on 8 May 1917: "If I can maintain my existence as a writer until the end of this year, I'll be content, won't hold any grudges, and will step out of the picture; i.e., take a job somewhere and disappear into the crowd. In the six years I've lived here, I've done everything humanly possible in the way of economizing. Good luck to anyone who wants to do the same."

Walser's fiction of the Biel period shows more stylistic diversity than any other. These pieces range in tone from the heavily mannered, mock-serious prose of "Der Spaziergang" ("The Walk"), to the nervous, manically repetitive stutters that characterize most of the contents of *Kleine Prosa* (cf. "Well Then" in this selection), to the lyrical, melancholy idylls that seem to long to have been written in an earlier century. He wrote one novel during this period, *Tobold,* based on his experiences in Zürich; it was rejected by Rascher Verlag and then either lost or destroyed.

Why Walser was unable to continue his writer's existence remains unclear. He lived a pauper's life, yes, but we know him to have received an inheritance of five thousand Swiss francs upon the death of his brother

Hermann in 1919, a considerable sum at the time, and ten thousand three years later when an uncle died. He later reported having experienced a crisis, a sort of burn-out at the end of the Biel years, where, after all, he had maintained a strict regimen of work for a virtually uninterrupted seven years. In 1921 he took the post of assistant archivist in the Swiss capital Berne, and thus, for the first time in many years, found himself in a steady job, his last, and even managed to hold it for several months before offending his superior with an "impertinent remark."

In Berne he achieved a level of productivity greater than in any other period of his career. The prose from the years 1921–1929 fills over two thousand pages in his collected works. The manuscript of a short novel, *Theodor,* from which Walser read publicly in 1922, and which was apparently based on his experiences at the Sezession in Berlin, went astray at Rascher in the late twenties. Though he still was able to place many of his prose pieces in the feuilleton sections of the best German-language newspapers and magazines, Walser's work was becoming increasingly difficult, which led to difficulties for the editors who accepted it. Eduard Korrodi, for instance, feuilleton editor of the *Neue Zürcher Zeitung,* remarked once that it was always an act of daring "to print a feuilleton by Walser in the *NZZ;* each time, I would receive letters from disgruntled readers threatening to cancel their subscriptions if the nonsense didn't stop." Walser also found himself unable to get book manuscripts accepted; after 1919 he published only a single collection: *Die Rose,* in 1925, with Rowohlt.

It is during this period that Walser immerses himself in the dream of language in a manner unlike any author before him. Writing about the style of the late work, Christopher Middleton observes in his essay "The Picture of Nobody" that Walser's "form of arabesque discourse can explore dimensions of verbal comedy which are inaccessible to any prose of a representational nature. Often what is said may be out of all proportion to what it is said about, but in such a way that the statement creates its own proportions, its own world of imaginative forms." His prose pieces become a box on the ears for anyone who has mistaken the literature of ideas for ideal literature. In them he championed a liberated language, the autonomous word. For one very recent example of the importance of Walser's late prose (and especially the *Räuber* novel written in microscript) upon contemporary German-language literature, see Friedrich Dürrenmatt's 1989 novel *Durcheinandertal.*

No one will ever know for certain what went on inside Walser during the events preceding his entry into Waldau Sanatorium in 1929, but of the myths surrounding his case history, the first that should be consigned to oblivion is the diagnosis of schizophrenia. In the winter of 1928-29, Walser, suffering from depression and attacks of anxiety, was taken by his sister Lisa to see Dr. Morgenthaler, a friend of the family, who advised Walser to enter Waldau. According to his report, Walser was aware that he was ill and was willing to be helped. These criteria should have excluded the possibility of schizophrenia, but unfortunately the report arrived a day after Walser had entered the clinic. Walser's statement to the doctor on duty was that he had been unable to work for several weeks, couldn't concentrate, suffered from sleeplessness, was depressed, and had had fleeting thoughts of suicide, though these were not to be taken seriously. The doctor asked enough questions to feel justified in noting: "Finally admits to hearing voices." When he heard of the Walser family history (Walser's mother suffered from mental illness in the last years of her life, and one brother died in Waldau), he left blank the space "Tentative diagnosis" on the admission form and wrote "schizophrenia" under the heading "Definite diagnosis."

By late summer of 1929 Walser began to write again and continued to do so until 1933 when a new director, Prof. J. Klaesi, came to Waldau. Klaesi considered the clinic a place for acute cases, not long-term residents like Walser. He suggested that Walser move to a farmhouse where a family could take care of him. Walser refused. Then Klaesi said that they would have to release him. For Walser, being released to work again as a writer in a world where the Nazis had come to power, and to look for a job at his age with the onus of the asylum, was not a promising prospect, especially since he had become accustomed to the security and comfort of Waldau. He would have liked to have gone to Lisa, but in the meantime she was doing her utmost to prevent this; she used her connections to get him placed in the Herisau clinic. Walser fought the decision all the way. After all, he had no guardian, was himself paying the costs of his institutionalization; the choice should have been his. On 19 June 1933 two attendants had to forcibly put him in the car that was to take him to Herisau.

The fact, then, that Walser was classified at Herisau as schizophrenic had nothing to do with any real psychiatric assessment of his condition, especially as, a few days previous, he had been considered ready to be released from Waldau. Bernhard Echte (from whose essay on Walser's clinical history the above information about Walser's asylum years has been drawn) states that "this transfer must have made Walser feel like someone deemed no longer capable of controlling his own life . . . in need of care and thus only a burden to others, someone whose personal autonomy could apparently be denied outright, and whose literary achievements merited no further attention." He withdrew into the tasks he was given to perform: picking over peas, sorting tinfoil and old paper, making twine and gluing together paper bags. The brief entries in the clinic records show him as a lonely, aging man who sometimes talked to himself in great agitation, but the picture presented in *Wanderungen mit Robert Walser* by Carl Seelig, who first visited Walser in 1936 and became his legal guardian, shows us a man whose mental vivacity and pleasure in walking had in no way lessened.

From his transfer to Herisau in 1933 until his death of a heart attack on Christmas Day, 1956, while on a walk outside the clinic grounds, Walser wrote no more.

The stories and letters selected here cannot provide a full picture of Walser's oeuvre; they are intended above all to give the reader unfamiliar with Walser a taste of his prose. Information on other translated work is contained in section II of the bibliography, "Walser in English." If readers encountering Walser for the first time here hie to their libraries and bookstores in search of more, this issue will have served its purpose.

The essays bear witness to the fact that Walser was a writer who resisted and resists all classification and reduction. He is, as Elias Canetti affirmed, "the most camouflaged of all writers." When we try to get closer to the essence of his work, we grope in the dark, clutching at points of seeming stability that he keeps whisking away like carpets from beneath our feet. The essays in this volume are attempts to ride these enchanted carpets. If only for his influence upon later generations of German-language writers, it can be said that this elusive, gentle, confounding author changed irrevocably the literature of our century. Now let literature, like the fairy-tale knight clad in invincible armor who was cut in two by the world's sharpest sword, shake itself and see what has happened.

Above: Walser in the late 1890s. *Previous page:* Microscript from early 1927 containing the continuation of a prose piece, two complete prose pieces, and three poems. (Reproduced at actual size.)

Top: Walser in Berlin, probably 1905. *Bottom:* Walser in 1927 or 1928, Berne.

Walser in 1944 or 1945. This photograph was taken by Carl Seelig on one of their walks.

Walser in Gais, which he visited with Seelig on Good Friday, 1954.

Prose Pieces and Letters

Robert Walser

Letter to Lisa Walser

Zurich, May 5, 1898

DEAR LISA,

I'm sending you two little books. I'd promised you something of the sort. How are you? Your first letter sounds a little mel-an-cho-ly. Well, what's got into you? If I were a stupid fellow, I'd say: ha, I don't understand that, but if I were really very stupid, I'd join you in your moonlight-pale lament. But since I am (let's hope) neither stupid nor very stupid, I'll simply shout: damnation, Lisa, yes, damnation and thunderation, and that's all. Cursing is excellent in such cases, let me tell you.

Alas, every evening I have reason to curse several times. Longing, o longing! Really, why do we have it? Who slipped it into our waistcoat pockets on the sly? Perhaps an angel, or else some gloomy zero.

As for me, I'm valiantly studying French, go to work each morning, come home insane in the evening, expect letters, don't write any myself but still expect, every evening, at the very least three letters. They should be lying there when I open the door, white, dazzlingly white, with the dear stamps upon them, the sweet postmarks and all the rest. And when there aren't any, I get perfectly stupid and can't work, and then I say to myself quite sensibly: you never write any letters, but you expect them! You blockhead!

It isn't precisely that I expect letters, but now I'm always expecting something as dear, as tender as a letter. Every evening there ought to be some uplifting little surprise waiting for me, just like a letter.

But one can live quite well without excitements, can't one, only one ought to be endowed with a bit less *poesie* and the like, should one not, should one not? What a babbler I am, am I not, am I not?

You're certainly going to experience a minor disappointment in me, as will the rest of Biel, at Easter I mean. You mustn't think of me anymore as some extraordinary artistic creature and make much of me in front of other people, for you know that at Easter and Christmas it's always quite an ordinary beast that comes home: me.

I can imagine it will be difficult for you at times to meet the demands of your present surroundings. One ought to be much colder, and you seem to me very soft. But it's downright lovely, all the same, for a soft soul to lie in

21

battle against all the world's harshness. And we "softies" fight the most beautifully.

Our dear Mama was like that, too. I often think of her. But you have a quite special right to think of her, for you were the one who was with her the most while she was suffering.

But, damn it all, it's certainly no good for you to think about her much, for her memory is a dark, oppressive one, and life demands cheerful faces!

But I'll stop all this business of faces and gloom, otherwise I'll wind up talking about eternity and love, God forbid.

Yes, I'm the one who sent Widmann the poems and it's my poems that are about to be served up for dessert in the Sunday edition of the *Bund*. Do you think I'll receive many compliments on the delicacy of my piquant culinary art? Karl's going to Berlin! I hadn't heard. I'm moving to a new room soon.

Adieu, you lonely creature! Warmest greetings from your lonely
brother Robert

Trans. Susan Bernofsky

Mehlmann: A Fairy Tale

Once there was a small, black-draped stage. White Mehlmann sprang upon this stage and danced. You couldn't hear his footsteps or heels, for the stage was swathed in thick rugs. Suddenly Mehlmann froze, rather foolishly put a finger to his sharp, ruddy nose, seemed to be thinking about something, then began to make faces. This was his custom. The spectators knew it all too well. They knew when it was coming; it came as punctually as a bill at the end of the month. A Mehlmann has twenty or so faces at his disposal. The stupid thing is that everyone knows them all by heart, just like the buttons on his waistcoat. Comedy is a narrow field, and well-bred comedians are rare.

Mehlmann was not well-bred. His family tree was full of teachers, but he himself represented a quite degenerate branch. His family, of course, despised him. Mehlmann once had warranted high hopes, but as things now stand he scarcely warrants anything but laughter. People find him more pathetic than funny. He seems constrained by his humor like a madman by his straitjacket. His performance draws laughs from the unfeeling alone; the tender-hearted are more likely to weep in rage.

Then Mehlmann stupidly zipped offstage, as though it were supposed to be a joke, his zipping off like that, but it was something of a faux pas. Poor, poor Mehlmann!

A boy entered! A slight, slender lad in a tight, snow-white suit. The suit with golden rips, slits and flaps! A deep red, great-petaled rose in his belt. A marvelous sight, and all cried *ah!* This *ah!* contained much love and esteem and great fascination. Women found the lad's garments, coupled with his bearing, magnificent. The rose swayed back and forth in his belt. Now, all at once, the boy flew through the air, apparently without pushing off from the ground, not like an acrobat, no, but like an angel. His descent from space to earth was particularly exquisite. When his feet first touched the ground, it was the first step in a softly undulating dance. What grace, people said. And yet how manly, said the ladies. How childishly simple, remarked a few great artists who were present. A baroness, Baroness von Wertenschlag, threw the dancer a bouquet of violets. He caught it in his mouth by its little stem. Everyone rejoiced at his sweet, sensitive dexterity. A young god, son of a goddess, they all kept saying.

Suddenly, from behind the scenes, shot a whizzing red sphere that rolled to the feet of the dancer; lightly raising his leg, he sprang upon it, and the sphere rolled off with the boy toward the backdrop which, it appeared, led into an abyss. Now one saw nothing.

It's the sun that's carried him off, a lady said.

No, the moon, said a man.

No, his heart, said a girl, and blushed.

The girl's mother looked at her with surprise and tenderness, took her head in her hands, stroked it and kissed it.

Meanwhile the waiters came around asking who wanted beer.

The scoundrels!

Then a tall, elegantly dressed lady came on stage and sang songs. A song is anguish! There are no happy songs, only happy dispositions, happy souls! That's what everyone felt, and then they all went home.

Baroness von Wertenschlag, dreaming with downcast eyes, climbed into her carriage. A poet made his compliments. The coachman rolled off. What a lout, that coachman!

(1903)   Trans. Susan Bernofsky

The Park

Soldiers on duty sit on a bench beside the gates; I walk in, dry fallen leaves fly and swirl and sweep and tumble toward me. This is exceptionally amusing and at the same time thoughtful; the lively is always more thoughtful than the dead and gloomy. Park air welcomes me; the many thousand green leaves of the immensely tall trees are lips that wish me good morning: so you're up already? Indeed, yes, I'm surprised myself. A park like this resembles a spacious, quiet, isolated room. By the way, it's always really Sunday in a park, for it's always a bit melancholy, and melancholy stirs up vivid memories of home, and the only place Sundays ever really existed was at home, where one was a child. Sundays have something parental and childish about them. I walk on beneath the high, beautiful trees, how softly and friendlily they rustle; a girl sits alone on a bench, poking the ground with her parasol, her lovely head bowed, absorbed in her thoughts. What might she be thinking? Would she like to make an acquaintance? A long, pale green avenue opens up; here and there a person walks toward me; the benches, meanwhile, are rather sparsely occupied. How it shines, the sun, for no reason at all. It kisses the trees and the water of the manmade lake; I examine an old railing and laugh because it pleases me. Nowadays it's fashionable to pause before old iron railings to admire their solid, delicate workmanship, which is a bit silly. Onward. Suddenly an acquaintance stands before me; it's Kutsch, the writer, who fails to recognize me, although I call out to him amicably. What's wrong with him? By the way, I'd thought all this time he'd gone off to the African colonies. I hurry toward him, but all at once he disappears; indeed, it was only an idiotic delusion on my part, the spot beneath the oak tree where I thought I saw him is empty. A bridge! How the water glistens and shimmers in the sun, so enchantingly. But there's no one rowing here, which makes the lake seem drowsy, as if it were only a painted lake. Some young people approach. Strange, how we stare into each other's eyes on a Sunday morning like this, as though we had something to say to one another, but we haven't anything at all to say, we say to ourselves. A small, charmingly slender castle rises before me between the trees, in the blue and white air. Who might have lived here? Someone's mistress, perhaps; I hope so, it's an appealing thought. The place may once have swarmed with high and the highest nobility, hackney cabs and carriages and servants in green and blue livery. How deserted and neglected this stately edifice appears! Thank God no one notices, for if an architect were to come and with the aid of his intellectual spectacles renovate it—with your permission, I'll swallow this notion unconsidered. What has become of us as a people that we can possess the beautiful only in dreams? An old woman and an old man are sitting here, I walk past them, and past a reading girl, too; no use trying to begin a romance with the words: What are you reading, miss? I walk rather quickly, then suddenly stop: how beautiful and quiet such a park is, it transports you to the most distant landscapes, you're in England or Silesia, you're a landowner or nothing at all. The most beautiful is when one seems not at all conscious of beauty and simply exists, as do other things as well. I gaze down for a while at the quiet, half-green river. Everything, by the way, is so green, and gray, that's truly a color for slumber, for closing one's eyes. In the distance, ringed by branches, one sees the bluish dress of a seated lady. Cigarette smoking isn't permitted here, either; a girl laughs brightly, strolling between two young gentlemen, one of whom has his arm around her. Again a view down an avenue of trees, how beautiful, how quiet, how strange. An old woman comes toward me, her fine, pale face framed in black, her old, clever eyes. To be honest, I find it magnificent when a solitary old woman walks down a green avenue. I reach a bed of flowers and other vegetation where, on a pretty, shady bench, sits a Jew. Should it have been a Teuton, would that have been better? Flowers surround a diminutive statue in a circular bed; I walk slowly around it, and here comes the reading girl again, she's now reading as she walks, studying French under her breath. This wonderful boredom that is in everything, this sunny seclusion, shallowness, drowsiness beneath the greenery, this melancholy, these legs, whose legs, mine? Yes. I'm too lazy to make observations, I gaze down at my legs and march onward. I mean it, Sundays only exist around the family table and on family walks. The single adult person is deprived of this pleasure, he might as well, like Kutsch, sail off for Africa any moment. By the way, what a loss it is to have turned twenty-five. There are compensations, but for now I want nothing to do with them. I'm on the street now, smoking, and step into a respectable pub, and here, too, I am at once master of my surroundings. I think: beautiful park, beautiful park.

(1907)   Trans. Susan Bernofsky

Laughter

I heard some heavenly laughter, child's laughter, a wonderful tittering, perfectly delicate, pure as silver. A divine giggle. Yesterday, Sunday, I was on my way home around seven o'clock, that's when I heard it, and I must definitely report on it now. How poor adults are, the grown-ups, in their seriousness, with their dry, serious looks. How rich, how great, how happy are the little ones, the children. Such a full, rich, sweet happiness lay in the laughter of the two children who walked along beside a grown-up, such an exuberant, delightful joy. They felt total bliss as they abandoned themselves to their laughter. I walked slowly on purpose, so as to hear them laughing a long time. It was a pleasure for them, they enjoyed the full deliciousness that can lie in a laugh. They simply couldn't stop laughing, and I saw how it shook them. They practically writhed with laughter. O, so pure it was, so utterly childish! What they perhaps laughed most boisterously and sweetly about was the severe face the grown-up young lady beside them thought necessary. The big girl's seriousness gave them the greatest grounds for laughter. But finally, carried away by so much charming merriment, the dignified one laughed too, the serious and grown one. She was conquered by the children and now laughed like a child with her victors, the two little girls. How the happy triumph over the grim! The two children in their innocence laughed about everything, today's and yesterday's matters, this and that, themselves. They had to laugh at their own laughter. Their laughter seemed to them ever more laughable, ludicrous. This I could clearly hear and feel. I considered myself fortunate to have been able to hear this concert of little bells, this concert of laughter. They laughed all down the street. They were almost ready to fall over, melt, dissolve out of laughter. Everything about them, these dear, happy children, was laughing, their heads, their limbs, their hands, feet and legs. There was nothing left of them anymore but their laughter. How the laugh-pleasure gleamed and glittered in their eyes! I almost think they must have been laughing so horribly, cruelly, persistently about a stupid little boy. It was so wanton and yet so beautiful, so moving and so dissolute. Probably the laughter had a quite insignificant cause. Children are artists in seizing hold of a reason to be blissful. A small, quiet incident it might have been, and they turned it into a major event and hung upon it such a long, large, wide, voluptuous laughter. Children know what makes them happy.

(1914)   Trans. Susan Bernofsky

Snow

Here, my dear friend, we have snow, as much as you like and could wish for. The whole countryside is buried in a thick layer of snow. Wherever you look, snow: snow here and snow there. It lies on every object, and the people of our city, big and small, throw snowballs at each other for pleasure. The children can sled as much as they want, and they certainly want to. Yesterday I climbed the mountain in the snow, and the higher I went, the deeper I waded in the deep white mass. Not only were the twigs and branches of the trees piled with this white burden, but the tall trunks as well. There had been a snowstorm, and the ferocious snow-creature had blown out of the west as though it wanted to pour whiteness sideways over the world. I'm surprised everything isn't covered, houses and all. I climbed higher and higher through the snowy forest. Not without a bit of groaning, it's not easy to walk in fresh deep snow. I pulled off my hat from my sweating head, as in summer, and my winter coat became a burden. Then I heard the blows of an axe. A young lad stood all alone in the white evening woodland seclusion, working on a fir tree. Onward, and then I came upon a strange, unexpected obstacle. Two great firs, torn down by the storm, lay with their full stately length in the middle of the narrow path, blocking it with their outstretched branches. But I valiantly made my way through them and walked on. Already it was growing dark in the white enchanted forest. I walked downhill, through all the snow. Once I was knocked down and sat in the snow as though I'd meant to take a seat at a table to have supper. I pulled myself up, couldn't help laughing, and hurried home.

(1914)   Trans. Susan Bernofsky

Well Then

A delightful, distinguished bourgeois family cheerfully sipping tea one morning, about four o'clock, in enchanting moonlight, while outdoors, right by the window, sunshine beamed and rain, what a pity, poured down in torrents—was sipping what? Tea!, and what was the beverage? Oh, for heaven's sake, tea! If this nicely numerous tea-sipping family drank anything other than tea, then to hell with me, and if this self-same, altogether lovable, tea-slurping family imbibed anything other than tea, then I cede the reputation as a smart and clever person that I have hitherto called my own.

Mister Author! Hey! What's the matter? Are you a fool?

What's the matter? Nothing, nothing. You're welcome. And I most certainly am not a fool. I beg your pardon a thousandfold for daring to claim that I'm utterly sound. I am completely normal and reliable in every way, although, strangely enough, I'm not as attuned and writerlike today as I usually am. Today I'm perhaps a little so-so or blah-blah, exceptionally mind you. Otherwise I'm quite healthy. Of that I can assure you. Wit belongs in writing, but today this very commodity known as wit seems regrettably, let's say, absent.

Odol mouthwash belongs on every modern washstand. To appreciate Odol means to appreciate oneself. There can be no civilization without Odol. Anybody who cares to be considered a cultivated individual rather than a mere barbarian ought to procure Odol right away. Odol is a truly delicious compound, a blend of the finest substances. Experts don't reveal the slightest hesitation in extolling Odol, on the basis of strictly scientific tests, as an accomplishment of the first order and a boon for mankind. Individuals or nations who reject Odol shall and indeed must be forced to pull themselves together promptly, so as to ensure its diffusion and frequent use. Odol is in every way an ideal substitute for all positive human qualities. The ladies of the uppermost bourgeoisie and aristocracy, apparently sensing a real need, use massive doses of Odol. For years, decades even, top dignitaries have doused their highly esteemed maws with Odol. Odol can fill each mouth or gullet with a pleasant, long-lasting fragrance, and it isn't entirely inconceivable that pleasant odors, no matter when or where they arise, are doubtlessly preferable to foul odors and stinks. Each day commodity traders, elegant spies, railway and oil barons, princes and princesses regent, admirals and field-marshals, deputies from all factions, and many highly esteemed personages besides, empty as much Odol as possible down honorable and, no doubt, eminently respectable gorges. A nation accustomed to Odol marches at the forefront of all nations in terms of intellect, progress, and the enhancement of mind and heart, and, moreover, any such nation—it should certainly be possible to say this much—exercises by virtue of historical necessity the right to dictate laws for all other peoples of the earth and exert unconditional rule over the entire globe.

Goodness gracious once again, tell me, are you utterly how now?

Gentlemen, my dear children, kindly calm down for God's sake and cease working yourselves up, since it's well known that those who work themselves up lose valuable energy working themselves down again, and that's a pity, because energy is valuable and valuables are dear, and dear things ought surely be handled solicitously rather than squandered or misused. Doesn't that seemingly clever and reasonable sentence sound a bit how-nowish? Besides, I have already said I'm just a little so-so or blah-blah today, exceptionally mind you, and maybe also a little oh well and how now. This is probably entirely sufficient for now, since I feel it's hardly necessary to add anything.

Bunion-ring users always enjoy the utterly requisite trust of European governments, since they are justly celebrated as harmless subjects.

Is that so! Well that finally does it. Begone with you. Got that? Pray grab your author's materials and tools and depart from this room, since only decent people are welcome here.

But which room? And why get so upset and expend such valuable energy? After all, you have received my calm assurance that I am utterly sound, although I am feeling just a little so-so or blah-blah today, exceptionally mind you, and also maybe a little oh well and how now. Calm down, calm down. Things will eventually look up; we always have to hope for the best, and, besides, those who work themselves up ultimately have to work themselves down again. So, by your leave, your most humble servant!

I went to the Yiddish Theater of the Brothers Herrenfeld, and must say I enjoyed myself enormously there. Afterwards, if I'm not mistaken, I sat in the Kaffeehaus des Westens, corner of the Kurfürstendamm, and guess whom I saw passing by? None other than a creature who calls forth aurochs, primeval forests, clashing swords, and bearskins: Wulff, the total Teuton. His full beard extended to the tips of his toes. He was arm in arm with a voluptuous, buxom, strapping, juicy capitalist. No cause for excitement! After all, I have said quite clearly that I seem a little so-so or blah-blah today, not to mention oh well, and perhaps also just a little how now. What's so bad about that? Well then! And now have a most pleasant day or good night and very best wishes, for I have done my bit, am finished, and can go out walking again.

(1917)   Trans. Mark Harman

Letter to Hermann Hesse

Biel, November 15, 1917

Dear Hermann Hesse,

Thank you for your kind letter, also for the Welti book you so thoughtfully sent me. Both were a delight. In the book there are very strange things.

You tell me you have wartime duties to perform. I've heard that Hans Muhlistein recently graduated from the military academy. For my part, I can assert, loud and clear, that my rifle stands, so to speak, ready for use, spick and span in the closet. I spent last summer in the Tessin [on military service]. The red wine was pretty good, we drank it like milk, a liter or liter and a half a day. Yes indeed, everyone is performing wartime duties now.

Your remark that writers could do something does not seem unusual to me at all. The thought does come to mind, of its own accord. It may be wrong to sit, as I do, for example, in an expensive overcoat, inside an old Venetian palace, allowing oneself to be waited upon by seven hundred nimble servants.

Word is going around that Robert Walser is leading the noble life of a dreamer, idler, and petit bourgeois, instead of "fighting." The politicians are dissatisfied with me. But what do people really want? And what great or good aims can be achieved by articles in newspapers and magazines? When the world is out of joint, the efforts of twenty thousand Hamlets are no use at all, or precious little. Every day I read a little French, because it is such a pretty language. Does that make me a rascal? And then I can't help walking around every day, a bit, in the winter countryside. Does that prove I'm indifferent to a great deal of suffering? I believe that you understand better than anyone why I like to live a quiet and thoughtful life. With friendly greetings from the marble palace I'm inhabiting,

yours,
Robert Walser

Trans. Christopher Middleton

Finally She Condescended

Finally she condescended. I gasp for breath already, I almost swoon. The sophisticate, in her bright and beautiful attire. At any moment he might expect her, in his home. He had summoned two servants, paid servants, you know, and they had cleaned everything. The furniture was aglow. On the table with its patched tapestry cover stood a bouquet of flowers, or rather, to be precise, it did not stand directly on the table but in a container placed upon the table. The window with its windowpanes, well, take it from me, it made a shimmering display of light. The room positively swam in sunlight, and now, suspicious of herself and of him too, she was coming up the staircase, which had been polished till it was virgin pure. Her heart knew not what it felt, what it really wanted. A wondrously opulent bijou, alluringly golden, with a splendor I'd willingly describe in much detail, was enthroned upon the sideboard, in an oblong case. The bijou was intended for the angel now quietly lowering her blonde head at the door, though she wasn't thinking of anything. She was grumbling at herself for not sufficiently grumbling about him. So one may say that while she knocked she was repeating her role of the indignant lady, the role she faithfully took through her life. A voice in the room called out, "Come in!" She went in, the room was empty. Not a leg in sight, let alone a person. She liked the decor, she was amazed how clean it was. Every object seemed to welcome her with a benediction. I am outraged to be writing about this; I must make it clear, for instance, that the rascal he seems to me had no sooner called "Come in!" than he hid in the wardrobe to irritate his ladyship. And irritated she was. "Well now, here's a to-do," she told herself in her childlike voice. There she stood. Then she saw the bijou. How on earth could she not have seen it? Now she was grumbling to the bijou, which appeared to want to make fun of her. "That coarse fellow is hiding," she said. I almost said "whispered," but the word *whisper* is a bit coarse, so I told myself to omit it, if I didn't mind. The bijou reveled in its beauty. That sounds like something out of a fairy tale, but I'd better let it stand. Fairy tales are ever in demand, in life as in bookshops. People everywhere are seeking experience, the real thing, wholesome, if possible. The best and most genuine people want simplicity to be restored. Well now, did he leap out? Ah! At this point I want so much to nose the right idea out. No, he kept quiet. He let her stand there. Not a sound in the street, nor in the room, either. This storybook silence is putting me to sleep. She harkened. Inside the wardrobe, so did he. I'd also like to describe in much detail how eager she was to embellish herself with the bijou. Really now though, he could stop pussyfooting around like this. A childish situation. It seemed interesting to him; she was irritated to be finding it tense. So she was the small child and he was the big one, or perhaps it would be just as well to think of him as the small child and of her as the big one. The difference is only slight. Once she had wasted a certain amount of time, she went away. "I'll never come again," she vowed to herself. Did she keep her vow? We do not know. We do know that he leaped out of the wardrobe now and delightedly capered around the room. He was radiant.

(microscript, 1924)   Trans. Christopher Middleton

Style

Style is a kind of manner. People who comport themselves well possess style. Once on the Nile a style prevailed: Ancient Egyptian. Note the pyramids and obelisks, their architecture and life-style. Without doubt Cleopatra struck the conqueror Caesar as stylish. Among architectural styles, we discern Romanesque and Byzantine, Gothic and Renaissance, Baroque and Rococo, Empire and Biedermeier. From certain Asiatic styles the Greeks derived their architecture and, perhaps, in part, their philosophy. The Romans, on the other hand, seem to have borrowed not a little from the Greeks. Then Roman manners and furnishings were, as it were, handed down to us. Possibly stylistic similarities exist between Iran and Mexico. The Italian campanile originated, it seems, in orientalisms. Each race evolves from its predecessors. A perpetual exchange, then—just like the giving and taking in daily life, in business and trade. There's style in one's appearance, style in politics, and, yes, style in writing. It's something many have failed to grasp and it will go on being misconstrued. Things of immense importance sometimes are either entirely overlooked or recklessly disregarded, as is likely the case with style. We speak of decorous servants, meaning those who possess adroitness, that is, manners. A person without a lick of style can still speak and write intelligently. Witlessness, on the other hand, can now and then be full of style. Of course there are various types of style. For example, we recognize early and late styles, a, as it were, spring style and autumn-of-life style. Gentle, delicate souls can display their own personal style just as well as some strapping colossus. Nonetheless, style implies a domination and, springing and emanating from this subjection, a contentment. From constraints can and must arise spontaneities. Those who submit to constraints can let themselves go. Someone unrestrained in his behavior will make people think he has himself in hand. In Goethe we see displayed a splendid, lovely, graceful early style. And who could deny that Schiller's prose is founded entirely on stylistic sensitivity? Adalbert Stifter, on the other hand, is, in matters of expression, almost girlish. I could cite many other examples. Japanese actors act in a manner far more stylized than Europeans. In the English theater acting was, perhaps, at one time somewhat Japanese; in any case, we feel entitled to assume, it was superb— that is, highly expressive. This question preoccupies me: why is there no longer any uniformity of style? Has some refined predilection, ability, strength, social grace, inventiveness been lost to us? What's really puzzling, though, is how, in early times, styles arose at all. Where did they come from? Who created them? Certainly each evolved from the last, but why is this no longer the case? Could mankind have mislaid its sense of style? Nowadays we construct in every possible form, conduct ourselves in a most piecemeal manner, both on the street and in drawing rooms. One person acts this way, another in a manner altogether different. The congenial, dreamy, bourgeois Biedermeier was the last distinct style the world saw fit to produce. With the invention of the railroad and the rise of industrial tumult, the urge to reproduce life in clear images disappeared. Was the necessary peace to develop a coherence-giving style now lacking in people? Or were all such possibilities already exhausted? Is style itself the expression of the will of something great and lofty, and has this greatness, this loftiness gradually diminished to the point of vanishing? Concerning the styles of gardens, we immediately conjure up the name Lenôtre and picture ourselves strolling about the parks of Versailles. If today, for example, a poet pursues his calling in a garret, one may assume he is sufficiently educated to call to mind the architect Mansard. Style means a sense of culture. With culture, history begins. Prehistorical man differs from historical man in that the former hadn't yet found a style for himself. How could he, since the prerequisites were not yet present? This earliest man busied himself primarily with the harsh and naked defense of his life. He dwelt in natural apartments; later he built himself crude huts. At any rate, he devised something miraculous: language. What incredible pains it must have cost him! It's hard for us to form even a roughly accurate picture of this. Centuries must have passed before he'd even learned to fan a fire. The tasks of the first men lay in acquiring the most elementary knowledge. Style, seen in this light, might have been a kind of disgrace, an extravagance. Or might we call it an affair or product of the mind, of order? Did it come from monarchs? Or did the monarchs simply occasion its development? In any case, I affirm that it's a pleasure to have a sense of style. I should know, since it's widely acknowledged I'm in possession of one. This may not seem like much to some people, but all the same perhaps it is.

(microscript, 1926)   Trans. Susan Bernofsky and Tom Whalen

I Contemplated Pride and Love

I contemplated pride and love. All this contemplativeness. When will I be free of it? And then I had the, no doubt, laudatory intention of writing about roses and flutes. Moreover, there arose in me the need to drive out my opinion on Bolshevism from, so to speak, the warehouse of my spiritual being. Drive it out? My, my, what energetic talk! It mustn't be forgotten that on the street today I encountered a woman whose appearance invited me to hope she might offer me the opportunity to wait on her hand and foot. I'll return to this hand-and-foot waiting in a moment, as soon as I've extricated myself, at least a little, from the rest of these handlings or formulations. Roses surround me with fragrance. How bewitching it is. Carl Maria von Weber, if I'm not mistaken, once composed a dance poem entitled *The Rose.* I once saw the title role performed by the dancer Nijinsky, who had real Renaissance legs to show for himself. Flutes turn up in Jean Paul as well as Friedrich the Great. The latter had somewhat too gunpowderish, spurrish, riding-bootish a name. Nevertheless, he was enchanted by French poetry, philosophy and art. Personalities like d'Alembert, Watteau, Voltaire, and so on appear dimly or distinctly on the horizon of this essay. I don't begrudge these figures the pleasure of emerging from the past. Flute strains and the perfume of roses can be superb together. A park would provide an appropriate setting. Who wouldn't love to inhabit a house situated in the midst of a large, silent garden? There exists a novel fragment by the poet Brentano, a story that makes reference to the flower I've now had occasion to mention several times. I read the above-mentioned prose poem in the journal *Die Insel*, which once came out of Munich. Islands and roses—things are getting better and better, more and more refined. Schröder, Heymel, Bierbaum are personalities who occur to one of their own accord when the talk is of castles full of the finest porcelain and boat trips along dreamy shores. Roses lie splendidly upon the bosoms of women. Doesn't this plant remind us instantly of the joys and beauties of existence? If only I'd gotten my report on Bolshevism out of the way already. It seems it torments me, but there's no escaping it, no escaping. Still, I'll doubtless speak of it only briefly. One, two, three, and it will be over. Flute strains drifting bannerlike in the morning or evening air, and a woman's hand upon a rose bush; I confess I'm feeling at home in my subject, which, I admit, demands, so it seems, the utmost attention, and I believe myself quite capable of giving it this. The *Rose of Stambul* and the *Rosenkavalier* seem to be matters which, in all politeness, request that I think of the theater and its cultural mission. Briskly I set about it. The German word for "flute," *Flöte,* rhymes, significantly, with Goethe, who possessed deep sympathy for an instrument that, with its linguistic peculiarities, occupied a generation we people of today consider interesting and thus worthy of our love, occupied them, one might say, down to the farthest reaches of their villages and souls. This age, after all, was so wonderfully sensitive, and perhaps we envy it for this luxury, out of which these people made a celebration. Tootling his flute, proud Vult, lost in his introspections, parted from his dream- and sleep-entangled little brother, Walt, at the end of Jean Paul's novel *Die Flegeljahre.* Regarding Bolshevism, I'd made up my mind to state I don't consider it an absolute novelty, that is to say, don't think it unprecedented. Collective strivings that have as their goal the elimination of personal tastes, idiosyncrasies, individual sensibilities, have always existed, I think I have the right to claim. But let's bring on some pride. Where's it been all this time? I mean, pride is allowed to be seen, and love is certainly no less entitled, perhaps more so. Pride often struggles conspicuously against love. Many, I'm convinced, will share my opinion when I declare that I consider, for example, girls beautiful merely because of their pride. When Beethoven, improvising at the piano in fine society one evening, at approximately nine or ten o'clock, smote an unfortunately rather too loud pair of lovers or spouses with a lightning-swift word of perhaps quite unsuitable content, of what else was he giving luminous, rattling, possibly even thunderous proof than his presumably inborn pride? The proud are always right, and yet also wrong, in their feelings, and if you were to ask me what a person should be, proud or humble, I wouldn't lose much time responding: both at once, now humble, now proud, depending on how I feel, how I find the circumstances, the other people, myself. Doesn't

Shakespeare's Othello stand out as an exemplar of pride before our litera-
ture-adoring eyes? Wisdom can preach for days on end to an individual
inclined to pride: "Be considerate and understanding"; the proud one's
pride demands, with a quite natural necessity, opportunities to make itself
felt. Who can fail to recognize that there were and are people who, on
account of the pride they couldn't and can't overcome, have languished and
crumbled to bits and still languish and crumble to bits, and who could be so
coarse as to have been and to be unable to perceive the beauty that
emanated and emanates from the behavior of such members of our society?
Thank God I'm capable of finding a bit of pride more interesting than all of
Bolshevism, though I have no objection if this rapid observation is assessed
wholly or in part as mere words. A writer may and must, in my opinion, let
himself go, to a certain degree. There are great masters of the word who,
now and then, seriously overstepped their bounds, but perhaps it turned out
that unfettered remarks are less disagreeable and do less harm than a
complete lack of temperament during the act of composition. Softly now, I
return to the jealous Moor, whom I once saw explosively portrayed by
Matkovsky. One could well believe that, with regard to Desdemona, he'd
swung in a hammock of contentment all his life. Yet it appeared this wasn't
entirely the case. Othello was proud enough for jealousy, but not proud
enough to spurn it. An absence of pride sometimes shows up in the proud.
On the other hand, someone who always acts insignificant and submissive
can still be filled with a joyous pride; that is, he can be proud he submits.
Admittedly this sort of pride is difficult to perceive, but what does this
matter? Despite his propensity for idolatry, Hölderlin possessed colossal
pride. No one who knows and loves his verses can doubt this. Let me
emphasize that, flutes and roses aside, which I by no means begrudge
anyone who has the time and desire to let himself be beguiled, I wish to
make some distinctions regarding pride. Pride and pride are two different
things, four different things. One person can be proud of this, another of
that. The author of *The Life of the Merry Schoolmaster Maria Wuz of
Auenthal* depicts this character as proud but not vain, a presentation that
can't be praised enough. If pride isn't rigid but rather flexible, adaptable,
one can give it one's approval; that is, I, for example, check to see whether
my pride benefits my health or makes me ill, whether it makes me cheerful
and courageous or irritable, rude and tired. I'm always ready to welcome
any sort of pride that invigorates me, but in the meantime where has love, to
which I promised to devote a few lines, gone strolling off? To Madretch or
Bözingen? I'll start out from the opposite direction, perhaps I'll meet up
with it. That lover of the word and mankind, glorifier of the City of Roses,
tracker down of fluting tendernesses, Jean Paul, was most definitely
acquainted with pride, for he created the figure Vult, who is among the
proudest novel characters I know. Just as Shakespeare could have understanding for both an Iago and an Othello, that is, for both a scoundrel and a

full-scale hero, Jean Paul showed understanding for both the all- and ever-loving Walt and the condition-setting flautist who to an absolute degree was conscious of the majesty of art. In Vult we have someone who played the flute but whose heart failed to melt beneath the flute strains, someone who was capable of ardent love but also cold calculation. I consider the woman I met today on the street one of those people who have no desire to belong to anyone but themselves. I confess I'd very much like to make the acquaintance of a woman who doesn't want anyone to touch her. I'd rather touch such a woman than anyone else. I'm almost impressed with myself for managing to speak, I think I can flatter myself, more or less successfully on the theme of pride. I find all pride rosy, warm, tender, dear, good, small and large and beautiful. The proud always give off a scent like that of fate. Introspections, spiritualities offer a drama for our delectation. But now to say a few more words about love: it's wrong, in my opinion, to spurn cold love in favor of warm. I consider the former more solid, more durable and reliable, and this element of reliability is essential in love, which contains so much selfishness, so much error. Cold love, in any case, never cools, for it—is cold. But many a warm love does.

(microscript, 1926)   Trans. Susan Bernofsky and Tom Whalen

Letter to Max Brod

Berne, October 4, 1927

Dear Max Brod,

I received your card. It indeed surprised me to learn you spent two years on your novel, since this really somewhat moving circumstance wasn't at all evident in the lines I once again thank you for sending me. Stendhal, what a great name that is today. Here in our idyllic Berne I experienced a night in which I was almost destroyed. But don't speak of this to anyone. It has such a romantic flavor. I'm most grateful for your friendship. Your colleague, Otto Pick, still has in his possession a number of my poems. In your office, too, a poem or two is still lying about, which you may still publish yourself, i.e., in the *Prager Tagblatt,* before you undertake any steps regarding that rascal Zsolnay to make the scoundrel take action. Zsolnay is quite simply a scoundrel of a novel editor who runs like a rabbit before the outrageous suggestion that he might print, i.e., publish, poems. All the same I would be pleased, i.e., in agreement, if on some occasion you would recommend me to the cur, who, like all the other snot-faced publishers, is terrified of poetry, which is, after all, understandable. If you write to the sorry bastard, I bid you do it briefly, earnestly, generously; better to be boastful than in any way beseeching. Writers, who are a pack of beggars in the publishers' eyes, should treat the latter like mangy swine. When dealing with this Viennese agent of culture regarding me, be proud, delicate, casual, pompous. For the time being I wouldn't send this stupid wretch any material for fear he would simply sink into his stinking arrogance. For you see, in my opinion, it very much depends on *how* one treats them. And then the idea of publishing a book seems lovely and interesting so long as it hasn't yet happened. Every book that has been printed is, after all, a grave for its author, isn't it?

   With sincere and respectful greetings,

Robert Walser

Trans. Susan Bernofsky

There Was Once, to My Knowledge, a Poet

There was once, to my knowledge, a poet who proved to be an exceptionally considerate escorter of women, for he took upon himself the both courageous and humane task of eliminating flies and so forth—that is, annoyances—which landed upon the blouse-draped backs of these sensitive creatures out for summer-evening strolls. If, one night in the middle of the scorching-hot winter, this poet addressed verses in a blithely icy and changefully monotonous tone to a room graced and enlivened by the most perplexingly soft, dear light of a yellow lamp, this by no means rules out the possibility of his producing, with casual ease, successful novels that seemed to be nothing but lyrical, sustained, Damascus-blade notes and ornamental arabesques, and thus a sort of spiderweb or carpet weave. The publishers were always quite hesitant to introduce these apparently epic products into their sales departments, since examining and reading these works cost them huge efforts, and they couldn't help considering the likelihood that the same would hold true for their potential, estimable customers. In a castle the poet composed novelistic poems, colossally delicate agglomerations of a thoroughly raffish sort that at times virtually shrieked with the sugar glaze with which they were salted and peppered. He possessed the nimblest pair of legs ever provided a member of the writers' guild, and with the help of this marching apparatus he occasionally conquered whatever stretches might be necessary to arrive at the source of his lovely essays, which were laced with expansivities into the realm of the novelistic as a roast is laced with bits of bacon to heighten its delectability. From time to time, he rhymed and hauled together a few stories that, with their crystalline truths, formed a stalactite cave of analysis. On account of all the wit-strewn pages composed by this poet who, the moment he began to poeticize, became a prose author, whereas writing prose turned him into a poet, ladies were overcome by fits of wistfulness, only, however, to allow themselves, by way of recovery, to joke about his seriousness, which apparently they found ridiculous to the same extent as his ridiculosities clasped or entwined them in contemplation, whichever one prefers. The odd thing was that everyone thought him peculiar, though they declared him exceptionally average, and that he never ceased to be a missing person, though no one attracted more attention than this fellow whose mouth gave out trumpet blasts. Himself he considered quite modest, and if the others saw him as other than he was, and he saw himself in a way such that no one else could ever have thought themselves in a position to look upon and judge him, it was only fitting he was once dubbed an enigma. Did he remain uncomprehended because he was too easy to comprehend? Was he impossible to grasp because it was easy to believe one had figured him out? The significant declared him a significant figure, while the insignificant found him insignificant, rather than the opposite being true; in any event, he signified something, it's just that no one knew what, and people reassured themselves by calling him a ne'er-do-well, though he was really no idler. He seemed to have produced his poems, which resembled ledger entries, in his sleep. He often behaved stiffly, but bestowed all the more fluidity upon his dramas, which at first existed only in his head, where, now and then, he imagined that, from time to time, people imagined this and that on account of him. His uglinesses were deemed beautiful; his beauties were insufferably ugly. Those who smiled at him became ugly, whereas those who hated him were permitted to believe themselves beautiful. Now that I've tried to make sense of him, he's a stranger to me, too. Constantly he seems to be lying in wait for himself, watching to see whether it's to his advantage to eavesdrop on himself, whether there's opportunity for him to suck himself dry. I'll call him his own vampire. He's been dissecting himself so long one hardly notices him anymore. Am I fantasizing, has he led me astray? That this astray-leading leads somewhere is demonstrated by this page, for I have the impression he wrote it. Because I've concerned myself with a lazybones, I'm sleeping; getting a grip on certain things signifies a waking up. Already he's exhausted any number of people. Anyone who wishes to wake him falls asleep. Only when no one knows him any longer will he arrive at self-knowledge. Those who know him swoon, as though he lay at the foot of a glass mountain. Why bother with him at all?

(microscript, 1927)   Trans. Susan Bernofsky

Maidservant Story

One thing you had to give her credit for: she never nibbled on the sly. This virtue alone was enough to make her despised. Her faithfulness shone like a sky full of stars. Here I seem to be speaking a bit sentimentally. At times she wrote poetry in the attic room to which she was in the habit of retiring and gave these more delicate than striking and more dainty than powerful or weighty proofs of her literary talent to her master, who sent off these poems for publication, having signed them with his name, to editors who assured him he wrote superbly. From time to time she received in payment from the kind sir, as she liked to call him, a lash of the whip. Having heard how she was treated, a girlfriend of hers, a member of high society with whom she kept up a regular correspondence, wrote that she envied her. In fact, well brought-up girls at times long dearly for rough treatment. "Wouldn't you like to pretend you were a man and entitled to mistreat me just a little?" she asked her friend, who modestly yet also offhandedly replied: "I haven't the least desire to do so; after all, it would be quite inappropriate." The children of her employers sometimes told her she stank, but knew perfectly well they were amusing themselves by lying, so as to take pleasure in an arrogance children know better than anyone how to relish. On the other hand, nobody was better at feeling shame than the one who once softly implored the mistress of the house, that is, fervently beseeched her, to tweak her nose. The latter didn't hesitate to advise her petitioner to speak in more refined a manner, that is, less bluntly; otherwise, much as she prized her, she'd send her packing. Gliding elegantly, it seems, over the question of whether or not her scent or fragrance was such that one could have exhibited it at an exhibition for sweet scents, let me just quickly mention her perhaps really quite beautiful eyes, with the aid of which she began a by all means serious, sometimes valuable, amorous friendship with her mistress's daughter.

I just ate a dish of soup, then a rather long sausage, then a scrumptious piece of cheese, then sardines, then ham, then an apple, then a few nuts, and this maid's kisses were never savored, for she never kissed; kissing *her*, however, had nearly a consuming effect, for she was a born kiss recipient.

She always played exceptionally, that is, unspeakably well with the accepted kiss; that's rather lazily put, since as I already mentioned, if I hadn't eaten a bit too much and weren't, more or less, so indolent at the moment, I might have been capable of depicting, with surely only a slight expenditure of effort, the way she dealt with this treat. She had a pale, moist face. Anyone who touched this face, which radiated submissiveness, felt unable ever to break free of it again. The maid had manners and naturalness, and her masters, despite certain cultural shortcomings, were cultivated, while as for me, I inhale and exhale responsibility, that is, aspirations to culture, with every breath, for which reason I am loved and unloved—in a word, respected. I wrote these lines coldly, as though I were heartless.

Sometimes my cheerfulness, that is, what one can call heart, is pale, sometimes ruddy.

I remember going years without laughing.

The maid most definitely deserves the honor I've accorded her.

(1927/28)   Trans. Susan Bernofsky

A Poet Apart: On Robert Walser

Martin Walser

> The lonely one. It's not certain if he sits or stands.
>
> —Robert Walser

IT'S ALL RIGHT TO BE enthusiastic about a writer for whom great and widespread enthusiasm already exists. But if one believes the writer has been assigned far too low a literary rank, then, alas, this enthusiasm can be harmful. Any serious reader can easily come to the conclusion: if this Robert Walser were really so important, I'd know more about him. So one has to proceed with pedagogical cunning, bring out the gilt-edged greats Kafka, Musil, Walter Benjamin, illuminate historically the literary rumor named Robert Walser and demonstrate the necessity of a revival so discreetly that everyone will feel compelled to read him at once. In view of this incredible situation, why worry about appearing didactic? Who else besides Kafka, for example, is as well suited for genuine dissertations as Robert Walser? He remains as enigmatic as ever. An untended literary grave. And it might be even more difficult than with Kafka to form intelligent opinions about him. A body of scholarship has emerged around Kafka. Even someone who approaches him warily will sooner or later be caught up in this discipline; he can become well-versed in Kafka's labyrinth. But Robert Walser again and again smashes the instruments by which we want to explain him. Joy and sorrow have been planted so close together; despair and ecstasy grow on the same branch and perpetually intertwine. And because we're accustomed to trying to picture our favorite writers, this Swiss kinsman of Kafka's will make us founder. Yet, like Kafka, he wrote almost exclusively about himself. I certainly wouldn't find his landscapes and nature subjects at all interesting, if it weren't for this confounded wanderer who reports how he sees himself on his alpine excursions. And there's no trusting how he sees himself. He keeps switching back and forth between Karl Valentin and Hölderlin. The beautiful surface of his prose has earned him the reputation of a sensitive miniaturist. To be sure, it's acknowledged that something lies beneath this surface. Eccentric, dreamy, always a sort of youth.

A gentle vagabond and accomplished idler, at least according to the rumor. Because it stops short before the dissonances that stipple his idylls, because it doesn't have the courage to venture into his office rooms where he lets Fate run the business, as though his bookkeepers were called Hamlet or Richard III. But this discrepancy—they are only bookkeepers, yet inexorable things occur—creaks with a dreadful comicality. He describes his insignificant incidents in an extremely rich language. Walser must have found it vexing that, according to a bourgeois ideology of art, tragedy was possible only in the past, in feudal times. And so he permits himself an alpine pathos for all sorts of trivialities, but laces his delicately elevated speech with words that hitherto had no place here. He himself, the organizer of this prose extravaganza, is always on stage. Gradually we can identify him as an exceptionally *real* character. Not by means of physiognomy, nor by rational judgment, but by his unmistakable way of simply being there, or existing. Unmistakable, yet not at all apparent, not distinctive, not fully delineated, of undefined temperament, inaccessible to all psychology. He represents the exact opposite of a lasting clarity, rather is more a medium in which everything is refracted fiercely, timidly, while the medium itself remains drenched in secrecy. It timidly, fiercely performs its function, but is afraid of depicting itself directly. For him that would entail a finality akin to madness. Everything in the books combines to form a bewildering pattern. Celtic. The change-obsessed author, his vanishing existence: this is what's bewildering about him. I can't bring myself to trust his ecstasy. He loves retelling things rapturously, so to speak. Above all, natural occurrences. And their greatest antithesis: visits to the theater. But in his retellings he refuses to let himself be seduced by conventional modes of understanding. He has no desire to be clever or pursue interpretations. He prefers to take his head in his hands, weep a little, or else give an occasional unexpected giggle. All he has to do is describe being at the theater, in nature, in a salon, and once more the world has been set to rights. Without his meaning to do so. Simply because this timid, good-natured, disappointed, contemplative, tremendously refined medium puts himself at risk and collects experiences. As far as I know, with the exception of Kotzebue, he's never approached anyone or anything with pronounced aggression (at the most Goethe's stability). He brings himself in as unobtrusively as possible, allows himself to be buffeted by the world and describes the colors in which it is refracted in him. And at the beginning he does this cheerfully.

He sets out with a capacity for devotion that is prepared to stop at nothing. Possibly he believed at the beginning that paradise had disappeared only because of a blunder made by an overzealous wallpaper hanger, and that he could restore it again by running his fingers over people and walls with a bit of enthusiasm. So it's possible he truly was ingenuous. But not for long. He must soon have perceived that everything is made of the same fabric, and that this has calamitous consequences. The rest is a series of attempts to adjust himself accordingly. By means of distance. If anything at all stands out in his discrete transformations, it is this withdrawal, this radical diminution, which he would like to have us and himself believe is harmless. As always, he's afraid to speak out. But still the roles he slips into almost mark out a trail that can be followed. Even if he still plays the harmless youth and walker, he's beginning to feel less and less at ease in his scenes. Finally it's immaterial what role he takes, for the language itself now can no longer be held within bounds, having perhaps simply lost track of itself. The beautiful surface has gone up in smoke. And indeed we can see him sitting there: equipped with the finest contemplative habits on the continent, he takes out a sheet of paper and is moved by his own gentle and orderly writing abilities, he is particularly well acquainted with the word *sweet,* now he'd like to start something in such and such a direction, and his hands, well versed in beauty, are willing. An initial sentence is written, of a gracefulness such as the German language rarely yields; really, how can one help but envy this prose piece the elegant munificence being lavished on it by its author. So now it can surely proceed flowingly to its end, no different than a firm glance that glides along an avenue in the certainty that in the end it will be able to refresh itself, as it were, in a fountain. But this isn't what happens. Suddenly a sentence jars. A second one thunders down. A weapon that's really out of the question here makes its appearance. What is to be destroyed? Is it still the same Ariel-like author sitting there? In no time, utterly out-of-place ideas come pouring in and grotesquely disfigure the work in progress; this he notices and valiantly tries to steer things back into a gentler sphere, but already the next noxious sentence comes pelting down, the author loses control over his prose piece, beautiful wreckage drifts about, good will can't be stretched any further, the author now makes an impetuous outburst, confesses his injuries, is ashamed of his confession, cancels it out with some horribly comical banality, quickly plays the youth again, the wanderer, the ardent miniaturist and attempts with, so to speak, professional strength to drive his prose piece back into the frame from which he created it, and appears to succeed; nevertheless: the final sentences of these prose pieces often tremble with exertion and astonishment.

Surely no one will ever be able to write more naturally and with such unabashed identification about Kleist, Lenau, Brentano, and Lenz. There's no question that Walser adopts these names, too, these careers that so resembled his own, as roles for himself. Shy as he was, he would never have dared say about himself what he said about Lenau, Brentano, or Kleist. But once he has a role, he flourishes in it. Not that this makes him any clearer. Everything timid and fierce within him is simply searching for material to express itself in without having to pin itself down, to acknowledge itself as this or that. Walser was truly afraid of this. He eluded every definitive picture of himself, everything stable, the dreaded paralysis of consciousness, anything that might become the basis for a final judgment. They say children start to sing in the woods. He tried to help himself with physical activity. In nature, for example. And in that epitome of unnaturalness: the theater. No one else has ever written so much and so idiosyncratically about actors and the stage, with so little essayistic and professional interest. He would have liked to have been an actor himself. To have become acquainted with his own face only in its transformations. Not to have had to be himself. Not to have been condemned to these eternal identifying characteristics. Every time you allow something to be pinned down in this world, you contribute to your own definition. Every relationship requires nurturing. So then he probably fled to the theater; is it an operetta or *The Magic Flute?* No matter, just so there are stage sets, wings. Or else he would go out for a ramble, and didn't mind the risk of being mistaken for an aficionado of landscapes. The consequences of remaining so alone, so apart, bothered him less than the fear of lasting relationships. This way, at least, he could always imagine that each momentary wretchedness would soon end in a change.

It surely isn't inadvertent or the result of pure ecstasy when he says that on the mountain meadow a "Hölderlinian freedom" prevails. After all, if he had been less distressed he might have garnished this sentence with William Tell instead. The maneuvers he used to talk himself out of marriage are highly reminiscent of Kierkegaard and Kafka. It almost seems that of all of them Walser was the one who stood the most apart. And then he was no longer living in a big city aswarm with distractions. Apparently he had all but accepted solitude as a profession. Once he wrote: "What else should I do with my feelings but let them thrash about and die in the sand of language? I'll be through with myself as soon as I'm done writing, and this pleases me. Good night." Or: "It is as if I stood at some central point. Life is languishing with thirst; it yearns for me. I simply gaze at it, carry it within me as a lover bears the portrait of his soul's delight." That might have come from Kafka's diaries. And stern Musil, with blind rationalism, criticized Kafka's first book for seeming like a "special case of the Walser type." As if there were nothing more to this similarity than imitative dexterity. On the other hand, where might a literary scholar place this sentence: "May we never be lost to the sacred"? No, it isn't a line from one of Hölderlin's hymns, but rather the last sentence of a prose piece by Robert Walser, whom the critics like to call a master of "short prose." That's where he belongs: among the poets who it's hard to imagine ever lived. Hölderlin is like this. Kafka, too. He is one of those writers whose books offer no insight into how their authors ever managed to behave acceptably. The reverse, though, is easily understandable: that they couldn't stand it for very long. Robert Walser once wrote a birthday prose piece for himself. In it, he admiringly tallies up the authors who failed to grow old in good health: Büchner, Novalis, Kleist. Of Hölderlin he writes: "Hölderlin saw fit, that is, found it tactful, to lose his healthy common sense in his fortieth year." Probably one should avoid trying to understand sentences that place one's health in such jeopardy. On another occasion he wrote of Hölderlin: "Will I succumb to the same thing?" Yes, it was, in fact, approximately the same. But no one can genuinely comprehend this. The misunderstandings possible with regard to this writer often seem of his own devising. But at the same time he asks, with a comic shrug, whether we really want to rest content with this misunderstanding. Such incredible things occur to him that he's obliged to resort to comic retractions. He surely would have seen it as impertinence if he had managed to talk himself into self-confidence. This is a trait that determines his following.

One can imagine that with this Swiss writer one has come into contact with something akin to pure pain. Yet his prose pieces, read aloud, are funny. There are always a few listeners who laugh aloud, because even the most dreadful experiences are compelled beneath his language-tamer's hand to trot around the ring like sheep. But if one wants to say something about the author himself, anything that occurs to one seems like a cinematic oversimplification. Right away one turns him into a person whose existence can be grasped without difficulty. Any involvement with this man can make one feel ashamed in more than one respect. So best let him contribute the concluding lines. In the mouth of one of his child personae he places this stern sentence: "No one has the right to treat me as though he knew me."

Trans. Susan Bernofsky and Tom Whalen

A Sort of Hero

Lynne Sharon Schwartz

MY HERO WAS BORN in a snowstorm; fast and furious fell the downy flakes round his pink young head as he uttered his first piercing shriek, to the delight of his stalwart lady mother, naturally somewhat in disarray from her recent efforts, but nonetheless overjoyed. Into the room dashed his six lively, rosy Alpine brothers and sisters, to be introduced and predict his illustrious future. One of the cleverer sisters, taking a first excited glance at the hushed infant, his eyes already bemused by the multiple wonders displayed before them, pronounced him "not of coarse enough cut for this life." As for the young fellow, he pondered already, as he was to continue to ponder: "What made life so? Is it going to stay as it is, or change? Why am I asking this? Why do so many questions come to me, softly, one after the other?"

Was there really a snowstorm, you may reasonably pause to ask, even at this infantile stage of our chronicle, as it was the month of April? Since I make up the story as it proceeds, I would have it an unseasonable snowstorm if you please, if I may beg your indulgence, for the simple reason, if I am not sweeping too far ahead of my story, like a train sweeping past the desperate passengers running tardily alongside, hanging on to their hats, that he was to meet his death in the snow. How comforting, isn't it, to have stories come full circle, as in the old high days of narrative? Perhaps if I draw a rounded circle instead of letting my tale evaporate like a little cloud, some lordly publisher will deign to print this frivolous enterprise and not float it fleetly back to me like a paper airplane on billows of wind.

Walser was the name of this fine hero of mine, and hero he was, for he was destined to follow the noble profession of servant, that is to say, writer. What is more noble than the servant who humbles his will and learns to present all things with deftness and agility, whether his task is to carry a whiskey and soda on a silver salver to his most dignified and wealthy employer, or to deposit bushels of harvested words in the ample lap of Poetry's exacting mistress? Indeed, our hero was schooled in humility from his earliest years when his mother loved him, let us say, adequately, but perhaps not quite to the ultimate degree.

On a smiling summer's day, a morning of gay birdsong and beckoning leaves, he set forth through the forests of his native land to seek his fortune. This he did not find so very quickly, it seems, as happens even to the best of lads. A handsome, clever youth was he, though perhaps a trifle eccentric or careless in his dress: he did not always replace his buttons as promptly as might be desired or iron his shirts and trousers; he could be seen in the villages with an odd assortment of hats of the most distressing colors— orange, blue, grassy green, not at all hatlike.

And yet he cut an amiable figure as he ambled through the streets on his everlasting promenades, observing each flower turn its luscious, colorful, tearful face to the sun, each pious shopkeeper open his doors to the gracious public, while the town stretched its limbs and blinked awake, preparing to endure yet another promising day.

He was unfailingly courteous to all he approached. He gazed with humility and appreciation at the bosoms and bustles of the ladies strolling by on their ladylike errands, some of whom gave back a puzzled glance. He would pause to stroke a peripatetic canine, that is to say, a stray dog, in the spirit of soulful camaraderie. So what if, as he reported, "Nothing ever happened! To be bored and to ponder how I can possibly break the boredom —that is what my real occupation is." Walking, he listened to the murmur of the soul, for "one listens to the murmur of the soul only because of boredom."

Bored or not, he was industrious; we cannot, no, we most certainly must not hint that he was unindustrious or—can it even be whispered?—lacking in ambition. He tried his untried hand at a variety of trades: he trod the boards of the stage for a time, he was amanuensis to an inventor, and on occasion settled briefly into the time-honored profession of clerk.

Ah, to be a clerk in a bank, ladies and gentlemen, indulgent readers! Imagine, for a moment, our gifted young hero admitted into the halls of commerce, to shiver to the rustle of bills and the clink of coins, poised at the magnificent center of the modern universe. To be a clerk is to perch on a high stool, pen in hand, and set columns of splendid numbers dancing elegantly across the luxuriant pages of a ledger, to the unheard music, like the music of the spheres, of investment and profits. To be a clerk is to wake in the morning in a small bare room, don one's dark clerkly garb, fervently swallow one's tea and roll, wave a friendly good-bye to one's tight-lipped landlady wrecked with loneliness, and set out briskly through the morning streets with a missionful purpose and energy! To be a clerk is to know life, to bow one's head to the inevitable, to the desk. Why, to be a clerk is hardly less august a role for a gay blade of a hero than to be a cockroach, if I may say so, and who among us can be unaware of the literary worth, the symbolic dimensions, of a cockroach?

Don't you think this story is coming along nicely? It is being written in a little house in the woods, before a stately mullioned window, as I eat a tuna-fish sandwich, unfortunately garnished with pickle. The servant girl at this establishment, a saucy, charming young thing with fetching carroty hair, is all too fond of pickles. Out of mere indolence I suffer them rather than complain. Outside, a badger shuffles aimlessly about the ashy trunk of a birch tree. I might even desert my desk and hyperpickled lunch to join him, for as our hero wrote at an advanced stage of wisdom, it is "just as fine a thing to be human and go for a walk as to sit at one's desk and successfully turn out books."

After his perky day of clerkiness Walser would stop in a local café and drink his glass of beer with his fellow clerks and upright citizens, eyes somewhat glazed from the glare of their ruled ledgers. He might smoke a cigarette, for he was very attached to his cigarettes, a symptom not uncommon in clerks of the modern age. "I know a brand of cigarettes that lets me play the grand seigneur and smell terrific," he remarked. "Yesterday, by the way, I went a whole afternoon without smoking: an exercise in renunciation. People who can't renounce things never get to know the deeper pleasures."

A cigarette is a curious object, a heap of weeds rolled cylindrically into a paper and set on fire at one end. All manner of people put it to their lips, virtually kissing it with ardor, to draw in the fumes. A foul-smelling habit, certainly, yet one that has left an indelible, possibly salutary, mark on civilization. If not for the cigarette to quiet the nervous nerves, who knows how many more murders and acts of mayhem might have been perpetrated on suffering humanity? What might one not write about the effects of cigarettes on human history? And the effects of their renunciation as well, for now, the pundits tell us, these sweet weeds are unhealthy poisons. Yet away in the lands of the spicy East, potentates and peasants alike indulge in this fumy, curly, misty habit, and seem none the worse. We must die of something, evidently. And a good thing, too. Wouldn't you agree?

After his glass of beer, or his several beloved glasses of the sparkly, inspiriting brew, our little clerk—little not in size but in worldly position—would return to his cell, I mean his room, to sit at another desk.

For, yes, there can be no more evading the subject: he was a clerk of another sort. He wrote: voluminously, incessantly, frivolously, profoundly, insanely, merrily, ambitiously, hopelessly. He wrote, he mailed his writings, though on occasion was known to burn them. Was he unhappy, you may well ask, when the mighty and learned editors of newspapers flew his pages back to him on billows of wind like flocks of paper airplanes? Unhappy because he was eternally poor and unrecognized? No, he was not unhappy. It would take more than such a mite to make our noble hero unhappy. "The apathy of an unappreciative public," he swore, "will never do me in." He was ever cheerful and fun-loving, amusing the good townspeople with playful antics on his never-ceasing walks. And yet once in a while, perhaps he imagined himself unhappy. "It seems," he concluded as a young, or youngish, man, "It seems one has only to imagine oneself unhappy to be so."

Still, for all his clerical fervor, our young man did not feel his deepest ambitions fulfilled. His taste for servility, that is to say, for knowledge, a prodigious, arrogant craving, was unsatisfied. Through forest and town he wended his way. Woodland creatures cavorted in greeting. The tops of trees swayed at his approach. Streets crackled and blistered with excitement. And what a high old time he had. Through the great metropoli of Switzerland and Germany, through the highfalutin salons of the literary and artistic he strolled. He shook hands, now and then, with the great.

One glistening morning he approached the gates of a famous castle, guarded by customarily fierce men-at-arms, spears raised, visors lowered. Young Walser had to plunge through a perilous moat to reach its portals, thereby arriving at his destination in a fairly wettish condition. Nevertheless he was received, taken in, welcomed, embraced, in short, hired as butler. He served a mere three months, but ah, in those three months he served enough to last a lifetime. What did he not learn about the habits of the aristocracy at work and at play? About how to dust the statues of heroes of myth in a high-ceilinged salon, grovel to the steward and carry steaming soup to the table? But as with all things, his service came to an end. Back to the city, to the desk.

How he lived is something of a mystery. Isn't there a mystery to all lives, come to think of it? Isn't the shape of a life a question mark, with its initial optimistic curve, its gradual descent, and its diffident little point at the bottom, nodding farewell? Didn't our hero love questions? "Questions are usually more beautiful," he said, "more significant than their resolutions, which in fact never resolve them, are never sufficient to satisfy us, whereas from a question streams a wonderful fragrance."

They say he was like a child, so innocent and simple. But have you ever known an innocent, simple child who wrote a thousand and one hundred prose pieces? What did he think, our nominally childlike Walser, all those decades at the desk, rich in poverty, writing novels destined to feed his fireplace? Did he wish he had married a lovely lady with bosom and bustle and plumed hat, one of the festooned ladies adorning the cafés, or possibly a brown-legged child of the forest, a woodland dryad living on nuts and berries? One way or the other, did he picture himself dandling a bunch of babbling babes on his knees? Oh, I don't know. People expect authors to know too much. I know he wrote, "The best thing will be to beget a child and offer the product to a publisher, who's hardly likely to reject it."

Do you think he longed for solace and recognition? I suppose he did. Who doesn't? Am I right or am I right? But he was an aimless sort of fellow, like my badger. Aimless, aimful. A cheery sort of melancholic fellow. "Aimlessness," he wrote in his wee, indecipherable script, upon a scrap of paper originally wrapping his bakery rolls, "leads to the aim, while firm intentions often miss. When we strive too zealously, it may happen that our strivings harm us. I would advise speedy slowness or slow rapidity. Still, advice can't be more than advice." How abundantly correct, friend Walser of the buttonless waistcoat.

At last this fellow grew so melancholically confused that he was taken to the hospital by his sister, an upstanding lady whom I have woefully neglected in my story. Neglect is the literary fate, alas, of some quite worthy characters. He was examined, scrutinized, so to speak, by the holy priests, I mean the doctors. Did he want to go, you ask? Well of course he did, unless he really didn't. He had a genius for bowing to the inevitable. "In renunciation of every sort," said he, "I became a great artist."

He went, and there he stayed, among the madmen whose words were as bizarre as pomegranates. I confess it embarrasses me—my face is all red; lucky no one can see me writing—to bring him to such a pass. I didn't want my story to wind up this way but what can a helpless author do? I wanted him to be a literary grandee, his name on the wet, greedy lips of posterical readers. A madman they called him, a madman he became. Or behaved, anyway. And with his gentle, serviceable temperament, even in the hospital he served—the doctors, that is, who always need to employ patients. Which is not to say he never smiled. As he was overheard to murmur, "there are moments, after all, when one feels compelled to smile although gripped with horror."

That is the last we hear from young Walser, nearly old by this time. His lips, as they say, were sealed, like a nun's body. And why did he not continue to write his frivolous, leafy, bucolic, terrifying little questioning, earnest, dissembling, skeptical, merry and artifactical prose pieces? Surely they would grant him pencil and paper, even in a hospital? Perhaps he had no more to say. Perhaps they convinced him he was nuts? "Trot, trot, trot," he wrote in his last prose piece, not really the last, only so called. "What's with me? Have I gone a bit nuts? What's going to become of me?"

Some say he was in despair, some say he was happy. I don't say anything at all. I hope you don't think this unfair. I certainly wouldn't want to be thought unfair by anyone, most of all by a reader. I can tell you, since you clearly thirst for more information, that he said, "I think the best thing for me would be to sit in a corner and be silent."

Silently he died in the snow, as foretold in the beginning. (Editors, please note the full circle!) Walking in the snow, painfully he parted company from this life. For as he once confided, "It is a very painful thing, having to part company with what torments you." Some children found him, as they gamboled on the slope with their dog. "Ho, ho, what's this, a melancholic genius-author lying in the snow!" they cried, and the dog barked, but Walser the friendly could not stroke him anymore. He could only lie in the embrace of the snow angel his body made as it fell.

Perhaps the children were horrified at the sight, or perhaps not; one never can tell with children. If they were, so much the better: "Why should horror not grip us modern people, slightly? It seems to me that we do very much need to be woken up, to be given a shake." In their horror or in the elation of discovery, the little ones ran off to alert their plump rosy mother, busy making a dinner of roast lamb and potatoes with succulent Brussels sprouts bathed in drippy butter, her face all asweat, her hair awry. The dinner, as you can guess, was late that night. Her husband, a sturdy bald farmer with a conspicuous wart on his left cheek, was considerably put out as a result. Marital disharmony ensued in the cottage after the children were put to bed. The mother shed a tear for the poor old man in the snow, for all mothers have tender hearts. So did the servant girl, or scullery maid as she was called, weep for him, a plain creature, I have been told, but with the most delicate white fingers and moonlike fingernails.

"Just one of those loonies from down the mountain," the farmer said, more harshly than he should. "Stop your snivelling and carry out the ashes." A boorish, heartless fellow who had never read a line of our illustrious hero. No doubt if he had, he would have remembered: "At least we should learn to understand our fellow beings, for we are powerless to stop their misery, their ignominy, their suffering, their weakness, and their death."

And the dog? Well, the dog just barked, musing silently—for he was an intelligent dog, a brown and white Saint Bernard who, unlike his crude master, had read a bit of Walserian prose in a newspaper long ago—" 'You and others expected much from the modern age. But it's not turning out quite the way you imagined.' "

The dead fellow was not to rest there in the snow, though, that glistening fresh mountain snow worshiped by skiers far and wide, its flakes settling like weary flowers on his brow. He was to be resurrected. And oh, patient readers, what the critics said of him! They could not bear to leave him a question mark. Their analyses and speculations are far beyond my gifts to recount. Our hero, the snow prince, could he read what they surmise of him, would laugh his melancholic laugh and say, "I was sparsely read, both at home and abroad, but even so there are people who think highly of me because of this."

And now what more to add? For when an author has taken her hero up to his death and even beyond it, surely she has reached the end of her little treatise, and may be granted surcease from sorrow. "Life, after all, writes such beautiful works. Isn't that enough for us?"

Translation as a Species of Mime

Christopher Middleton

WHAT I HAVE TO SAY here will be partly chronicle and partly conjecture. First, I should like to say something about the moods and places in which I have translated Robert Walser's quite peculiar prose. Then I should like to ask some questions about where the imagination of a translator situates an author. To conclude, I shall make some speculative remarks on mime—on translating Walser as a performance with analogies in mime.

I was introduced to Robert Walser's writings in 1954 by Ernst Nef, at that time a student at the University of Zurich. I cannot remember if he showed me a book in the corridor outside the English seminar, or if he knocked at the window of my Zeltweg apartment and passed a book through the window when I opened it. Anyway I was immediately spellbound. I was spellbound by the unliterary, even counterliterary, character of the writing. Soon I wanted to see how this writing would look in English, so I started to translate "Der Spaziergang." At the same time I ransacked antiquarian bookshops and combed catalogs for original editions of his books, which were hard to find, but their rarity put ginger into the search.

When the translation was finished, I wrote to Carl Seelig—Walser's legal guardian—and he invited me to visit him. He showed me some manuscripts, including some of the microscripts. We drank tea and cognac. I remember how graciously he received me—and how he called the cognac a *surrogat* for an honorarium. This was in the spring of 1955 and Walser was still living. For me he was living not only in his books and in the Herisau asylum, but everywhere in Zurich and in the bony faces of young peasants I saw in the train to Sankt Gallen one day. People on the streets, normal or eccentric, suddenly assumed identities, all of which, however variously, I measured against my image of Robert Walser or of his characters. I thought I could perceive a *spiritus helveticus* lurking under all the orthodoxy. As a maker of mischief, my Walser was enveloping everyone in a Walserian aura. His prose was affecting me like Merlin in the Dark Ages, like Hermes in antiquity: my mind was projecting a spectacle in which all figures and events were essentially Walserian.

In 1961 and 1962 I spent some time teaching at the University of Texas at Austin. There I met another Englishman, Kim Taylor. Kim's wife, Aya, was Swiss-German. Aya read some Walser, on my suggestion, and so did Kim. In 1963, after I had returned to London, Kim wrote and asked me to translate some Walser pieces for the *Texas Quarterly,* a respectable university journal. Kim's friend Cyril Satorsky, an exuberant Polish lithographer from Cockney London, was commissioned to illustrate the translations. So it was in London that I translated "Pierrot," "Herren und Angestellte," and "Helblings Geschichte." The room where I worked in London, like the room in Zeltweg, looked out on a street, but I did not see any Robert Walsers walking in the street, because this was in south London. Besides, I never could fathom the English or put auras around them. Even then, I managed to tear the London sky apart and provide an English basis for the astonishing, furtive, dithering, anxious, micro-nihilist, and somehow Laforguian Helbling.

In 1966 I returned to Austin. One evening at supper I met a lady of (I believe) Austrian descent, who happened to be an editor at the University of Texas Press. She knew of Walser's work. She said, "Why not translate *Jakob von Gunten?* We'll publish your translation." I had recently finished translating a selection of Nietzsche's letters. The idea of translating *Jakob von Gunten* excited me. (It was only later that I heard that Max Brod once said, "Nach Nietzsche mußte Walser kommen.") I worked on the translation during the summer of 1967, in a very small house not far from the lake. Again I was looking out of a window. This time I was seeing a green mountain laurel bush, a conical cedar tree, and a roughly built wall of stones, limestone, with singing birds, perilous insects, and deadly snakes housed among them. When I translate, I work like a maniac. So I had soon finished a rough draft of *Jakob von Gunten.* Then, in company with a friend, Ann, I traveled south through Mexico to the Yucatán. We were hoping to find a totally strange world down there. I took with me my big notebook with Walser in it. We did not find any strangeness, and it was July in the tropics down there, people begging in the streets, sweating in hammocks, pyramids, and enormous pools into which princesses had once been toppled as a translator topples into an original text. Yet—in Merida, we found a hotel where D. H. Lawrence had stayed once. I scribbled revisions into the draft while lying on a big white bed. Later, I almost got drowned inside a shoal of goldfish off the coast of Isla Mujeres, but surfaced just in time to lunch off the flesh of a barracuda, later to finish the translation of *Jakob von Gunten.*

Back in the Yucatán, in a Merida hotel, Jakob and Herr Benjamenta are still traveling in search of adventures, in search of strangeness.

After a lapse of ten years I began to receive letters from Tom Whalen, a young American writer. In the forests of Arkansas he had discovered the Walser translations, and he was now reading them excitedly with his students in Louisiana. He visited me in Austin and persuaded me, over glasses of bourbon and after several games of pool, to translate some more short prose by Walser for a little magazine which he was co-editing. Walser subsequently appeared in New Orleans, to inspire several small authors, hardly more than infants, and some of them won prizes for their inspired writings. In 1980, I believe, I began to edit *Selected Stories.* Susan Sontag had spoken about Robert Walser to my English publisher, Michael Schmidt; at that time he knew nothing of my work translating Walser, for I had never thought to mention it. So, still in Austin, still in the small house, no, by now it was twice as big, but I still worked in my dusty room among the singing birds. I translated many more short prose pieces for the new book. I was still looking through the window at bushes and stones and great gliding black swallowtail butterflies.

The question arises: When you translate a writer's work, where is the writer? Obviously he is not there, in the place where you walk around or lie or sit, wringing your hands, translating what he wrote, murmuring the words. He is not to be seen through the window. He is not in Zurich, London, the Yucatán, or River Hills (Texas). Yet, afterwards, *he has been there.* Afterwards, I say, he has been there. He has been where you translated him. The work, and the passion of translating, place him there *afterwards.* Not physically, not altogether fantastically either, but in a sense that we invoke, in all honesty, when we say that rays of feeling surround, penetrate, and situate a particular object. This work of translation, as a kind of sensitive passion, unfolds through two successive moments of *Einfühlung.* First, obviously, you enter into a relationship with the writer as a presence which pervades the original text—a presence, that is, rather than a personality. Second, from that relationship, as your translation comes into the open, the writer as a presence is released into the place in which you worked—he steps out into it, that presence.

The bond which guarantees that presence in the place is now your translation, the text you have conducted out of the original. This means that the place, too, has changed. It has become the dwelling, transitory enough, of a presence which would not otherwise have been there. If, as some suppose, the signs in writing gather momentum only to defer final signification, then the act of translating, if not the final translation, carries the movement of deferral a stage further. The translator in the act is catching what the writer threw. Even if the catch is not a complete one, the act restores to presence the writer and to that writer's signs a glow of immediacy. If the act is formally completed in the translation as text, then there is reason to think that the translation is not a copy in another idiom but a creative transcription which has ensued upon a deep assimilation of the so-called spirit of the original text.

Perhaps this isolation of the act from the text is merely an attempt to put a limit around a field of variables. But in proposing that such a limit is not inconceivable, I mean to propose three ideas. (1) The catching of what is thrown is almost certain to be an asymptotic movement—no finality. (2) A circuitry between the signs establishes itself and ushers into imagination a presence, which, being imaginary, is manifold. (3) We arrive here in a borderline area—or a liminal area—where a concept like "magic" passes across from discourse about the imaginative power of the original into discourse about the act of translation. The magical is a thorny issue. Possibly discourse about translation is often inhibited by cautionary ideas about a creative magic so mysteriously enshrined in the original as to be unhoped for in the translation. The caution is mandatory. Despite crass or cunning pretensions on the translator's part, no translation substitutes for its original (least of all, perhaps, the truly vital translation). On the other hand, there can be, I think, in the ongoing act of translation, in the translator psychology, if you will, a belief which exhilarates the translator, bears him up, so that he feels he might be reweaving the original spell. The notion of magical process —*katexochen:* transrational—on both sides of the threshold between original and translation, is not as vain as it might often seem.

I am talking about the fertility of the spirit to which a writer may give birth in his writings. Into this fertility the translator inserts his own language roots. Latency and actuality, the imaginable to be converted and the translation text, somehow conspire. Somehow this spirit I have called "presence" fecundates places and persons, and translation can disseminate the spores, the signs, the traces, of that presence. Transformed into another language, the signs are set free to become otherwise fertile (in a different value code, which is the *proprium* of the translator's language). Becoming otherwise fertile, the converted signs modify the confines and constraints of the other language, so that English, say, may actually undergo a local change. At least, translation can re-situate its expressive range, once the Walser presence comes to life in it. This will happen as long as the other language learns to play by rules which had not been recognized, had only been latent. Well, but everyone acknowledges that translation negotiates intercourse, not just discourse, and that large mutations in cultural morphology may slowly occur as a result of the going-between that translation does—witness southwestern Europe during the twelfth century.

I mentioned play a moment ago. This is where Walser is eminently important to his admirers. I shall not go into particulars about Walser's ways of playfully, but also critically and often fiercely, subverting linguistic norms and behavioral codes. I shall not even explore the ways in which his "ludic" writings spring from and make hay with a defensive angst which is foisted upon civilized people by their desires and, no less, by their torturers. What I shall do is offer some conjectures on mime. It seems to me that quarrels about equivalence in theory of translation, not to mention arguments about possible varieties of literary translation, are inclined to be stymied by a failure to pass from notions of imitation to notions of mime.

The manifold presence (in my case, Walser) is released into a place and comes to dwell in it. This release is negotiated by an act of translation conceived as miming which is not imitation. In practice, imitation copies appearances. Imitation reproduces the self-evident, it takes a cast of the statue, it tries to replicate. Mime, on the other hand, formalizes a profound— and rebellious—need of the central nervous system, a need of which imitation is no more than a passing shadow. The need formalized in mime is a need to become one with that which is not-self, that which is utterly beyond what self is or was. Mime actualizes a desire for union with the "other." It embodies more than contact with the other, more than inclination toward it. This is not so odd, after all. We are mimes more often than we realize, from babyhood on. Our first efforts to speak are miming, rather than imitation; you only have to watch the face of a one-year-old to see that. A passionate love-relation is perhaps the first real step toward an authentically poetic or dramatic miming. Lovers will often mime one another. Lovers hope to achieve a fullness of insight into the other person. Each dreams that the other person is a living presence, not a mere skin-coated bundle of nervous and bodily reactions. (And so many loves founder because they are, at root, narcissistic.) Love is what makes the other person seem like a spirit who makes life happen, who inaugurates life. The beloved person means the beginning or the refreshing of life. Think what festive inaugurations they are, the moments that lovers enjoy. If the love is reciprocated, this miming for insight is countermimed. With imitation there is no such intense reciprocity. There is less *Einsicht,* as one might say in German, there is *Zweisicht* and *Vielsicht* instead, and these go on multiplying, never completing the clean mimetic circuit, only augmenting—as in Kafka—the labyrinth of angst. This does not imply that the clean mimetic circuit of reciprocity is less than catastrophic. Bland lovers can be boring ones. It does imply that the mime's ecstatic self-surrender, by which a naked insight into the other is achieved, is not part of the experience of imitation.

In the field of representations occupied by mime and imitation, the interval between them may be no more than a hair's breadth, or it may be greater. Both are, inescapably, modes of representation. Yet with imitation you recognize the original through its representation and judge whether the imitation is good or poor by measuring it against the original. The original is what you are reminded of. With mime, certain traces of the original may be implied in the act, but the act itself is originative. If the act is powerfully originative, the traces may be reduced to a mere ghostly scaffolding.

This, I realize, is an as yet insufficiently considered distinction. To suggest the scope of it, rather than grappling with Aristotle and his heirs, I shall furnish a small but extreme instance. At lunch in a leafy arbor on a hillside near Itschnach east of Zurich in 1956, one of my fellow guests was a deaf-mute, in his early twenties, an engaging and high-spirited person. He had learned to simulate Swiss-German speech patterns, several, and despite the oddity of his sounds he was able to get by, even amusingly so. After lunch, urged by our hostess and other guests, he stood on the terrace tiles and showed us how a hatted middle-aged man might trundle to his place of work. The showing was, to some extent, an imitation of something quite commonplace—but it differed in kind from the simulation audible in his speech. The performance had an outline and distinctness that set it apart, it was sui generis. It projected an image that surpassed mere impersonation. It had a quiddity that was all its own. The energy blocked on the level of speech had been conducted into another area, that of the deaf-mute's motor-muscular system. His act of miming, with its intense empathic hyperbole, set *this* hatted man's trundling altogether apart. The act condensed all rigmaroles, revised and reframed all routines, to project a creation as singularly "inscaped" as anything by Chaplin or Marceau.

What does a mime do? He imitates, yes, but not the actions, gestures, idio-syncrasies of one individual, isolable, human or animal subject. Rather, he takes possession of a total structure by bringing countless small and subtle perceptions into an imaginative configuration. This distinction in effect sub-ordinates all imitation, subordinates it to a spellbinding, independent, and creative action. That action has an air of being its own principle, and of being positive, as opposed to derived or secondary as an imitation is. And surely it is the "absolute" aesthetic and the coherent style of his performance that distinguishes a creative mime. So imitation is only his sketch. What's more, once his synthesis is varied enough, profound enough, he distances himself from the integral image he has created. Next, out of the aura provided by the distance achieved, he leaps into life with a performed "total structure." Technically, the breathing matters most—and the breathing is a matter most intimate. With the breathing, an essential image springs into the mime's whole body and actively occupies it as a breath of life. For a translator, an essential image springs into his language to animate it, often as a voice or grouping of voices. A translator's body-mind is, after all, his language. Voice—character and quality—is altogether crucial in literary translation and not only in poems. What is language, when all is said and done, without voice?

Two more thoughts. (1) For a mime, the key to his performance is the rhythm of his breathing (as for a dancer). The rhythm of his breathing is the ghostly system through which his essential image is channeled, to become the dynamic of his gestures, his individual body articulated as motion. For the translator, this breathing is the syntax which makes the words ring true. Without the right syntax, even the rightest words can lack appropriate bonding. (2) The mime seems to exaggerate. In motion or motionless, his body projects the dynamic of his image in hyperbolic ways. Why this hyper-bole? Does expressive language have to be exorbitant, as Gottfried Benn once proposed? Does hyperbole, as Mallarmé conjectured, track the true oddity or profile of a spirit which would otherwise choose to remain mute? I cannot say. But I do know that in the sacred miming dances of central and south India, this hyperbolic expression is required, required by the myth which is danced and by the veteran dance instructors.

Even the tiniest children, learning the temple dances, are disciplined to quell their mortal pride and to express humbly—in hyperbole—the satisfactions of divine desire, *Ananda.* Without the exaggerated gestures, without the hyperbolic facial expressions, the myth would remain indistinct, and so would the gods that the myth invokes. The god being danced does move as humans do, but his movements and gestures are made doubly distinct. The double distinctness projects all the distance the god preserves in the very midst of his dancing immediacy. The distance sustains, it would seem, the numinous. It is precisely the distance of the numinous that calls for the hyperbolic gestures, which make, as it were, the points and edges of the numinous perceptible under and through its aura, like the peaks of a mountain range (to adapt Walter Benjamin's description of aura). One might also suppose that the distance has to be sustained in order that it should absorb the shock—the mortal danger—that divinity would otherwise present.

There are relations, I think, between mime so conceived and the task of translation. There is at least a workable analogy here. As the mime performs hyperbolically the distant god, so too does the translator perform the presence he divines in the original text. The dancing mime's breath is matched by the translator's syntax—syntax, the nonapparent part of language, as Mallarmé said. As for hyperbole, it comes into play as the translator raises into profile the animating impulse, the speech-as-play in Walser's case, which fashions the text. Sometimes one has to lift up this impulse, having sensed it fathoms down, higher than Walser might perhaps himself have done, but with tact. Why? Because Walser like any writer was unaware of himself as a spirit (or "god" in the Indian analogy), let alone as a presence. He was self-aware in quite another way—as an incorrigible, fragmentary, impecunious, mischievous, or forlorn person. Here, presumably, is a domain of high risk. The translator responds to a spirit. Believing that he perceives it, he performs it. He thinks and laughs and wrestles with a spirit as language. Moreover, in translating Robert Walser, a very trickster, an architect of liminalities, you have to be keenly mindful of the iridescent switchings of his language-gestures—one moment subverting stereotypes, and the next embracing them, though coyly, or fiercely; one moment distant, and the next point blank.

This spirit, this manifold configuration in all its mobility, which the translator tries to mime, is of course not identical with the spirit he performs, or hopes to voice. Precisely that discrepancy is the area of risk which provokes the translator as mime to grapple with the manifold, now insightfully, now blindly. A translation can only achieve so much, no more, of a manifold spirit which persistently disseminates itself. The spirit a translator hopes to have voiced is never more than one that has been there and probably got away. It is fugitive, it is afterward. "Anyway," as Vladimir Holan put it in his poem "A Night with Hamlet,"

> . . . that is the moment
> when you are still expecting guests
> and they're already here, for they came earlier.

Five Letters from the Brothers Quay
and Stills from The Comb

2 December 1988

DEAR SUSAN,

There are four Walserites on this train from Zurich à Basel. We have been with Herren Frölich, Echte, und Morlang—in Walserien white chocolate that melts down to Mister Happy, Mister Real, and Mr. Longer, and that's another reason we're not making the translation—UND SO— this is why we're writing to you. They've told us that you have a publisher at work on your translations and of course we're impatient to see this book. Can you tell us if it's true you have a publisher, and when you think it will be published? Or better yet, do you have fotocopies of these translations and are any of these the Microgrammes? We are headed for Basel because a German friend of ours has a Swiss friend making decors for one of his theater pieces. When we talked in August to both of them we of course mentioned that we were preparing *Jakob von Gunten* for Channel 4 London. The Swiss fellow's mouth dropped because he was making the decors for *Jakob* for a Swiss friend of his in Basel—which is why we're on the train to Basel. So we've coincided the Basel trip with a visit to the [Carl Seelig] Stiftung [and Robert Walser Archives] where we heard you were in residence for some time. We gather that since everyone there wears glasses, you must too. So—please write to us with details of your book—we four are Keith Griffiths, colleague and Producer; Alain Passes, Writer; and the Brothers Quay, who would like to perpetrate this onto film.

Gebr. Quay, Keith Griffiths, A. Passes.

23 December 1988

Dear Susan B. and Tom W.

Carumba!! What a fabulous package to have found elegantly propped up on our 3rd floor landing on the eve of Christmas Eve. Bless the English postal system, and grand himalayou identical bows from the two of us here in Kilburn where we thank you from the bottom of our little wooden hearts for this immense cadeau. A flurry of questions are in order, but maybe it's best we obscenely swoon into these pages. So we salute you both and wish you the very warmest Christmas Greetings filled with unending flurries of snow and snowdrifts to bruise our lips against if only as sleepwalkers.

Our very best to you both and New Orleans

Quays

20 March 1990

Dear Susan and Tom

We've been silent and we're sorry!! The filming goes well but despairingly slow and for weeks upon weeks we exit, our foreheads so low and hunch-backed, but it also seems to be going well, but one's always working in a sort of incompleteness—that's to say, lack of sound effects, voice, and music which gives these naked images a thicker orchestration (god, how we need thick orchestrations!). So one has to navigate these months to come on the thin drool of imagining-it-all-working and "hope."

Listen, you two, could you not find a way to send copies of everything you've written on Robert W.? We're hungry and insatiable. The interview with Bernhard [Echte] and Werner [Morlang] was marvelous as was the little essay.

Have you any thoughts on the "quality" of an "imagined" voice for Walser—we're thinking of a voiceover voice? For instance, an "Appen-zeller" voice, we were told, would sound quite risible. But, then, should it have a slight "woodenness" to it? And then, how to score an element of the fairy-tale, but one edged in darkness.

Is the *Räuber-Roman* absolutely impossible to translate? Can you be challenged?

Warmest regards

Quays

17 June 1990

Dear Susan and Tom

How fine to return home and find stuffed, hammered and powerfully wedged through our economical mailslot, a handsome package from you "duo" which could only promise further "Walseriana" for our poor deprived and hungry souls and I don't think we've ever begun to thank you enough for your last fabulous bundle of "Walserings." So once again deep watery baroque flourishing bows and scrapings so beautifully low you could almost willingly drown. It comes—your package, as we go into our final two weeks and the film *must* be completed—Channel 4 is screaming, so is Keith—even us a little, but we are pleased (in the most petrified and smallish way) so far, and naturally on the desperate hunt for a title which, for us, can "evoke" all the Walser we've read (and for all the Walser we might not ever be able to read) —mindful of the fact that this short film (now to be 15 mins) was originally meant to be a pilot for our *Jakob von Gunten* feature film project and *is* power-fully informed by a "Lisa," and a sort of fairy-taleish "Jakob" and then again we just went off wildly for a long walk through Walserland willy nilly and trespassingly happily scoring a moment here and a moment there, plus weav-ing a few silly ideas of our own—hopefully you won't see the stretch marks.

Basta!!

Quays

10 September 1990

Dear Susan and Tom

Thank you for your letter and the "brief report" from the front.

We just completed the dubbing of the sound for the new film and it's now all over—only the gruel of grinding out a good print which always takes up so much time. The details are as follows:

TITLE: "The Comb"

SUBTITLES: "From the Museums of Sleep"

           Fairytale Dramolet to Scenes and texts by Robert Walser

TIME: 18 mins.

      Black and White and Colour

      Live Action/Puppet Animation

All the very best from us two here

                  the Quays

(EDITORS' NOTE: *The Comb* premiered at the London Film Festival on 20 November 1990.)

Walking Wounded:
The Moral Vision of Robert Walser

John Biguenet

A CONNOISSEUR OF exquisite moral dilemmas, Robert Musil, in his review of Robert Walser's *Geschichten* (1914), reduces his complaints about the collection to a single formulation: "In sum, although people will not actually say so, it seems to me that what will irritate them deep down is that these stories lack ethical depth."[1] On the other hand, Musil's fellow Austrian and anti-fascist Elias Canetti is ready to canonize the Swiss writer and "madman": "One cannot read him without being ashamed of everything that was important to one in external life, and thus he is a peculiar saint. . . ."[2] What are we to make of an author who seems to one great moralist an ethical dilettante and to another a venerable martyr?

Walser himself is too truthful to be of much help in sorting out such contradiction. Late in 1917, for example, Walser responds to a letter in which Hermann Hesse alludes to his own wartime duties:

> Word is going around that Robert Walser is leading the noble life of a dreamer, idler, and petit bourgeois, instead of "fighting." The politicians are dissatisfied with me. But what do people really want? And what great or good aims can be achieved by articles in newspapers and magazines? When the world is out of joint, the efforts of twenty thousand Hamlets are no use at all, or precious little. Every day I read a little French, because it is such a pretty language. Does that make me a rascal? And then I can't help walking around every day, a bit, in the winter countryside. Does that prove I'm indifferent to a great deal of suffering? I believe you understand better than anyone why I like to live a quiet and thoughtful life.[3]

It is not difficult to understand how a moral monumentalist like Musil might grow impatient with such an attitude. But neither does it seem incomprehensible that a writer like Canetti, nearer the end of our bloodstained century, might discover an ineluctable ethos in Walser's gentle words. Canetti, in fact, tells us what he has learned: "I am not yet even a human being."[4] Who is this writer who teaches such a rigorous morality?

No one speaks of the death of Robert Walser without mentioning its circumstances: on Christmas Day, 1956, the unremembered Swiss writer collapsed while taking a walk on the snowy slopes near the asylum at Herisau where he had passed the last twenty-three years of his life. Improvised out of his private tropes—the melancholy of a holiday afternoon remedied by a walk among the ordinary marvels of nature—no more fitting death could have been prepared for a man who had constructed an entire aesthetic out of strolling.

That a writer whose long sketch "The Walk" has been hailed finally by even *Time* as a masterpiece of twentieth-century literature should die forgotten in a madhouse will not surprise Walser's readers. His taste ran to the undistinguished. "We don't need to see anything out of the ordinary. We already see so much."[5] And nothing was less extraordinary than himself. "The striking thing about me is that I am a very ordinary person, almost exaggeratedly so. I am one of the multitude, and that is what I find so strange. I find the multitude strange and always wonder: 'What on earth are they all doing, what are they up to?' I disappear, yes, disappear in the mass."[6]

The ordinary, though, need not be the simple. Christopher Middleton suggests in "The Picture of Nobody," an essay published just after its subject's death, that Walser "seems to be a stranger to the realm of ideas." Rather, he "brings a new world of sensibility, an unmediated vision of experience, an image of reality seen without the interference of a concept."[7] Walser is full of emotion that is capable of expressing itself with a quiet (and sometimes quirky) eloquence, but as with such poets as Rainer Maria Rilke and Heinrich Heine, the emotion and its inspiration survive the mind's consideration. As Walser delicately puts it in "Thoughts on Cezanne," "The things he contemplated became eloquent, and the things to which he gave shape looked back at him as if they had been pleased, and that is how they look at us still."[8]

If to develop a sensibility means to discover one's humanity, then Middleton and perhaps Canetti are right. Walser's talent may be verbal, but his genius lies in the humaneness of his vision. " 'Is the peacock not a little uneasy? Does this Adult Gentleman who goes about so beautifully not feel in any way whatsoever concerned when he sees dirty speckled little children? It seems to me that no mature man ought to want to appear all elegance as long as there are children who have no finery to wear at all.' "[9] Had Walser stopped with this indictment of bourgeois vanity and indifference, Musil might well have championed him. But Walser always tells the truth, the whole truth. And thus his humanity is evident not only in posing such a question but also in recognizing that we, poor humans, are incapable of answering. "This is of course asking too much. And if anyone were to wait content and enjoying life until finally the world should contain no more poor miserable people, then he would be waiting until the gray impenetrable end of all time, and until the ice-cold empty end of the world, and by then all joy and life itself would in all probability be utterly gone from him" (97). One begins to sense Walser's wisdom about the human predicament and to understand Canetti's homage to his morality. But in what is such a morality grounded?

Earlier in "The Walk," from which the preceding meditation is drawn, Walser echoes the opening lines of Dante's *Divina commedia,* when the poet prepares to undertake the long walk from hell to paradise. Walser confesses that " 'Not long ago I came into this region out of cold, forlorn, and narrow circumstances, inwardly sick, completely without faith, without confidence or trust, without any finer sort of hope, a stranger to the world and to myself, and hostile to both' " (66). But walking about this "wandering curious planet," he discovers the "flowering present":

... I dreamed of nothing but this place itself. All other fantasies sank and vanished in meaninglessness. I had the whole rich earth immediately before me, and I still looked only at what was most small and most humble. With gestures of love the heavens rose and fell. I had become an inward being, and I walked as in an inward world; everything outside me became a dream; what I had understood till now became unintelligible. I fell away from the surface, down into the fabulous depths, which I recognized then to be all that was good. What we understand and love understands and loves us also. I was no longer myself, was another, and yet it was on this account that I became properly myself. In the sweet light of love I realized, or believed I realized, that perhaps the inward self is the only self which really exists. The thought seized me: "Where would we poor people be, if there was no earth faithful to us? What would we have, if we did not have this beauty and this good? Where would I be, if I was not here? Here I have everything, and elsewhere I would have nothing." (90)

This is no simple moral system to castigate improprieties. Rather, it is the ecstatic mysticism of a Saint Francis. Whence does Walser's authority arise? From the unblinking contemplation of the present, this moment in this place. Middleton is quite right to call him a stranger to ideas. Walser allows no metaphor, no concept, no system of belief to intervene between him and the world. He declines the veil of conventional perceptions, the blindfold of accepted explanations. The questions upon which his morality is built are simple to the point of stupidity. His answers are as obvious, and as certain, as the ground we walk upon. I will not be so foolish as to offer an explication of the mystical. But I will suggest, with Canetti, that if we are to become those mythical creatures of whom we read so much—those human beings—we must read Walser.

NOTES

1   Robert Musil, "The *Stories* of Robert Walser," in *Robert Walser Rediscovered,* ed. and trans. Mark Harman (Hanover: University Press of New England, 1985), 141.

2   Elias Canetti, *The Human Province,* trans. Joachim Neugroschel (New York: Continuum, 1978), 229.

3   Robert Walser, "Prose," trans. Christopher Middleton, *Lowlands Review* 3

(1976): 15-16; rpt. above, pp. 28-29.

4 Canetti, 230.

5 Robert Walser, "A Little Ramble," trans. Tom Whalen, in *Selected Stories* (New York: Farrar, Straus and Giroux, 1982), 31.

6 Robert Walser, "Helbling's Story," trans. Christopher Middleton, ibid., 32.

7 Christopher Middleton, "The Picture of Nobody," *Revue des langues vivantes* 24 (1958): 405-6.

8 Robert Walser, "Thoughts on Cezanne," trans. Christopher Middleton, in *Selected Stories,* 190.

9 Robert Walser, "The Walk," trans. Christopher Middleton, ibid., 96; hereafter cited parenthetically.

Reading Geschwister Tanner

Peter Bichsel

ON CHRISTMAS DAY 1956 Robert Walser was found dead in the snow above Herisau. He had died on a solitary walk. Robert Walser was and remains a legend, a sad fairy tale. His death is a poet's death, that of the poet he himself described fifty years before, at the age of twenty-eight in his first great book, *Geschwister Tanner* (The Tanner Siblings): "Perhaps Sebastian collapsed here out of an exhaustion too great to be borne any longer. He had never been too terribly strong. He always walked with a stoop, as though he couldn't bear to stand up straight, as though it hurt him to hold his back and head erect. Looking at him made one feel that life and its cold demands had been too much for him."

Whether we like it or not, the young Walser described his own death here. I am convinced he knew that writing is a serious business and that one can't make things up with impunity. This frightens him, too. He never pins himself down when he's writing, he takes things back, offers variants; he's afraid to put names to things; he resorts to humor, which perhaps he doesn't have, but which he needs.

His Sebastian in *Geschwister Tanner* is an unsuccessful poet—and not only unsuccessful, but bad as well—untalented and vain. This is how he's presented to us, the readers, and we have no trouble understanding the author's ridicule of him. Simon's brother Kaspar, the painter (Simon is the real "I" of the novel, though it's not in first person), tells the conceited Sebastian with regard to his poems: "Leave that for when you're fifty." But fifty is when Simon—who after all is none other than Robert Walser himself—gives up writing forever.

Not Simon but his sister Hedwig stands up for the unsuccessful Sebastian: "If I were a painter, I'd truly be brother to a poet." Robert Walser's brother Karl was a successful painter, and he was his friend. So Walser had it better than Sebastian. And the sister Hedwig, who corresponds to Walser's real sister, also says: "Poets are so easily hurt; oh, one should never hurt poets."

So which should I believe, Walser's ridicule of the would-be author or his sympathy for him? For, whether it's his brother speaking or the sister, it's really always Walser. Ridicule of whom, sympathy for whom? Surely ridicule of himself, as well as sympathy for himself, for Robert Walser.

Simon decides not to inform the police about Sebastian, who has frozen to death: "I don't want to notify anyone. Nature looks down upon her dead man, the stars sing softly above his head, and the night birds screech; this is the best music for someone who no longer hears and feels."

From the dead man's jacket Simon takes a notebook containing poems which, bad as they are, he intends to deliver to the nearest publisher. He tosses them into the mailbox, having written on the cover: "The poems of a young man found frozen to death in the forest, for publication, if possible."

It seems to me that with the publication of *Geschwister Tanner* we once again toss the poems into the mailbox with the humble hope that it will be "possible."

Possible is a key word for Walser. It signifies not only the possibility, the subjunctive, the alternative—it means much less than this, and more: the polite query coupled with an apology for the intrusion. (Another writer from Biel of the same generation used this word as well, though in a different sense: the clown Grock. A coincidence? In any case, let me point this co-incidence out.)

Who was this Walser? Everyone who reads him will argue this point with everyone else. Was he intelligent, educated, refined? He was. Was he naive, prejudiced, bourgeois, petit-bourgeois? He was. Was he insane? This is probably the only thing Walser fans can and will agree on: no, he wasn't insane. He was a gentle, cautious, quiet, reserved, sensible, reasonable author. He demands nothing, he simply apologizes. Simon is apparently lazy when it comes to work, but it's not a point he insists on, he apologizes for it. Who was Robert Walser? Anyone who tries to answer this question with his biography willfully avoids answering it. There is doubtless no other literary oeuvre of this size as autobiographical, line for line, as Walser's. The real events behind it can be traced for the most part; yet, oddly, this proximity of biography and work gets in the way of understanding the real person.

But all of us who argue out of love for him will agree on this: a poor devil, a sad life. And he, the writer, was determined to move us. He succeeded in this: Walser admirers tend not particularly to like one another, out of jealousy, but they agree with each other.

One mentions his biography only out of helplessness. Work and biography alike tell us blessed little about him. And this is what's made him a legend.

All the same: Robert Walser was born in Biel in 1878. In 1894 his mother died. In 1895 he completed his apprenticeship at the Bernische Kantonalbank in Biel. From 1896 to 1906 he lives in Zurich, working without much enthusiasm at various jobs, and sometimes not at all, and to his own astonishment survives. We have to imagine the novel *Geschwister Tanner* as taking place in this Zurich; he wrote it in Berlin in 1906—very quickly, in my opinion. He lived with his brother Karl Walser there, not yet the famous painter but all the same a prominent member of the Berlin bohemia. For the insiders, Robert Walser was no longer an unknown quantity. He had already published a small book that admittedly had failed to raise a furor among the reading public but still was popular with insiders: *Fritz Kochers Aufsätze* (Fritz Kocher's Essays), a collection of very short prose pieces that formed the basis of his reputation as a writer of short prose.

Walser always remained a short-prose writer, and his novels were written using the techniques of short prose, without real structure, and with a great deal of trust in the patient and good-natured reader.

It's my impression that with *Geschwister Tanner* Walser wrote what amounts to his residence permit for the Berlin bohemia. I mean by this that the motive for its writing was first and foremost an external one—simply to bring off a book, to produce something, to do something, to want to do something, to become involved in something. Walser does this with a great deal of trust in his own abilities and with a great deal of trust that once again something, quite by chance, will occur to him: a sprinter strong enough to maintain his same technique for the long stretches.

The book begins like this: Simon walks into a bookstore, asks to speak to the owner and convinces him, with a loftily enthusiastic speech about the book trade, to offer him employment. The reader soon knows (as does Walser) that it won't work out. Walser writes this enthusiastic speech *against* himself, as it were, and it is followed directly by his disappointed farewell speech to the bookseller, his apology. (I have a son who often switches jobs; I love him for the enthusiasm he works up and expresses at great length each time he takes on a new post. As for the rest, he benefits from the fact that I have read and love Walser.)

But Walser's biography? I'm all for taking the one offered to us by the young (twenty-eight-year-old) Walser. Of all the Walser biographies I know, this is the best one, and the only one written in ignorance of the whole course of Walser's life. Did he write out his life in advance? A sort of kismet? By no means: Walser knew himself, that's all. Walser had no desire to become anything, do anything, change anything. And, as a moralist, he knew what happens to people who live the way he did.

Perhaps it would be appropriate to mention here Kafka's famous sentence about *Geschwister Tanner:* "and in the end nothing comes of him except that he provides amusement to the reader." Yes, Kafka liked Walser. This is important to Walser's propagandists. They think they need a chief witness. But the original quote and the circumstances surrounding it are much more Walserian: in 1909 Kafka writes to Ernst Eisner that he knows *Jakob von Gunten* (the third of Walser's novels within two years). Kafka describes it as "a good book. I haven't read the other books, for which you are partly to blame since, in spite of my advice, you did not want to buy *The Tanner Siblings.* Simon is, I think, a character in that book. Doesn't he run around everywhere, up to his ears in happiness, and in the end nothing comes of him except that he provides amusement to the reader?"[1]

Apparently Kafka hadn't read the book, but he'd heard about it. I'll even assume people read passages aloud to him—Franz Blei, perhaps—for the statement that nothing comes of Simon except that he gives the reader pleasure is surprisingly accurate. As for the "up to his ears in happiness," Kafka doubtless would have revised his opinion after having read the book, but what for me is even more surprising and accurate is the other sentence, the one that's never quoted: "Simon is, I think, a character in that book."

That he is. The title of the book is an unkept promise. It isn't about siblings at all; for Walser this would be far too novelistic an endeavor and would destroy his prose. The book is devoted, almost monomaniacally, to a single person among his siblings. Who are these siblings?

A brother Kaspar (in reality Karl Walser) who is a painter—a fascinating painter ("The next morning the painter unpacked his portfolio of land-scapes, and an entire fall tumbled out of it, then a winter"). A brother Klaus, the successful bourgeois who worries about things and is constantly reproachful (Simon's bad conscience); his real name was Hermann and he taught geography in Berne. A brother Emil whose real name was Ernst and who really was interned in Waldau Sanatorium. And the dearly beloved Hedwig, really the dearly beloved Lisa who was a teacher in Bellelay.

Simon lives among his siblings with a bad conscience: a bad conscience with regard to his brother Klaus, a righteous man who reproaches his brother (these are reproaches the author himself thinks up, that he is capable of thinking up); a bad conscience with regard to the brother in the sanatorium who's less well off than he is; a bad conscience with regard to the self-sacrificing, utterly loving Hedwig; and great admiration for his brother Kaspar, a real painter.

Walser makes up everything the siblings say. They speak in Walser's register—both sides of the conversation—and it's touching the way he occasionally has them praise him and describe him affectionately. That's the woman's job in his book, to describe him affectionately. Simon is embedded in his siblings. In fact, this seems to have been true for Walser as well. But here Walser elevates it to the realm of the fairy tale: everything succeeds, even if it succeeds in sadness and poverty.

Geschwister Tanner is a fairy tale, and for me the most astonishing one ever written, since no other fairy tale takes place so close to reality. It's the only fairy tale that could actually be produced in the real world—if fairy tales can be produced at all, or in Walser's words: "if possible."

One fairy tale I'm sure Walser knew and loved and was impressed by is Andersen's "The Little Match Girl." This fairy tale, too, takes place close to reality; for Walser it became Simon's tale, and there's a beautiful varia-tion on it near the end of the book—a winter's tale. Did it also become the tale of Walser himself?

The biography of Walser? The fairy tale of Walser? When he wrote this book he was living in the midst of the Berlin bohemia of the turn of the century. Bruno Cassirer, an influential man, was his publisher. He may have been a starving poet—his great productivity during this period was related to his financial worries—but he was neither unimportant nor unknown. There are also reports that the two Walser brothers raised quite a ruckus in this bohemia. But in this matter, too, I'd rather stick to Walser's book, which bears witness to something different: it is the book of an unhappy poet, of a man with a heavy burden, and it is already—and this is what's moving—the book of an old man trying to write about a young one.

Perhaps with this book Walser wrote in advance what he might have written later. Perhaps he gave up writing later because he'd already done it. "A poet who doesn't love life is lost," he once wrote. Perhaps he wrote the description of his life before the fact because he knew he wouldn't have the strength to love life long enough.

In not a single line by Walser, who wrote an enormous amount in this period, do I get the impression of a passionate writer who felt a compulsion to write. Almost every line contains the melancholy undertone: one could also give it up.

Though Walser scholars may spend years on the question of why he gave up writing at fifty, I'm more fascinated by the question of why he didn't do it sooner—this question has no answer, which makes it more important.

Back to Kafka's oft-quoted sentence. It is the chance remark of a man who knew the book only from hearsay. But Kafka's sentence has a double meaning. I assume that Kafka later read *Geschwister Tanner,* and I'm sure he had no reason to take back his statement afterward. It's true that almost nothing whatever happens in *Geschwister Tanner*—a bit of life, that's all; and there's no story in this book that might drive the reader on—all that's driving the book is language. But in the past few weeks I've pestered all my friends with *Geschwister Tanner;* I had an uncontrollable urge to talk about it. The book isn't suspenseful, not suspenseful at all, but it makes one want to talk about it, and everyone who hears it described—like Kafka—finds others to pass it along to. Why? Perhaps because there's nothing being told, or because everything is *only* being told, the book makes me think not "story" but "life." Someone whose life isn't worth recounting tells the story of his life.

I'm very grateful Walser was discovered. It's not something that could have been taken for granted, since you really do have to be disposed toward him from the beginning if you want to read him. He needs the reader's trust in advance because he's too quiet to solicit it himself.

Joseph Viktor Widmann, author and an editor at the Berlin newspaper *Der Bund,* whose feuilleton section was internationally acclaimed at the time, introduced Walser's first publication in the paper in 1898: "A twenty-year-old office worker in Zurich, Robert Walser, who left school at the age of fourteen to become a clerk and thus was unable to profit from any regular sort of higher education, recently sent the editor of this paper a notebook containing approximately forty lyric poems, his first."[2]

Widmann, a sensitive connoisseur of literature, had discovered an important author. Franz Blei became aware of Walser through this publication—of poems, by the way, that today seem perhaps to reflect all too clearly the prevailing tastes of the time—but Blei discovered more in them, remained faithful to Walser and did a great deal for him.

Something surprising: the very first sentences about Walser (Widmann's) determine the tone in which the entire Walser legend is told to this day: the petty clerk who writes poems, the naive talent, the man from outside the literary sphere. I can imagine that he himself didn't mind this misunderstanding. He knew quite well that he was much more consciously literary and wrote far more skillfully than people realized.

Still, even these lines of mine cannot shake off the tone of this legend. Legend and oeuvre have become so closely entwined that it would be a suppression of information not to pass them on together. I've been called on many times to comment on Walser. I never have. This will be the only time I do so: here and now.

For when all is said and done, Walser belongs to me alone. This, too, is a feeling that Walser fans share, and which makes it so difficult for them to communicate. Everyone who reads Walser discovers him—and discovers him for the first time, and for all time. I discovered him in 1954, in a second-hand shop. I spelled out his name without knowing there was anyone else who knew him. I didn't even know he was Swiss. He was still alive in 1954, but I didn't know this either. I even remember that it was 1964 before I learned he had died in Herisau. In 1964 I visited his monument there—people are quick with monuments.

But, as I said before, I'm not the only one Walser belongs to completely. Walser probably doesn't have any critical readers: either one goes along with him or one leaves him alone. You have to identify yourself with him, with his grief, his melancholy, with his often peculiar philosophy, and you have to get used to the fact that it's not really stories you're reading but sentences, not three hundred pages but thousands of sentences, almost every one of them worth quoting, self-contained and beautiful sentences—the reader's pleasure.

Under these conditions it's hardly possible to analyze Walser; it's difficult to decide when he's being serious, what's meant as humor, where he's presenting his own opinions and where he's quoting. And even in the places where one could do this, it wouldn't be right to him, for he has no interest in such analysis, what matters is the work as a whole. The key word here is irony—it may well be present in Walser's work, but it can't be localized. He can be funny, terribly funny and playful, but still we're afraid of doing wrong by him with our laughter.

There's really only one voice in Walser's work. No matter who's speaking—whether it's Simon, the men in the copyist's bureau and employment agency, a brother, or the kind, beautiful woman—they all speak in Walser's tone. This, it seems to me, is the technique of estrangement we find in fairy tales. No matter who's doing the talking in a fairy tale: in the end it's always the gentle storyteller's voice that speaks, the voice of the mother.

There are hardly any real conversations in Walser. Walser's characters (Walser himself) speak in extended monologues. They make speeches to one another—very written-sounding speeches—and these monologues comprise the story itself. On one hand this is certainly a skillful, deliberate trick, but above all it creates an apologetic tone: it's with a bad conscience one begins a monologue.

If one wanted to reduce *Geschwister Tanner* to a single theme, it would be the idler's grand lament over his own uselessness, the helpless apologia of a man who is actually something of a moralist, who is driven to work by his conscience, but whose will is unable to obey it and often stubbornly refuses to try—a quite up-to-date theme. (I myself learn to understand my son a little better when I listen to Simon, for Simon forces me to love him—and thus I learn to love my son.)

A second theme—and I think the author hardly notices it, it shows up of its own accord—is that of the woman: the tall, beautiful, strong, all-understanding woman: deliverance. Women provide Simon with a place to live without rent, they lend him money, let him eat without paying at a restaurant; he offers them his complete submissiveness and now and then lets them figure in sadomasochistic daydreams. But Simon is anything but a ladies' man; he doesn't really, and doesn't only, want women's hearts, he wants their compassion: deliverance. By means of this, by means of the woman, he might become someone. And the book ends in the anticipation of this fulfillment. Of course the reader knows, as does Walser himself, that nothing would come of it if the story were to go on—that's doubtless why it breaks off where it does—and so, by the last sentences of the book, everything becomes a fairy tale, a winter's tale.

There's a third thing Simon and Walser have in common. Simon goes for walks, and as a walker is no idler but an almost professional, compulsive walker. No other theme appears so consistently in Walser's work, and one of his most beautiful stories is entitled "The Walk." No one else can describe a walk in its own right the way he does. For him, it's neither a matter of wandering nor of observation. The things around him are almost fortuitous, they have no names, the trees are called trees, the flowers flowers, the lake lake. (In this case it's unquestionably the Zürichsee, Lake Zurich, and the region where he goes walking, on the Zürichberg, can be traced with a bit of biographical research. People's curiosity about this is understandable, but it doesn't take one far. Walser's landscape is always just somewhere or other, his walks are walks in their own right. When all is said and done, he isn't writing landscape at all, he's writing walk.)

Walking became the rhythm of Walser's life, and Walser writes in the rhythm of his own heartbeat like a blues singer. His entire oeuvre is one great, long walk, and if *Geschwister Tanner* has a structure, a construction at all, it is the principle of the walk: one thing leads into the next, the themes appear before the author without his help, so to speak, without his having to move at all. He often describes things—a farmhouse, an angry dog he's afraid of—in such a way as if they were going to take on meaning for the story, then sweeps them aside with, for example: "Onward!" And this means nothing else but "leaving something behind." The narrator, the walker, never deliberately approaches anything, but he always deliberately leaves things behind.

"Onward"—that is the gesture of the walk. It shows up in many forms in Walser's work: "Then it was Italy's turn . . . then England's. . . ." Or: "It was Klara Agappaia." Or: "The next day, Klaus was gone again."

Now, these aren't really typical Walser quotes. The typical Walser is the man of the interior monologue, the walker making speeches to himself, and the cold little sentences scattered about like "It was Klara Agappaia" are when he remembers he has feet. When Simon meets this wonderful, strange, singular woman again, it apparently doesn't occur to the author until after he's described her that she might be Klara Agappaia showing up again. And the reader smiles. "It was Klara Agappaia"—that is the principle of ambulatory coincidence, the principle of "onward."

Simon's (and Walser's) narrative principle of driving the story on with the walk is reminiscent of another literary character and another author—Eichendorff's *Taugenichts,* his *Good-for-Nothing,* and *Geschwister Tanner* has often been compared with this book.

The comparison, I think, is justified, so long as it's a question of narrative technique. But the figure of Simon isn't equivalent to the good-for-nothing, and Walser can't really be compared to Eichendorff. The author Walser resembles Eichendorff's character, the good-for-nothing. He takes whatever he happens to need at the moment. The coincidences are there when the story requires them. Simon is by no means lighthearted like the good-for-nothing, but the author Robert Walser has a lighthearted way of writing. The good-for-nothing rarely carries his fiddle around with him, but it's always there when he needs it.

But the biggest difference between the good-for-nothing and Simon is the difference between wandering and walking; wandering is lighthearted, walking is melancholy. Moreover, I can't imagine that Eichendorff himself was a wanderer—but Walser was a walker. He doesn't invent walking, it's quite simply what's nearest at hand—when he wants to describe himself he has to describe a walker.

And when he wants to describe himself he has to describe someone Swiss. Not much occurs to me in this regard, and I'd find it difficult to try to prove this decisively, but I have the impression that behind this book there stands a bourgeois Swiss citizen constantly mindful of his own self-defense, constantly mindful of not making all too poor an impression on his neighbors.

He's rarely courageous, more likely to be playful, and his anger, suppressed, can only be guessed at—for example, when he informs the bookshop owner of his disappointment in him. He can be extremely bourgeois and sees no reason to declare this bourgeoisness to be irony or parody. It stands there just the same as everything else—simply written, recounted, strolled.

The fifteenth chapter of the book is the philosophy chapter. Here, too, one can't tell for certain if these are really all Walser's opinions—but one thing is certain: these are all things that occurred to him, and he was glad of it. Simon on the theme of the homeland: "I'm an odd character in my own country." It's really very Swiss to connect one's own peculiarity with one's homeland, and something else very Swiss is the need to justify one's presence there: "I'm staying here and will no doubt continue to stay. It's so sweet, just to stay. Does Nature go abroad? Do trees travel to acquire greener leaves elsewhere and then to come back and show themselves off?" A lovely thought, and doubtless Walser's opinion. But he's in Berlin, enjoying Berlin. So is it homesickness? I don't think so. Or is it perhaps the statement, made before the fact, of the old man, the old Walser, who really will stay? In any case: the homeland as a source of vexation, a theme of contemporary Swiss literature, never shows up in Walser's work. The homeland comes naturally.

There's something almost religious about this naturalness, but of course Walser isn't religious; still, the subject does occupy him: "Religion in my experience is the love of life, heartfelt devotion to the earth, joy in the moment, trust in beauty, belief in mankind, lighthearted revelry with friends, the desire for meditation and the feeling of being without responsibility when misfortunes come." This isn't exuberance or humor; it's gentleness and a challenge, and it fails to meet this challenge, and then it's also sadness.

And the Swiss citizen goes on to say: "but I won't sacrifice the pleasure I take in the world for anyone's sake; at the most I'd sacrifice it for my sacred fatherland, but so far I've had no opportunity."

Does he really mean this? I don't know, but there's reason to assume Walser was a conservative—at least a social conservative. It's just that this sentence is far less suited for use in a civics course than would be, say, similar statements by Gottfried Keller. When Walser is undecided, he exaggerates, and by exaggerating makes his statements unquotable. He thinks in Swiss-German at such times, resorts to the noncommitalness of Swiss-German, and tops it all off with the stiltedness of High German. Walser was perhaps the first among the Swiss to discover that, as Swiss, one can employ the somewhat foreign and pompous High German as an artificial, role-playing language, and that the Swiss, unaccustomed to High German, have the advantage over the language—they can use it deliberately. I have no desire to try to figure out which Swissisms in his work are deliberate and which inadvertant. And he definitely overcompensates at times—often he writes even more "High Germanly" than necessary. But this balancing act pleases him. If High German had been his mother tongue, he could never have become the Robert Walser he did.

Artificial language—it can exist in long monologues that are more like letters than normal speech. Genuine conversation would require a greater familiarity with colloquial German speech. (An aside: our abilities have less effect on us than our inabilities—what other profession should the walker, the idler, have taken up?)

Walser plays, he plays out roles. And now and then I have the impression he's playing himself—he isn't a writer at all, doesn't want to be one, he's just playing one—a tightrope act that one day must fail. But this Simon, the reader constantly suspects, simply has to be a writer. Walser uses every means in his power to keep him from being one. He has someone else write—Sebastian—and write poorly. After Sebastian's death in the sixth chapter, Simon himself begins to write in the seventh—but casually, out of boredom. The reader now expects, with reason, that he will become a writer. But he doesn't, Walser won't let it happen. Does this contain, perhaps, the seed of Walser's later refusal to be a writer?

So did the twenty-eight-year-old author describe his entire life here, a life that was to last another fifty years? Did the young author write an old man's book? And was the old man then unable to do it himself, since the young one had already done it for him?

In 1929, at the age of fifty-one, Robert Walser is admitted to Waldau Sanatorium outside Berne. Four years later he's transferred to the asylum at Herisau, in Appenzell-Ausserrhode, the canton whose citizenship he holds. He abandons his literary work altogether, can scarcely be approached on the subject. He wants to have nothing more to do with literature; the walker Walser has left the writer, too, behind him. Gradually he is forgotten, and isn't really rediscovered until after his death in 1956. He spends the last twenty-seven years of his life in the asylum. There aren't many records of this time. Only a single person—the Zurich journalist and writer Carl Seelig—actually keeps in contact with Walser for a period starting in 1936, and later becomes his guardian.

People are still puzzling over his illness today; our understandable attraction for the legend, the sad fairy tale of Walser, makes us keep wanting to doubt his mental illness. There is also the testimony of visitors who report that one could have a perfectly reasonable conversation with him and that he only played the madman in front of the asylum staff.

We'll never be able to clear this up. In any case, it's not inconceivable that Walser voluntarily left literature behind him, whereas it's hardly conceivable he could have performed any other sort of work.

In 1956, on Christmas Day, a man who had once been a respected and critically acclaimed author died in Herisau. For the few faithful readers who hadn't forgotten him during this period, he was a man who sought in his work to make others share his grief, a man one learned, in his work, to love.

This Walser lived thirty years longer than his work and rejected all sympathy, all public, all literature.

The walker Walser outlived the writer, and must—for whatever reasons —have chosen walking forever. If an illness is to be seen in this, what sort of illness? Simon, in any case, can be seen in it.

Geschwister Tanner ends as a fairy tale, a winter's tale. The lady who loves this Simon at first glance and for no apparent reason, who ordains that he needn't pay for his food, who crops up all of a sudden, written into the book by the author, says: "No, you won't go under. It would be a shame if this were to happen, a shame for you. . . . You must learn to whisper into an ear and return caresses. You'll become too delicate otherwise. I'm going to teach you: I'll teach you everything that's lacking in you. Come. We're going out into the winter night. Into the stormy woods. There's so much I must tell you. Do you know that I am your poor, happy prisoner? Not another word, not another word. Come."

Not another word, not another word: this is the entry into silence. A very young Walser described it, an old Walser carried it out.

It would make sense if *Geschwister Tanner,* his first great book, had been his last. No other book of Walser's, it seems to me, looks so much like a last book.

We go out into the winter night: this is the proclamation of silence—the silence we know from fairy tales.

Trans. Susan Bernofsky

NOTES

1   Franz Kafka, "Letter to Director Eisner," trans. Richard and Clara Winston, in *Robert Walser Rediscovered,* ed. Mark Harman (Hanover: University Press of New England, 1985), 139.
2   *Der Bund,* 8 May 1898.

Der Gehülfe

Hermann Hesse

REREADING TODAY A WORK of literature that enchanted us thirty years ago, now that the world has changed so much, is a curious experience; not many of the novels that were famous at the time can withstand this test. Walser's *Der Gehülfe* (The Assistant) holds up splendidly. Although the mood of the novel clearly belongs to the early part of this century, the story wins us back at once by the timeless charm with which it is presented, by the delicate and casually playful magic with which it insinuates everyday matters into the realm of the spirit and mystery, and we can see even more clearly today that it is by no means the conflicts and the way they are perceived that have made us love this work, but rather its atmosphere, its poetic substance, its timelessness and play, its legendary quality.

The "Gehülfe" is a young man, Josef Marti, who comes from the city, where he's presumably been living in poverty, to take a post in the country. The town of Bärenswil reminds one of Wädenswil or one of the other small towns on Lake Zurich. He is hired by the engineer Tobler, a man who was earlier employed in a factory but now hopes to make his fortune as the inventor of an "advertisement clock," a deep-cutting drill, a vending machine for bullets, and various other carefully planned novelties. It is spring, and we follow the story until winter, up to the point where the assistant abandons his position and leaves the Tobler household, and at the same time we experience a year in the fate of the Tobler family, who were still living a splendid upper-class life in the spring, but in whose home changes have begun to creep in—demands for the repayment of debts, anxiety, and sorrow. The assistant spends the year in a house that is collapsing, in a "business" and family life that are becoming more and more muddled and neglected. What is so delightful and charming about this assistant and this writer Walser is that throughout the decline of the Tobler home and way of life, amidst the sorrow, deception and sham, a light nonetheless glimmers everywhere; everywhere there is a sound, a color that gives us pleasure. The assistant never receives his salary, he's never paid, but still he gets his daily bread, and the food isn't meager or grudgingly doled out, but rather abundant and cheery, they like to eat well in the house of Tobler, and the assistant is allowed to smoke *Stumpen* (thin cigars) in the office while he works, and in the evening everyone plays cards together over glasses of wine, the August 1 festival is celebrated in style, and the stubborn

77

boastfulness of Herr Tobler (who, already up to his neck in water, has a fantastic artificial grotto built in the garden to show the Bärenswilers what's what) is right out of Keller's Seldwyla.

Like all Walser's works, *Der Gehülfe* isn't without its playfulness; Walser takes decided pleasure in something nicely phrased or calligraphically written; there are sketches by him whose gaiety, lightheartedness, and playful grace remind one of Japanese art. This playfulness, however, this satisfaction with the aesthetic even when the ethical is in question, isn't simply a case of someone's indolently distancing himself from morality; he also modestly and lovingly gives up all right to pass judgment or preach. Here and there, behind the appearance of play, one can see an aestheticism not make-believe but genuine, the stance that says yes to the whole of life because it is a beautiful, magnificent spectacle if one observes it objectively.

This unforgettable book is written in a peculiar language wielded with great confidence and art. No other Swiss of Walser's generation wrote a German so beautiful yet at the same time so Swiss in its sensibility and tone. Language is Walser's great love, a love he sometimes openly confesses, sometimes ironizes. He writes out of the pleasure of language, a true musician, and this gives each of his works the magic of an art that has almost become nature again, of a virtuosity almost childlike and naive. Undoubtedly our time is even less receptive to this great magic than the period around 1900 when the book was written. One reason more for the friends of this writer to feel grateful and proud.

(1936)   Trans. Susan Bernofsky

Robert Walser on the Battle of Sempach: A History Lesson

Tamara S. Evans

LIKE MAX FRISCH'S *Wilhelm Tell: A School Text,* Walser's "Battle of Sempach" is a critical contribution to Swiss self-awareness and to the historiography of his country. Six centuries ago, on 9 July 1386, near the small town of Sempach, the Swiss Confederate infantry won a decisive victory over the Hapsburg cavalry that had been drawn up in great numbers and reinforced by allied contingents. According to tradition, this victory, marking the decline of Hapsburg hegemony in Switzerland, was owed to the self-sacrifice of one Arnold von Winkelried who, in the thick of the battle, thrust himself into the solid wall of enemy lances and thus opened a gap for those who followed him. The battle left a deep and lasting impression, not only on contemporary witnesses but also on generations to come. To this day, Winkelried exemplifies ideal soldiering as well as ideal citizenship, and his place of honor in the pantheon of Helvetian history has remained essentially uncontested. To tarnish the aura of a legend is risky business, as the following anecdote proves: On the occasion of the six-hundredth anniversary of the Battle of Sempach two sculptors created a gigantic Winkelried in styrofoam to be used during the festival. The sculpture, vaguely resembling King Kong, aroused such public outrage that it had to be hurriedly removed from the festival site during rehearsals.[1] Robert Walser was luckier than the two sculptors. Unlike them, he specialized in understatement, and thus his critique of ideologizing historiography in his story "The Battle of Sempach" was simply overlooked.

Walser toyed with the notion of writing a play about the Battle of Sempach as early as 1899, but he was advised to forget about historical topics and write from his imagination.[2] Nevertheless, the plan evidently kept haunting him, for in January 1907, he wrote to Christian Morgenstern that he had submitted a sketch on the Battle of Sempach to a German periodical, *Die Zukunft,* where it was published the following year.[3] Robert Mächler, Walser's biographer, is of the opinion that Walser could not possibly have planned anything more unsuitable than a play about a battle, and goes on to speculate that Walser's personally very militant mood may have tempted him to consider such a venture at that particular time. According to Mächler, Walser succeeded in giving the topic his own idiosyncratic stamp only with the 1907 sketch.[4]

"The Battle of Sempach" was written in the years between "The Fatherland"—one of the essays in Walser's earliest published prose collection, *Fritz Kochers Aufsätze* (1904)—in which Walser assumes the role of the naif dreaming "of stepping out into public life" and dedicating and sacrificing himself to the fatherland "in holy earnest," and *Jakob von Gunten* (1909), in which the protagonist settles accounts with conventional history lessons for good, leaving Western culture behind in order to strike out into the desert and abandon life within the historical process. As an investigation "on the advantage and disadvantage of history for life," in chronological as well as ideological terms, "The Battle of Sempach" stands between "The Fatherland" and *Jakob von Gunten.* I would like to show that "the personally militant mood," which according to Mächler may have motivated Walser to consider a battle play, did not simply dissipate; rather it left a deep imprint on the 1907 prose version and anticipated the deconstruction of Confederate myths which we encounter so frequently in Swiss literature after 1968.

Contrary to Walser's own remark on the sketchy quality of "The Battle of Sempach," it is actually a text governed by a rigorous pattern of antitheses. The first part of the story, in which Walser describes the approach of the proud and self-confident Austrian army in the sweltering noontime heat, is balanced by the fourth and final part, in which, until late in the night, the slain men of both armies are retrieved from the field of battle and buried by torchlight. The second part describes the beginning of the battle and the terrible losses suffered by the Swiss, while the third part focuses on the turn of events brought about by Winkelried's self-sacrifice and on the pitiful demise of the Hapsburg knights. The principle of antithesis also seems to determine the relationship between the structure of the text and its message: the former suggests construction, the latter destruction. The structure reminds us of Walser's original project in the tradition of historical tragedies, complete with a plot development that adheres to the three unities, with climax and catharsis; the message, however, riddled with alienation effects as it is, discourages empathy and forces the reader to assume a distanced position towards the events described. Yet on closer examination the Aristotelian benchmarks prove to be rather brittle, too. The unity of time as well as the unity of place are subject to a peculiar disintegration and transmutation: "The landscape no longer had contours; sky and summer earth merged into a solid whole; the season had vanished, had become a place, a fencing ground, free space to fight in, a battlefield."[5] It is as if the devil had botched the storyteller's trade. Is this still Sempach on 9 July 1386, if spatial relations are abandoned? If time becomes a spatial concept? To be sure, Walser calls the climax of the battle, i.e., Winkelried's willingness to sacrifice himself in order to create a breach, "a noble thought"; yet clearly he also denigrates Winkelried's heroism by referring to it as a "trick" (40). Not only do time and space become blurred; the figure of the hero, too, loses its contours: the infantrymen do not step on their valiant comrade but on a body that has become "a bridge . . . a noble thought meant to be stepped on" (40). Even the name of the slain hero, a name sacrosanct in Swiss history, is revealed only much later, when his body is recovered after dark. As far as catharsis is concerned, peace and quiet are indeed restored; but in light of the concluding remarks about the days that followed the battle, Walser hardly suggests that the battle brought about the purgation of the soul or the prospect of a better future. In short, in "The Battle of Sempach" categories pertaining to classical tragedy are put into play intentionally and ironically in order to be treated like stage props that have ceased to serve their purpose.[6]

Words, too, are juxtaposed in order to create harsh contrast. In an essay on "The Battle of Sempach," the Austrian writer Alois Brandstetter notes that the Hapsburgs and their allies are portrayed as silly, anachronistic knights paralyzed by their strong armor; in contrast, Walser calls their opponents neither "Confederates" nor "Swiss," but "people," "shepherds," and "mountain and valley men," because he wishes to attribute more humane qualities to them.[7] According to Brandstetter, Walser's sympathies therefore lie with the victors. Is Walser perhaps a historicist? Hardly—at least not if one keeps in mind Walter Benjamin, who asked: who is it with whom historicists usually empathize, and then said: "The answer is, inevitably: With the victors."[8] Brandstetter's interpretation misses the point. I consider it most significant that Walser calls neither the Swiss nor the Austrians by their name or nationality.[9] The word *people,* in the sense of *human beings,* is applied to both; and we surely cannot accuse Walser of humanizing the victors with his choice of words, for at the beginning of the third part he put *people* in quotation marks ("Menschen") precisely to prepare us for their inhumanity: "these light mountain and valley men" resemble "tigers ripping apart a defenseless herd of cows" (40).

Walser is least of all interested in playing off one army against the other, sympathizing with "one bunch of people" (as the original German has it) and scorning "the other bunch." Rather he is concentrating on a different dichotomy created at one point by the idyllic introduction of the approaching cavalry, the courtly and decadent manners of the knights, and the fruit trees in the meadows, at another by the brutal evocation of the din of battle and the slaughter of men. The text bristles with crude vocabulary, with nonchalant phrases and callous comments that are aimed at both armies. Some telling examples: a soldier is flung on the ground, "bleeding pitiably from his breast, tumbling head over heels, face down into the dusty excrement left behind by noble steeds" (40); "Something like a hundred handsome noblemen died a watery death, no, were drowned in nearby Lake Sempach, for they were tossed into the water like cats and dogs" (41); "one handsome youth . . . sank to the ground where, mortally wounded, he bit the dust with his half-shattered mouth" (41); "They'd all gladly have scoffed, had they been capable of scoffing" (41); "A few shepherds who'd lost their murder weapons . . . threw themselves . . . upon the necks of the knights and throttled them to death" (41).

Two world wars and many other wars lie between Walser's "Battle of Sempach" and today's readers. Countless documentaries and photographs have been released to remind even those who had the fortune to remain unafflicted of the horrors of war; exposed to this constant flow of information, we have become used to it. However, once we compare Walser's terse battle story with the thick novels and large canvases of the *Gründerzeit* (i.e., the period around 1871 and the founding of the Second Empire) and its renaissance around 1900 that were meant to glorify war and warriors alike,[10] and once we juxtapose Walser's sobering lesson to the jingoism of the Wilhelminian era, the modernity of Walser's treatment and its concomitant protest are all the more striking.

"Paradox," as Agnes Cardinal put it in her Walser monograph, "destroys the comfort of traditional and commonsense thinking and gestures towards new and uncharted possibilities of thought and understanding."[11] The incongruous and therefore disconcerting metaphors Walser uses to describe details of the battle scene fulfill a similar function: "The bright sun . . . blazed down on stirrups the size of snowshoes" (37). The Hapsburg cavalcade resembles a serpent, a giant lizard, or a lady's train "ceremoniously drawn along" (37). In the thick of the fight "iron men held out their lances; you could have gone for a buggy ride across this bridge of lances" (40). Or: "those on horseback were flung down like paper, with a crack like that of a paper bag blown up and burst between one's hands" (40). Footwear for other seasons, other latitudes and other guilds; shimmering animals and precious fabrics; holiday outings and children's pranks: *they* present themselves as comparisons with an Armageddon removed from its eschatological context; as metaphors originating in a world as yet unharmed, they force us to take cognizance of the abyss that opened between them and the "wild, infernal turmoil" (41) that they describe.

We are left in the dark as to the specific incidents leading up to the Battle of Sempach. Walser could not possibly have counted on readers familiar with Swiss history; his text was not written for a Swiss public, and when it came to the details and consequences of a medieval Swiss battle, most Germans would have been at a loss. In other words, Walser was simply not interested in providing his readers with historical and political explanations. He also leaves it open what the defeat of one party and the victory of the other might finally have signified. Territorial losses? To make Switzerland safe for freedom? We are never told. Did he mean to commemorate the weak who fought for a just cause and emerged triumphant? A point he does not make. The lessons to be drawn from this historical event are of an entirely different kind. As far as the defeat of "one bunch of people" is concerned, Walser has the following to say: "Actually the Battle of Sempach is a lesson in how terribly stupid it is to muffle oneself up. Had they been able to move, these jumping jacks: well, then they would have; a few of them could, having freed themselves from their unbearable garments" (41). Such a lesson is relative, offers itself only in retrospect, and may well turn out to be useless the next time round. The military equipment on the losing side proved a failure: in this case it had been too heavy. Another lesson, however, might be drawn from another battle, for example, that the equipment was too light, that supplies were slow in reaching the troops, or that winter arrived earlier than predicted (see Alexander Kluge's *Schlachtbeschreibung*). As a matter of fact, the lesson to be learned from the Battle of Sempach self-destructs: the tautological conclusion—"Had they been able to move . . . well, then they would have"—says little about the possibility that, given other circumstances and lighter armor, victory would have gone to the Hapsburgs. In any case, Walser merely comments that some knights were able to move once they freed themselves of their armor; he does not tell us whether they also survived.

Faithful to the very end to the antithetical structure of his story, Walser also implies what lesson "the other bunch of people" were to draw from the Battle of Sempach:

No festivities were held in their honor (well, in a small way, perhaps, as they entered Lucerne): all the same, the days went passing by, for the days, with all the worries they bring, would have been coarse and rude even then, in the year 1386. A great deed cannot obliterate the laborious succession of days. Life doesn't stand still on the day of a battle, far from it; history alone makes a momentary pause, and then it, too, impelled by imperious life, must rush on. (42)

Dulce est et decorum pro patria mori: no allusion is made to this dictum, although it had been proclaimed—with slight irony, to be sure—in Fritz Kocher's "Fatherland," to which I referred earlier.[12] Nor is there mention either of newly gained independence. No victory parades, no cheers, no posthumous fame—at least not according to Walser. Life moves along in its petty pace, and if we strike the balance, the days, "coarse and rude" as they are, make up the sum total of our lives, rather than the exceptional events Fritz Kocher had been longing for. Stronger yet: Walser presents the great deed as mass slaughter; far removed from heroic or religious idealization— of the kind we encounter with the apotheosis of Schiller's Joan of Arc, the *imitatio Christi* in C. F. Meyer's *Temptation of Pescara,* or the eschatological overtones in Gerhart Hauptmann's *Florian Geyer*—Walser's Battle of Sempach is fought under the banner of stupidity and bestiality.

"The Battle of Sempach" is a chapter of historiography filled with ambiguity and irony. Walser does not refer to cause-and-effect relations within the larger historical context, since they reveal nothing about the daily plight of the individual and because he has lost faith in the meaning and value of "monumental history" which, according to Nietzsche, portrays "the high points of humanity . . . linked throughout millennia," concentrating on the "great moments in the struggle of individuals."[13] According to Jost Hermand, the fascination with great individuals, so typical of the *Gründerzeit,* manifests itself in painting and literature of the time as follows: "most heroes are mythological or historical giants, persons of superhuman, classical beauty or tragic significance; besides, the fact that they are portrayed in close-up, that we are coerced to look at them, turns them into significant figures. This unremovable nearness is all over, and we cannot get past it."[14]

Considering that the renaissance of the *Gründerzeit* took place in the first decade of the twentieth century, it also becomes clear to what extent Walser distanced himself from this ideal of the "great individual." Arnold von Winkelried has not been given heroic or saintly dimensions; his sacrifice lacks tragic significance, and at the decisive moment he remains anonymous. We see him from afar when the Confederate infantrymen trample over his body or when they recover him from among the slain. To me, Walser's Winkelried represents a counterportrait to one of Switzerland's icons, namely, Hodler's famous 1903 painting *Tell,* in which the legendary founding father, upright, self-confident, and bursting with strength, seems to be looking us straight in the eye, ready, so to speak, to step out of the canvas in order to confront us.

Besides the implicit criticism of prevalent views of history and of late nineteenth-century predilections for pompous exaggeration, Walser also distances himself to some extent in "The Battle of Sempach" from the concept of "Life" as represented in German literature around 1900. As Wolfdietrich Rasch explained in his history of German literature at the turn of the century, "life is the key word of the epoch, its central concept," including in its totality also cruel, unscrupulous, and destructive elements.[15] It was an emotionally heavily charged concept with ecstatic overtones that encompassed "not only individual life . . . but all life, i.e., superindividual, preindividual, eternally flowing currents that penetrate each and every living being."[16] To be sure, Walser ended his story with a reference to the omnipotence of "imperious life"; his tone, however, is not emotional but altogether objective and sober. People who returned from the battle "were . . . working, serving, tending shop, looking after business, taking care of necessities" (42).

As Rasch has demonstrated, postimpressionist tendencies in art and literature—*Jugendstil* being one of them—created signs and language that celebrate the eternal secret of the linking of all earthly life. Certain stylistic features, such as the predilection for serpentines and two-dimensional structures reminiscent of woven textiles, are all meant to symbolize Life.[17] Both the serpent and weaving are motifs we also encounter in Walser's "Battle of Sempach." For example, prior to describing the outbreak of the battle, Walser writes: "Something ominous, in any case, [was weaving] eerily about the figure of the duke" (38).[18] And later we read: "Nature is always annihilated in a battle, where the course is dictated by the roll of the die, the weave of the weapons, the two opposing armies" (39). For Walser, then, weaving signals the destruction of life and nature; his text does not weave a "carpet of life" but a carpet of death.[19]

His transmutation of favorite motifs of the period is even more striking in his description of the Austrian army slowly moving ahead on the dust-covered highway, "often resembling a long, shimmering snake . . . often a large piece of cloth woven in a rich pattern of figures and colorful shapes" (37). Relying on the discrepancy between appearance and reality, Walser's play with *Jugendstil* ornamentation is highly ironic: the serpentine line of the army and the splendid colors of interwoven figures of knights and steeds, this long line of living creatures, is moving towards its own destruction. At the beginning of the battle the moving serpentine freezes into a straight line of knights seemingly "fused together" (39f.), a formation dictated by an art of war that Walser calls "idiotic," "the most prejudiced kind there is" (40).

Robert Walser belongs to those authors who, in the words of Max Frisch, did not reconcile themselves a priori to the history and the present of his country.[20] This is surely one of the reasons why Peter Bichsel, who—iconoclast that he is—doubts that the Confederates of old were more ideal fellows than he or his next-door neighbor,[21] is such an admirer of Walser. However, Walser's quarrel is not only with an idealizing and hence unproductive interpretation of Swiss history; it also transcends national borders. By deconstructing the legend of Winkelried, he also deconstructs both the portrayal of the past under the influence of historicism as well as the all too fanciful manifestations of the view of "Life" around 1900. The "great individual" receives new proportions that are more in keeping with everyday reality; effigies of our adversaries are dismantled; turning-points in history appear almost irrelevant in view of the universal process of life; no hymns are sung to war or to death on the battlefield. The destruction of historical contents and the transvaluation of the celebration of "Life" are reflected on the structural and stylistic level of the text: time and again, as I have shown, Walser brings into play ironies, antitheses, and paradoxes. "The Battle of Sempach" encourages the reader to think about how the past is treated and transmitted. To be sure, Walser never questions whether Winkelried existed or not. But he does question the relevance of the Winkelried legend in his own time, and offers an interpretation that runs counter to collective memory. Who knows: historiography Walser-style might awaken even Jakob von Gunten who, alas, had fallen asleep during one of his history lessons.

NOTES

1   The incident was reported in several dailies, among others in *Tages-Anzeiger,* 9 June 1986, 10.

2   Robert Walser, "Die Knaben," *Das Gesamtwerk,* ed. Jochen Greven (Zurich: Suhrkamp, 1978), 8:283.

3   Robert Walser, *Briefe,* ed. Jörg Schäfer and Robert Mächler (Zurich: Suhrkamp, 1979), 49.

4   Robert Mächler, *Das Leben Robert Walsers* (Frankfurt a.M.: Suhrkamp, 1976), 51.

5   "The Battle of Sempach," in *The Masquerade and Other Stories,* trans. Susan Bernofsky (Baltimore: Johns Hopkins Press, 1990), 39. All page references in the text refer to this translation.

6   Regarding Walser's treatment of traditional genres and their rules, see Jochen Greven, *Existenz. Welt und reines Sein im Werk Robert Walsers: Versuch zur Bestimmung von Grundstrukturen* (Cologne: Diss. phil. 1960), 172.

7   Alois Brandstetter, "Robert Walsers Österreicher: Überlegungen zu 'Die Schlacht bei Sempach,' " in *Über Robert Walser,* ed. Katharina Kerr (Frankfurt a.M.: Suhrkamp, 1978), 2:48.

8   Walter Benjamin, "Über den Begriff der Geschichte," in *Gesammelte Schriften* (Frankfurt a.M.: Suhrkamp, 1974), 1.2:696ff.

9   Only two names are mentioned in the text, each of them once: Duke Leopold of Austria and Arnold von Winkelried.

10   See Richard Hamann and Jost Hermand, *Gründerzeit: Epochen deutscher Kultur von 1870 bis zur Gegenwart* (Munich: Nymphenburg, 1971), 1:109.

11   Agnes Cardinal, *The Figure of Paradox in the Works of Robert Walser* (Stuttgart: Heinz, 1982), 48; 96.

12   I am reminded of the young Brecht, who declared in a school essay written during World War I: "The saying that it is sweet and honorable to die for one's country is sheer propaganda. The farewell to life is always difficult, in bed as well as on the battlefield, and surely most of all for young people in their prime." Quoted in Klaus Völker, *Bertolt Brecht: Eine Biographie* (Munich: Hanser, 1976), 16.

13   Friedrich Nietzsche, *On the Advantage and Disadvantage of History for Life,* trans. Peter Preuss (Indianapolis: Hackett, 1988), 15.

14   Hamann and Hermand, 67.

15   Wolfdietrich Rasch, *Deutsche Literaturgeschichte der Jahrhundertwende* (Stuttgart: Metzler, 1967), 17ff.

16   Rasch, 21.

17   Rasch, 210; 213-17.

18   This emendation of Susan Bernofsky's translation is mine. I would simply like to indicate the original German wording.

19   *Der Teppich des Lebens* ["the carpet of life"] is the title of a collection of poems by Stefan George, published in 1900.

20   Max Frisch, "Switzerland as *Heimat?*" in *Max Frisch: Novels, Plays, Essays,* ed. Rolf Kieser (New York: Continuum, 1989), 343.

21   Peter Bichsel, *Des Schweizers Schweiz* (Zurich: Arche, 1969), 16.

"The Walk" as a Species of Walk Literature

Phillip Lopate

A CURIOUS LITERARY phenomenon, the walk story. In roughly the same era, the surrealists Louis Aragon (*The Night Walker*), Philippe Soupault (*Last Nights of Paris*) and André Breton (*Nadja*), the Irishman James Joyce, the American Henry Miller, and the Swiss writer Robert Walser were all composing epics of perambulation. What was it about the times that led authors to pick the walk, that most transient, most seemingly formless of activities, as their subject matter? Was the walk's very shapelessness an inviting challenge to the fragmentary, lyrical, stream-of-consciousness aesthetic of early modernism? Or was this outpouring a twilight celebration of the *flaneur* (whose profile Walter Benjamin was busy working out on a theoretical plane), in the last decades before urban public space would become privatized, and lose much of its theatrical/agoric resonance? Finally, how significant was it that these writers were still relatively young men, whose restless, feet-conquering relationship to the city compensated in part for their bohemian poverty and powerlessness? Whatever the reasons, the streets beckoned as a free, inexhaustible source of entertainment and inspiration—a muse.

"The Walk" is Robert Walser's longest and arguably greatest story; certainly it is one of the best pure walking-around stories ever written. Unlike the other aforementioned samples, it takes place not in a metropolis but a small, unnamed city (Zurich?) which shades into suburban countryside. Just as the setting meanders from urban to semirural and back, so the mood traverses a continuum of emotional inscapes, each brightly lit. The "plot" (such as it is) consists of the narrator leaving his claustrophobic writing room for "the open, bright and cheerful street"; commenting on various passersby; entering a bookstore and asking to be shown the most successful book of the season, then walking out without buying it; stopping at his bank (where he learns that a thousand francs have been deposited by philanthropic ladies to support "the existence of a poet held repeatedly in contempt"); lunching with a patroness who frightens him with her teasing demands that he stuff himself; arguing unsuccessfully with a tailor; visiting the tax bureau to protest a raised assessment; having various epiphanies and anxiety attacks along the way; and finally settling into night, with its concluding personal illumination (which we will get to later).

"The Walk" begins (in Christopher Middleton's translation in *Selected Stories*):

I have to report that one fine morning, I do not know any more for sure what time it was, as the desire to take a walk came over me, I put my hat on my head, left my writing room, or room of phantoms, and ran down the stairs to hurry out into the street. I might add that on the stairs I encountered a woman who looked like a Spaniard, a Peruvian, or a Creole. She presented to the eye a certain pallid, faded majesty. But I must strictly forbid myself a delay of even two seconds with this Brazilian lady, or whatever she might be; for I may waste neither space nor time.

This opening locks in the self-reflexive tone of a twofold dialogue: (1) between the narrator and reader, and (2) between the main character and himself. The self-command to "waste neither time nor space" is particularly ironic: as Susan Sontag has astutely noted in her introduction to Walser's *Selected Stories,* "he had the depressive's fascination with stasis, and with the way time distends, is consumed; and spent much of his life obsessively turning time into space: his walks. His work plays with the depressive's appalled vision of endlessness: it is all voice—musing, conversing, rambling, running on."

Depressive or not, a person who walks is compelled to talk to himself, to carry on a soliloquy in his head. The walk itself is a continually changing field for meditation. It does this partly by throwing up one problematic stimulus after another. Thus, at the start of his walk Walser's narrator sees the unsmiling Professor Meili and, invoking the topsy-turvy principle that appearances deceive, concludes that "men who do not smile in a sweet and beautiful way are honorable and trustworthy." Many of the observations are paradoxes like this, which serve Walser's perspective that the first shall be last. He declares himself the enemy of everything that is "morbidly puffed up, offers a ridiculous tawdry show of itself." This antagonism extends to the "clumsy triumphal" automobile, which Walser is prescient enough in 1917 to see as the foe of walkers and nature:

To people sitting in a blustering dust-churning automobile I always present my austere and angry face, and they do not deserve a better one. Then they believe that I am a spy, a plainclothes policeman, delegated by high officials and authorities to spy on the traffic, to note down the numbers of vehicles, and later to report them. I always then look darkly at the wheels, at the car as a whole, but never at its occupants, whom I despise, and this in no way personally, but purely on principle; for I do not understand, and I never shall understand, how it can be a pleasure to hurtle past all the images and objects which our beautiful earth displays, as if one had gone mad and had to accelerate for fear of misery and despair. In fact, I love repose and all that reposes. I love thrift and moderation and am in my inmost self, in God's name, unfriendly toward any agitation and haste. More than what is true I need not say. And because of these words the driving of automobiles will certainly not be discontinued, nor its evil air-polluting smell, which nobody for sure particularly loves or esteems. It would be unnatural if one's nostrils were to love and inhale with relish that which for all correct nostrils, at times, depending perhaps on the mood one is in, outrages and evokes revulsion. Enough, and no harm meant. And now walk on. Oh, it is heavenly and good and in simplicity most ancient to walk on foot, provided of course one's shoes or boots are in order.

This passage, simple and lucid as it appears, is characteristic of the difficulties Walser poses to the reader, who is always kept off-balance. The sentiments seem unassailable (particularly to an urbanist like myself), yet the voice is slightly "mad." The narrator is part scamp, part Holy Fool. What is most noticeable is the artless tone, the complete absence of worldly expertise with which most professional belles-lettrists would armor themselves against the charge of naive cliché. Quite the contrary: Walser uses terms such as "beauty," "truth" or "simplicity" without qualification, almost as a challenge to the jaded literary establishment. I think it would be a mistake to assume that his childlike candor is merely another ironic pose. What makes reading Walser so tricky is the knowledge of his subsequent severe mental illness. Thus, the temptation to call various passages of his *faux-naif* must be tempered by the possibility that he was genuinely naive, naive in the way that emotionally disturbed people often are who hold on for dear life to some banally simple truth during those instants when the fog clears. At the same time, one does not want to release from considerations of literary standards— i.e., treat as a primitive—a writer whose narrative strategies were so complex and sophisticated.

Throughout the story, Walser addresses the reader like a paid companion trying to keep a bored dowager's attentions from wandering. These "digressive" asides to the reader are actually a unifying element in a genre desperate for them (the walk story); and he manages the technique with a comic, exaggerated politeness bordering on cheekiness:

Now, as will soon be learned, I shall on account of this haughty bearing, this domineering attitude, take myself to task. In what manner will also soon be shown. It would not be good if I were to criticize others mercilessly, but set about myself only most tenderly and treat myself as indulgently as possible. A critic who goes about it in this way is no true critic, and writers should not practice any abuse of writing. I hope that this sentence pleases all and sundry, inspires satisfaction, and meets with warm applause.

Here is Walser having his cake and eating it too: the grown man asserting that he has mastered literary manners and the claims of maturity, while the child-self (always obstinately strong in Walser) laughs at the rhetoric of responsibility as just another self-serving mask. As elsewhere in "The Walk," a comic effect is achieved by excessive loquaciousness (reminiscent of Gogol's runaway speakers) and a slightly archaic tone that presents the author as someone out of fashion and the hustle, amiably harmless, marginal. In this sense, Walser's patented brain-fever style is part of a tradition, which looks back to Sterne, Lamb, Dostoyevski's *White Nights,* and forward to Thomas Bernhard's hyperventilating narrators.

A walk, described on paper, becomes an opportunity to chart the movement between interiority and outward attentiveness, like the rack focus in movies that pulls first the background, then the foreground into sharpness. Many modern poets—Whitman, Apollinaire, Neruda, Frank O'Hara, Charles Reznikoff, Paul Blackburn, among others—have recorded this mental shift in walking-around literature as a keystone in the art of perception. Walser goes them one better, by approaching the walk not just as a perceptual but a spiritual exercise: a meditation in the Eastern religious sense, dissolving ego and promoting surrender and compassion. Of the good walker, Walser writes:

"He must bring with him no sort of sentimentally sensitive self-love or quickness to take offense. Unselfish and unegoistic, he must let his careful eye wander and stroll where it will; only he must be continuously able in the contemplation and observation of things to efface himself, and to put behind him, little consider, and forget like a brave, zealous, and joyfully self-immolating front-line soldier, himself, his private complaints, needs, wants, and sacrifices. If he does not, then he walks only half attentive, with only half his spirit, and that is worth nothing. He must at all times be capable of compassion, of sympathy, and of enthusiasm."

On the one hand, Walser has his narrator think that "perhaps the inward self is the only self which really exists." On the other hand, to fall "away from the surface, down into the fabulous depths" of the inward self, one must first attend faithfully to the external world. This entails pulling oneself out of solipsism into sympathetic awareness of others. Walser shows himself quite willing, exhibiting a kindheartedness toward all living creatures, though there are moments when a skeptical reader may be inclined to wonder whether the person or thing being tenderly apostrophized is indeed concretely seen, or is merely a pretext to release the author's tenderness. There is a sort of syrup of sad-eyed oneness which Walser seems willing to pour over landscapes, cows, houses, children, etc., which—to my mind, at least—does not entirely contradict a solipsistic position, or at least a distortingly aestheticizing one. But this is one of the dangers of the peripatetic genre, which invites a walking eye to bestow reactions willy-nilly on perfect strangers and any and all phenomena.

Another problem for the recording walker has to do with the inexhaustible detail presented by the external world. Walser faced this daunting infinitude of sense-details head-on—both by copious lists (see the page-long sentence that begins "Perhaps this is just the place for a few everyday things and street events, in turn: a splendid piano factory and also other factories and company buildings; an avenue of poplars close beside a black river, men, women, children, electric trams croaking along"), and by defending himself against further inventory-taking with the statement, "If one were to count until everything had been accurately enumerated, one would never reach the end." However, his main defense against cornucopic dizziness was to turn up the volume of receptivity, giving all his observations such a powerful emotional thrust that everything falling under his scrutiny seems germane— if only as the record of borderline hysteria.

One moment he comes across a gloomy giant, straight out of a fairy tale ("His woeful, gruesome air, his tragic, atrocious appearance, infused me with terror and took every good, bright and beautiful prospect, all joy and gaiety away from me"); two paragraphs later he confesses to "an inexpressible feeling for the world . . . a feeling of gratitude." These whiplash changes between rapture and terror do help keep the reader on his toes. It is interesting how frequently words like *terror, fear, courage, bravery, misery, dread* occur in the text, often about daily events one would not think required much heroism. When the walker is not delighted or ecstatic he is frightened to death—so much so that he seems almost boastful of his capacity for cowardice. The scene of lunching with his patroness, Frau Aebi, with its undertones of cannibalism and anxious erotic avoidance, illustrates Walser's tendency to give descriptions of normal social occasions a grotesque, Grimm-like twist: "Obviously, it moved her deeply to watch how I helped myself and ate. This curious situation astonished me. . . . Quite secretly I began to be terrified in Frau Aebi's presence." This fear extends even to "the reader, of whom I am honestly afraid." One is tempted to think he is pulling our leg. But again, who is to say what is appropriate grounds for fear in a writer who was "probably the victim of a quietly paranoid 'mixed state' " (Martin Seymour-Smith)? If he seems less frightened in the open street than indoors, he has moments of sidewalk panic as well. It must be said, though, that Walser was not alone in this street-paranoia, which infuses the paintings of Munch and Kirchner, and German silent films of the era.

Walser placed an immense importance on walking: nowhere is this made clearer than in the crucial scene where the narrator appeals to the tax inspector not to raise his rates. After pleading poverty as an impoverished, hard-working author, he is told by the inspector: "But you're always to be seen out for a walk!"

This offhand remark unleashes an eloquent defense of walking which is unique even in peripatetic literature. " 'Walk,' was my answer, 'I definitely must, to invigorate myself and to maintain contact with the living world, without perceiving which I could not write the half of one more single word, or produce the tiniest poem in verse or prose. Without walking, I would be dead, and my profession, which I love passionately, would be destroyed." Walser goes on for three more pages to spell out the necessity of walking: it is crucial for gathering literary material, for ensuring his mental health, joy and pleasure, for putting him in contact with edifying Nature, for inspiring him to philosophical heights, for teaching him spiritual surrender. Moreover, these walks are a form of study which "touch the fringes of exact science. . . . Although I may cut a most carefree figure, I am highly serious and conscientious, and though I seem to be no more than delicate and dreamy, I am a solid technician!"

From the passion of this peroration, it would seem that the bourgeois inspector's comment has touched a narcissistic sore point: we see how connected the activity of walking is with the *amour-propre,* the very identity of the writer. (In this respect, Walser resembles another proud, touchy literary loner given to monumental walks, Cesare Pavese.) Walser almost seems to be trying to elevate walking into an independent profession.

All along the author has shown signs of conflating writing and walking in his mind. This is not surprising; countless writers have testified how the rhythms of walking released their composing mind (think of Gertrude Stein working out the elephantine paragraphs of *The Making of Americans* in her jaunts through Montparnasse.) Walser escapes his writing room, which he calls the "room of phantoms," only to enter another fantasy milieu, with its giants, beautiful milliners, and so on. "All this," he tells himself as he strolls, "I shall certainly soon write down in a piece or sort of *fantasy,* which I shall entitle 'The Walk' " (my italics). At one point Walser directly compares the two: "But one realizes to be sure to satiety that he loves to walk as well as he loves to write; the latter of course perhaps just a shade less than the former." It was to be his fate, once he entered the mental hospital, to give up the weaker of the two habits.

Walking also stood for freedom. In this story, the walker has no sooner completed his defense to the official and continued on his walk, when he declares: "Raptures of freedom seized me and carried me away." Walking is the activity of the free human being—particularly when one is without destination or time-limit. Released from bureaucracy, Walser's narrator experiences a sudden effusion of "sorrow's golden bliss" and rhapsodizes: "Spirits with enchanting shapes and garments emerged vast and soft, and the dear good country road shone sky-blue, and white, and precious gold. Compassion and enchantment flew like carven angels falling from heaven over the gold-covered, rosey-aureoled little houses of the poor, which the sunlight delicately embraced and framed about. Love and poverty and silvery-golden breath walked and floated hand in hand."

The sugarcoated euphoria of this long passage resembles accounts of people on LSD, mescalin, or some other chemically induced high. Such a passage also suggests how close Walser felt himself personally to be (however much we try to make him out a modernist) to the nineteenth-century German romantics. Indeed, he is soon meditating on Brentano, medieval castles, the poet Lenz, and other lofty romantic subjects.

The tax inspector scene is essentially the climax of the story, and after

that the piece begins to lose steam: the descriptions of rosey-aureoled landscapes, architecture, street events and inns, the arguments against cutting
down trees, the raptures over poor children, seem redundant, water-treading.
Walser is enough aware of this to feel obliged to defend his right to repetitions: "The serious writer does not feel called upon to supply accumulations
of material, to act the agile servant of nervous greed; and consequently he is
not afraid of a few natural repetitions." Walser seems to have lost his way,
to have gone on too long—typical pitfalls in walking-around literature.
Then, suddenly, it all comes together.

However amusing or poignant the observations along the way have been,
there would still be a thinness to the story if it did not plunge to a deeper
level. The end brings a thematic darkening, consonant with the actual
arrival of night, and the walker comes to terms with what he has been
evading. It is a truism of meditation practice that the mind will first throw up
all manner of petty worries and sideshows before settling down to the heart
of the matter. In this case, the digressive reverie that went before has helped
clear the field for thoughts that the walker had been resisting:

> It was now evening and I came to a quiet, pretty path or side road which ran under
> trees, toward the lake, and here the walk ended. In a forest of alders, at the water's
> edge, a school for boys and girls had assembled and the parson or teacher was giving
> instruction in botany and the observation of nature, here in the midst of nature, at
> nightfall. As I walked slowly onward, two human figures arose in my mind. Perhaps
> because of a certain general weariness, I thought of a beautiful girl, and of how alone
> I was in the wide world, and that this could not be quite right. Self-reproach touched
> me from behind my back and stood before me in my way, and I had to struggle hard.
> Certain evil memories took control of me. Self-accusations made my heart deeply
> and suddenly a burden to me. . . . Old, long-past failures occured to me, disloyalty,
> hatred, scorn, falsity, cunning, anger, and many violent unbeautiful actions.
> Uncontrolled passion, wild desire, and how I had hurt people sometimes, and done
> wrong. Like a packed stage of scenes from a drama my past life opened to me, and I
> was seized with astonishment at my countless frailties, at all unfriendliness and
> lovelessness which I had caused people to feel.

He thinks again of the girl he knew, who had probably loved him, while his
own doubts

> had obliged her to travel, and she had gone away. Perhaps I would still have had time
> to convince her that I meant well with her, that her dear person was important to me,
> and that I had many beautiful reasons for wanting to make her happy, and thus
> myself happy also; but I had thought no more of it, and she went away. Why then the
> flowers? "Did I pick flowers to lay them upon my sorrow?" I asked myself, and the
> flowers fell out of my hand. I had risen up, to go home; for it was late now, and
> everything was dark.

In this powerful ending, note the quiet tone of voice, the complete
absence of giddy hysteria, or undercutting mock addresses to the reader, or

florid language. Note, too, the collapse of that system of defensiveness, so endearing in its way, by which Walser elects to portray himself as one of life's powerless victims, too childish and madcap ever to hurt anyone. Finally he is taking responsibility for his misdeeds. Finally, too, after so many confessional throat-clearings, he is giving us something truly personal.

It remains to ask whether this beautiful final passage is the crowning touch of a carefully controlled artwork, or a last-minute trick—pulling the Lost Love out of the hat, as it were, thereby rescuing a composition verging on shapelessness. Perhaps the truth lies somewhere in between. In any event, Walser has managed to solve in his idiosyncratic way some of the problems endemic to walk literature. The very fact of his narrator seeming slightly "cracked" keeps us suspensefully engaged through the otherwise random events of the walk. By presenting a voice of such charm and panicked surprise that we are willing to follow it anywhere, by handling the alternation of inward and outward focus in a rich, self-aware manner, and by structuring the meditation as an emotional arc with a payoff at the end, Walser convinces the reader that the trek has been worthwhile.

The Singular Bliss of the Pencil Method: On the Microscripts

Werner Morlang

IN JANUARY 1921, a financially strapped Robert Walser gives up his garret at the Hotel Zum Blauen Kreuz in Biel to move to Berne, where he is to take up the post of assistant archivist in the Office of Public Records. He loses no time informing the readers of the magazine *Die Weltbühne* of his move in a series of four prose pieces, assuring them: "And in general, it feels quite good to be in Berne." But a few months later, this final attempt on his part to hold a steady job fails. Walser is once more forced to realize that a normal bourgeois life is irreconcilable with literary work, as he laconically suggests that same February in a letter to his friend Frieda Mermet: "I don't have much to report. People who work experience precious little." What has here begun so inauspiciously is the third of three consecutive and curiously symmetrical periods of Walser's career defined by his place of residence. After eight years each in Berlin (1905–1913) and Biel (1913–1920), he manages, despite increasing difficulties, to continue to work as a free-lance writer for another eight years, until January 1929, when, as the result of a crisis that today can be only vaguely reconstructed, he is admitted to Waldau Sanatorium.

The puzzling chiaroscuro that constitutes Walser's biography as a whole is particularly troubling in the Berne years, for in this period more than any other, our quite limited knowledge of his life is overshadowed by a massive quantity of literary work in which his day-to-day experiences, though confusingly fragmented and distorted, are still recognizable. We know, for instance, of his many moves from furnished room to furnished room (there is proof of fifteen different addresses from 1921 to 1926 alone), and of his walks, including one two-day trek that took him all the way to Geneva. Isolated anecdotes have come down to us as well, the basis of his reputation as a now mischievous, now surly eccentric. One, for instance, tells of his receiving the publisher Hauschild in his garret: first, in the guise of a servant named Caesar, he opens the door to him in his shirtsleeves, only to present himself to the waiting guest a moment later, respectably clad, as Robert Walser.

Such episodes are no doubt welcome to the biographer struggling to find a few splashes of color in the uneventful Berne years to help create the typical picture of the artistic outsider. Still, they have little bearing on the monotonous daily routine of the solitary writer: work, walks, time spent in pubs. In restaurants and cafés Walser sees his last possibility for contact with others, but here, too, he tends to remain a silent observer and sometimes brusquely rejects drinking companions who try to get closer to him. Relationships to his colleagues are few and short-lived. His love affairs with waitresses, as reflected in the recurring figure "Edith" in his work, are probably more imagined than real. The appeal of idleness and walking, which he praised in his 1917 novella "The Walk" as a necessary inspiration for his work, decreased as the social acceptability of his literary career became less self-evident, and more and more suspect even to himself. Rightly or not, he felt the life he led was an easy mark for the disapproving, sometimes scathing glances of his fellow citizens: "For a time the people here thought I was insane and would say aloud, in the arcades, as I was walking past: 'He should be in the asylum'" (letter to Therese Breitbach, mid-Oct. 1925). Or in his room: "Here in Berne I enjoy the reputation of a lowly scribbler since the people strolling on the street past my writing room constantly see me scribbling poetry or prose, and these people feel a profound need to criticize and find fault—never with themselves, of course, just with others. At times I feel eaten up, that is to say half or wholly consumed by the love, concern, and interest of my so excellent countrymen" (letter to Therese Breitbach, 26 Sept. 1927).

The aggressive irony with which Walser twists the indifference shown him by the public into oppressive sympathy also finds expression in his claim (which he now makes periodically) that everyone keeps expecting him to write another novel. He manages to conceive and complete a novel (*Theodor*) in the early Berne years, but the manuscript is rejected by several publishers and then lost. With the exception of the prose collection *Die Rose* (The Rose)—his last book, which appeared from the Rowohlt publishing house in 1925—all his book projects of the 1920s fail. Still, for the time being, the feuilleton business continues to flourish: editors Otto Pick and Max Brod of the newspapers *Prager Presse* and *Prager Tagblatt* remain steady customers for his short prose and poems, and a few German and Swiss newspapers and magazines print his contributions on a more or less regular basis. But when at the end of 1928 the feuilleton editor of the *Berliner Tageblatt* advises him to stop writing for half a year, Walser sees this suggestion as a final condemnation. "I was in despair," he later tells Carl Seelig. "Yes, it was true, I was completely written out. Burnt out like a stove. I made an effort to go on writing despite this warning. But they were all foolish things I forced out. . . . At the time I made a few clumsy attempts to take my own life, but I couldn't even make a proper noose."

In view of the many internal and external obstacles threatening Walser's *condition littéraire,* not the least of these being his social isolation, one wonders at the perseverance that keeps him working far into the period of his confinement at Waldau. The surviving prose texts, poems, and dramatic scenes from these twelve years alone fill a good 1500 pages in his collected works, even taking into consideration that a good deal of what he produced in Berne was lost by publishers or in newspaper offices, or destroyed by Walser himself. But this is only the tip of the iceberg, the fraction of Walser's enormous late work that he himself authorized, wrote out in fair copy. Walser's most illuminating work from this period is at the same time his most private. He seems never to have told anyone, neither in person nor in writing, that in 1925 he wrote a long prose text that was later transcribed by Jochen Greven and published in 1972 as the *"Räuber"-Roman,* the "Robber" novel. Walser took his childhood fantasy role of the robber Karl Moor from Schiller's play *Die Räuber*—an 1894 watercolor portrait by his brother Karl captured him in this disguise—and projected onto it that side of his Berne existence that could no longer be dealt with through literary work: his descent into asocialness, which he suffered with increasing anxiety. In all likelihood Walser never seriously considered trying to publish this text. It was notated on a mere twenty-four sheets of art print paper in a minuscule German script that looked so strange to Carl Seelig, the first curator of Walser's literary estate, that he took it to be a "made-up, indecipherable secret code" and saw it in the context of Walser's "mental illness."

As we've since learned, these 526 slips of paper contain the first drafts Walser wrote of his texts during the twenties and late into the Waldau period. Most, though not all, of the texts from the Berne years have corresponding drafts in the microscripts, from which Walser prepared the fair copies with a varying number of revisions. In addition, however, these microscripts contain a vast store of previously unknown texts whose total length can be estimated at around two thousand book pages, making them considerably more extensive than the works Walser wrote out in fair copy.

Although Walser often talks in his texts about what went on in his workshop, he makes reference to the micrographic process on only a few occasions: he comments on it at some length in a letter to Max Rychner, and includes cursory remarks in "Bleistiftskizze" (Pencil Sketch) and "Meine Bemühungen" (My Efforts). In each of these, he mentions having suffered a crisis involving his pen that prompted him to start composing his first drafts in pencil. In the Rychner letter from 20 June 1927, he wrote:

The writer of these lines experienced a time when he hideously, fearfully hated his pen, I can't begin to tell you how sick of it he was; he became a complete idiot the moment he made the least use of it; to free himself from this sickness of the pen he began to pencil-sketch, to scribble, fiddle about. With the aid of the pencil I was better able to play, to write; it seemed this revived my writerly enthusiasm. I can assure you (this all began in Berlin) I suffered a real breakdown in my hand because of the pen, a sort of cramp from whose clutches I slowly, laboriously freed myself by means of the pencil. A swoon, a cramp, a stupor—these are always both physical and spiritual. So I experienced a period of disruption that was mirrored, as it were, in my handwriting and its disintegration, and when I copied out the texts from this pencil assignment, I learned once again, like a little boy, to write.

This letter contains imprecise statements as to when the micrography started, for while Walser's "breakdown" with his pen occurred in 1912 in Berlin, he writes earlier in the letter that he had begun to write his drafts in pencil "approximately ten years ago" (i.e., around 1917). Since the earliest microscript we have is thought to have been written in 1924, we must assume that the micrographic works from the late Biel and early Berne years have been lost.

For an observer today, it seems curious that all of Walser's remarks on his first drafts fail to take into consideration what is perhaps their most conspicuous feature, the minuteness of the script, but rather focus on the writing instrument itself. "Pencil method," "pencil system," "pencillation" are his designations for this unprecedented development in his modus operandi, his need to write a rough draft before the fair copy. In fact, his 1906 and 1907 novels *Geschwister Tanner* (The Tanner Siblings) and *Der Gehülfe* (The Assistant) were written in pen, each in a single stretch of a few weeks. As the manuscripts, which have an almost calligraphic quality, show, Walser interrupted the flow of the writing in only a few places to make isolated, minor corrections. He apparently needed this physical act of executing a neat, uninterrupted piece of writing in order to engage his creativity. Perhaps there were also visually aesthetic ambitions associated with his use of the pen that no longer could be satisfied in the first stage of composition. The "cramp" from which Walser suffered relaxed only during the revision of the text, which, thanks to the pencil method, once again allowed a fluid script.

One can also observe in the letters Walser wrote during the initial stages of micrography a tendency for the writing to decrease in size. If we take this striving to make things small as an additional motive for the emergence of Walser's micrography, we can easily understand the transition from pen to pencil as the pragmatic adoption of a new medium that permitted a much more radical minimalization of the script.

The calligraphic standards of the writing done in pen, the grace of composition displayed in the fluidity of the script, are preserved in the pencil system, though in different form. No one who sees a microscript can fail to notice its aesthetic qualities: the graceful regularity of the script itself, the strictly maintained horizontals, the purity of the line, the collagelike juxtaposition of different genres, the arrangement, sometimes dovetailed, of texts on the page. It almost goes without saying that Walser neglected this strong graphic element in his "commentaries." It must have been extremely difficult for him to accept this bifurcation of his creative labors, and the many determining factors in Walser's micrography probably also included some degree of shame (beneath which the tiny letters seem to cringe) at his admitted inability to compose a presentable-looking text in pen. It's likely this sense of literary inadequacy Walser is referring to in his letter to Rychner when he says he has his pencil system to thank for some "real torments." But this is only the bleaker side of the new method; Walser also had occasion (in "Bleistiftskizze") to point out its advantages: "Among other things, it seemed to me I was able to work more dreamily, peacefully, cozily, meditatively with the pencil, I believed that the process I've described above was developing for me into a singular bliss."

One other fascinating peculiarity of the microscripts Walser never mentions is the variety in the types of paper he used. Among the 526 recovered drafts there are two groups of homogeneous sheets that each comprise a chronological unit: 117 octavo sheets of art print paper that were used between fall 1924 and the end of 1925, and 158 halved pages from the 1926 *Tuskulum* calendar, 8 x 17.5 cm, which date from 1926 and probably the beginning of 1927. This was the paper Walser preferred (but didn't use exclusively) for his first drafts during this period; in later years it was joined by an increasingly diverse assortment of paper types that he always cut to size, into tiny rectangles. There were single-sided advertisements from magazines and books; envelopes, cards, and stationery from his personal and business correspondence; galley proofs; scrap paper of unknown origin, tax forms, etc. Despite the "unexplainable" oddity inherent in the use of these kinds of paper, one can definitely see an illuminating connection between them and Walser's late work. Their physical form shows a now exuberant, now roguish playfulness, while they display with oppressive concreteness the obstacles Walser had to battle in composing his late work. Just as the pencil script represented the attempt to take refuge from the public and internalized literary tribunals through a miniaturization of the calligraphic pen script, the decision to use small formats and scrap paper was also clearly a move in the direction of the inconspicuous that had always been part of Walser's aesthetic program.

In any case, the new modus operandi proved a suitable means for Walser to preserve the continuity of his work for a good sixteen years. Now and then the use of certain pieces of paper seems a sort of trick, a good-luck charm to influence the publication of the new texts. Instances of this invocation are, for example, thirty-eight honorarium-notices from the *Berliner Tageblatt* or a smaller number of advertisements from the magazine *Sport im Bild* and forms from *Simplicissimus* and *Die Weltbühne,* not to mention a 1932 postcard from Eduard Korrodi confirming his acceptance of two prose pieces for the *Neue Zürcher Zeitung.* The extent of the courage that kept the "prose piece business" going, despite the constant threats to its existence, can best be seen in the texts Walser wrote in direct defiance of the original contents of the draft-paper, for example this note from the editors of *Simplicissimus:* "Most esteemed sir, we have taken note of your submission with interest, but unfortunately do not find it suitable for our journal."

At times these "charged" materials egged Walser on to all sorts of pranks, humorous exclamations and remarks. Once he added a "vielmal" to the fee stamp "Mercy" on an envelope from Prague to make a Swiss-style "many thanks," then surrounded it with monosyllabic interjections. Another time he inscribed a postmark with the question: "About done scribbling now?" and added a terse "sessa" (which probably should be read as the French "c'est ca"). A good example of a direct connection between micrographic text and paper is a card from the Paul-Zsolnay publishing house. In fall 1927, Max Brod had his Viennese publisher send Walser a review copy of his latest novel, *Die Frau, nach der man sich sehnt* (The Woman One Longs For), and Walser used the enclosed card to draft his "review" "Hier wird kritisiert" ("Some criticism here")—only loosely based on the book—which appeared in July 1928 in the magazine *Individualität.* The inspirations his writing material offered were doubtless one of its attractions. His poetic/ethical principle—that each everyday thing, no matter how seemingly unimportant, is worthy of poetic discourse —is in keeping with his letting chance determine the type of paper he would use.

A cursory glance at the microscripts does not make a tangible impression of their motifs and themes, because, with few exceptions, Walser left his drafts untitled. The reader of these texts must also keep in mind that these drafts are provisional and thus are subject to spontaneous impulses and writing errors, irritating and appealing at the same time. Although the individual texts seem perfectly coherent and complete as drafts, it's often quite difficult to make a critical assessment, particularly with regard to the poems, as to whether certain peculiarities of form and content should be attributed to Walser's individuality of style or to the unpolished nature of the draft itself. There are some texts that, either because they are artistically unsuccessful or expose all too openly Walser's "private" obsessions, he probably never would have published. But however things stand with regard to their success or failure, it's precisely the trickiest, unruliest texts that are most strongly imbued with the moment of their making and thus afford a singular insight into Walser's workshop.

One expectation often brought to the microscripts should be put to rest right away: despite their confessional aspect, they contain *no* undisguised diary-type entries, much less sensational disclosures. In both content and form they largely resemble the known works of the middle and late Berne periods. Several of them also stand in direct, mutually illuminating relation to known texts, either constituting strongly divergent variants to them, or— as in the case of the prose sketches "Emil und Natalie" and "Ich las damals vielleicht zu viel" (Perhaps I read too much then)—forming full-length stories out of isolated marginal references. Sometimes correspondences appear in the form of identical sentence patterns or thoughts. Even the individual microscript page displays a network of relationships that weaves the various texts and genres together with shared words and motifs. Certain pages read like palimpsests among which, at certain points, the course of a day becomes visible. An obituary for Anatole France, for example, begins: "It's six in the evening, and I want to go to the opera, and there's so much on my mind, and now all of France is mourning beside a coffin, how awful," and further down there follows a report entitled "Hohe Oper" (High Opera) that apparently records the rest of this evening.

Walser scholars will be gratified to learn that certain lost texts whose existence we've known of from references in Walser's letters will henceforth be accessible in first draft. Among these are the essays mentioned in letters in 1925/26 concerning a "Zäzilie oder Agathe" and the city of Berne, as well as a study on "Stil" ("Style") and the poem "Nasenflügelbeglückender Duft von sauren Mocken" (The wing-of-the-nose-pleasing fragrance of Bernese sauerbraten). One can also learn more about an acquaintance of Walser's known only as Fräulein H. (as he addressed her in his letters) and her family of five grown daughters in a microscript where Walser describes with great psychological subtlety the absence of communication between the family members, each of whom, waiting to be entertained with conversation, maintains a strict silence.

A biographical puzzle of a special sort is provided by a story Walser describes as "more comical than lovely and more ordinary than true, though I'm telling it just as it happened." In it, Walser presents a five-man cast whose individual members form the most ridiculous alliances with and against each other, only to dissolve them again. This disorienting interplay begins: "Waterglass was delicate and so refused to let a temperament like Crocodilowski's consider him meek. Strictly speaking, Crocodilowski found it fun to think it child's play to shatter Waterglass so as to intone a dirge over his shards." The other characters are styled as Misters "Picknick," "Ofenrohr" (stovepipe), and "Weltmann" (man of the world). Although Walser concludes this witty scene with the assurance, "With this story I went astray in unknown territory," the reader would do well to look up his 19 April 1926 letter to Frieda Mermet in which the feuilleton editor of the *Neue Zürcher Zeitung* is parodied as "Krokodilödeli of the Neuen Höseli- or Zürcher Zeitung" ("Höseli" is the diminutive of "trousers"). One finds the other necessary explanations here as well. Walser had just succeeded in placing a contribution rejected by Korrodi in Otto Pick's ("Picknick") *Prager Presse,* which he then, with great pleasure, pointed out to Korrodi. Also around this time, Walser had complained to a representative of the Orell-Füssli ("Ofenrohr") publishing house about Korrodi, who then demanded a formal apology. "Weltmann" refers to the then famous literary review *Die literarische Welt,* which on 20 January 1928 published an interview with Korrodi in which he dismissed Walser as an ornamental writer.

Even in the pencil method prose, reality is seldom disguised quite this fantastically, but biographical elements can probably be found in all the microscript texts. Everyday Berne, in particular, shows up wherever one looks: the seasonally changing picture of the city with its streets, arcades, used book shops, pubs and cafés. The panorama of the mountains, which are sometimes figuratively invoked or otherwise make unexpected appearances in the course of a story: "Jungfrau, Mönch, and Eiger and the other exalted figures of our mountain world shake their mighty heads, as though they were annoyed at Emil and Natalie's pensiveness." Then of course Walser's own immediate situation: his various furnished rooms with the flowers the landladies leave on his desk, his walks, for example a nocturnal one that leads through Villmergen and finally to Zug, of which he says: "And then past a castle, Hallwil, with swans in its tower-reflecting moat. Oh, if only you could have seen me eating a calf's head with fried potatoes in Baden and heard a hostess in a Bremgarten inn say to me: 'Well well well, leaving so soon?' In my beloved Zürich I've stood, full of understanding, before the entrance to many a public garden."

And then come all sorts of day-to-day encounters and observations, pub visits, his avid reading, and the various concerts and performances that sometimes he carefully avoids. He once writes to Otto Pick: "In Berne you're never at a loss for new impressions, it's a city full of top-notch activities." Some of the most successful pieces are in fact the ones in which Walser puts some chance occurrence into literary form, as when he becomes witness to and participant in the "Ueberglücklichkeit" (Elation) of a group of children and a "foolish little dog" occupied in rolling and chasing beer coasters down the street. His constant readiness to coax all sorts of platitudes from outside literary boundaries and revitalize them appears when he writes of the most ordinary objects and casual thoughts. In "Mist, Jammergestalten und Tyrannen" (Dung, Wretches and Tyrants), he seeks in an act of surrealistic spontaneity to restore to these three disdained words the dignity they lost merely as a result of "ultra-respectable wing-of-the-nose recklessness, conversational thoughtlessness."

Walser is now working to such an extent with the ideas and words that happen to come to him through the grace of the moment that he's taken to beginning his prose pieces by making reference to the circumstances surrounding their composition and doesn't suppress even the most muddled thought if it helps to get the flow of the writing started, even though he sometimes drops it a moment later. Often Walser's imagination needs to be kindled two or three times while he gradually feels out his theme. Here are the opening sentences that finally lead into the tale of a young acquaintance and a thorough description of four book covers: "*Mon repos*-castles slumber in my renovation-shy head. I reside at the moment quite nicely in a nest full of girls who, one might say, twitter all day long. In this room that I requisitioned, there lived for twelve years an ingenuous *Gotsch*. '*Gotsch*' signifies an affectionate and thus most incautious soul."

Despite his euphoric claim that he'd never run out of material in Berne, Walser reported increasing difficulty in making his experiences bear literary fruit. It probably wasn't only out of weariness with the prevailing literary standards but also to compensate for the dearth of raw material that Walser began to read more *Trivialliteratur,* penny dreadfuls, in the Berne years. It's to be assumed he read these books in the way he explained to Therese Breitbach: "I read a wonderfully beautiful book, that is to say I read the book in such a way that for me it became wonderful." To be sure, Walser also saw this "acquisition by reading" (his phrase for this practice) as a threat to his artistic originality, and thus, despite his constant hunger for new reading material, he generally didn't allow himself to explore the contemporary literature of his colleagues. There was little risk of "influence" from these newsstand paperbacks, and so the microscripts contain numerous retellings of the plots of penny dreadfuls. This sort of material, as opposed to other sources precariously close to home, gives him much freer rein to manipulate his characters with complete confidence within the framework of a predetermined story line, and to bring out his narrative presence, his idiosyncratic humor. Often he speaks of his location or other circumstances that controlled or influenced his reading. And no sooner has he gotten started with his ostensibly faithful report than his addressees, who show up both singular and plural, formal and familiar in a single text, are playfully deceived on all levels. Besides his frequent use of the subjunctive forms, Walser occasionally pleads ignorance as to how things stand with regard to certain fictional circumstances. He indulges in the constant renaming of his characters or the alternation between pairs of names: "Her name was simultaneously Lotte and Käthe, and we'll run back and forth between these two appellations till we collapse from exhaustion."

Naturally Walser is careful to maintain a roguish complicity with his characters throughout his digressions, and once, in feigned helplessness, even calls on his writing tool for support: "Pen, if you let me down, I don't know what I'll do with you. 'I'll stick to my promises,' it replied, thereby putting my mind completely at ease." But even in the midst of what seems the most light-handed treatment of material taken from other sources, Walser can be seized all at once with a deeply personal consternation that may have its roots in his childhood. In the first of three "Tragische Geschichten" (Tragic Stories), a young man struggling to decide between his German father and Italian mother (the "lovely, undeniable one") chooses suicide. The same unresolved mother-son relationship is likewise reflected, quite strikingly, in the account of an opera production that Walser would have liked a "dear friend" of his to see so that it might have been an instructive example for her. It is a celebration of the union between mother and son, "plant and fruit," against which the son's sweetheart vainly struggles. Walser sides with the "beloved who loved his mother . . . who failed to soar up to the ingloriousnesses of desertion, nor to the glories of the Eternal Masculine."

Of course the microscripts also contain many love stories: anecdotal tales (sometimes patterned after penny dreadfuls), made-up letters to lady-friends as well as some addressed to himself, digressive monologues that, going beyond the love theme, are enriched with Walserian maxims. At the same time, in between all these vividly depicted love affairs, stand passages that deny all such exertions of the imagination, for example this dispassionate confession: "No one loves me, thank God. I don't want to state this with certainty, but still I think it likely that I've never been loved. This conjecture makes me happy." At the center of Walser's imaginative strategies for love and its prohibition lies a fear of being touched that makes erotic fulfillment possible only at a distance from the object of desire. The best-case scenario for this paradoxical sort of romantic bliss is described in a text in which *both* lovers are driven so far apart by the close contact of a kiss that they thereafter avoid one another: "He had hidden from her so as to be able to gaily embrace her, which in accordance with his opinions and the rather odd orientation of his principles could be carried out only in her absence, whereby it scarcely occurred to him to consider what she might be thinking of him in the meantime, but he was by no means mistaken when he told himself she didn't tell herself anything at all but simply went on loving him." For the most part, though, this need is one-sided, and the lover's sweetheart shows no understanding for his withdrawal. Walser then likes to take concrete examples designed to give rise to more appropriate behavior on the part of his ladylove. An ongoing love crisis may have been the source of one of the oddest, most private microscripts, in which the letter writer calls upon the "mistress of my heart" to treat him "roughly." Sadistic tortures come to mind as being potentially appropriate for purposes of instruction, methods used, for example, on runaway slaves; then he chooses a Dominican priest as his spokesman to describe to a medieval heretic in living color the horrors of the death by fire awaiting him. But no matter the painful, obsessive realms into which Walser's romantic pedagogy occasionally strays, it brings him back again to the confession: "That'll cost me an epistle chock full of atonements! For here I stand, poor devil full of faults, before your inexpressibly dear sweet delicate face."

Perhaps it's in the micrographic poems that the many nuances of Walser's experience of love are given their most formally interesting expression. Their formal artificiality, even when it consists in nothing more than a loose rhyme scheme, makes it possible for Walser again and again to abruptly interrupt a "frivolously" playful speech held in an intentionally humorous, chatty tone with startlingly frank "confessions." Often it's impossible to tell at these points what is to be ascribed to emotional consternation, what to artistic originality, and what to the provisional nature of the draft itself. A commentary in verse that Walser wrote outside the brackets in which he'd enclosed a poem he judged inadequate bears striking witness to this peculiarly fluctuating language:

That must be
better said.
But really I mean it
seriously.
I made you small
and boldly laughed at that.
It happened as if
of its own accord.
Presently
I'm so talentless
in poeticizing
it's horrifying.
It's in my head
but won't come out.
Someone once told me: you always want sweet speeches.
All these essays I wrote
are why I wasn't true to you.
While losing sight of you
I grew up into a European.
But enough for today.
Today I'm really no nightingale.

Trans. Susan Bernofsky

Robert Walser's Räuber *Novel*

Bernhard Echte

"I'VE DECIDED TO WRITE a novel, which will have to be psychological, of course. It will be concerned with vital questions," Robert Walser wrote in his prose piece "Am I Demanding?" that dates from February or March 1925.[1] Despite the irony in this bow to psychology and the mock pomposity of the announcement that "vital questions" will be dealt with, the intention itself still seems serious. Walser was all too well acquainted with the publishers' and the reading public's lamentably unilateral opinion that an author could only prove himself by writing novels; he had suffered too long under this restriction to have had any interest in awakening such expectations without good reason.

If we take this passage to attest to the fact that Walser had had a new novel in mind for a long time, the assertion at the beginning of the *Räuber* novel that he's constructing a "contemplative" book acquires an additional, more literal sense: he most definitely "contemplated" for four or five months before tackling the book's composition in July 1925. This might also be understood as the first indication that the compositional structure of the text and its curiously associative and discontinuous mode of narration isn't the result of a pathological flight of ideas or an uncontrolled literary mania, as a number of reviewers surmised upon the novel's first appearance in 1972, but rather is based on a well thought-out method and pursues specific intentions. Martin Jürgens made this point in his afterword to the first edition which is still well worth reading today.

That the formal conception and the execution of the novel are by no means the product of blind chance or the author's derangement can be further clarified by examining the texts Walser wrote in the year or so preceding the composition of the *Räuber* novel. Here one can trace the gradual development of the narrative techniques that account for much of the novel's originality. Numerous leitmotifs from the *Räuber* novel can also be seen, particularly in the texts that have survived only in microscript.

"More on this later"—phrases such as this are among the book's most conspicuous features. Walser first employed a similar technique of delay and concealment in the microscript text "Damals war es, o damals" (It was then, o then), which was probably written around the same time as the announcement of a new novel in "Am I Demanding?"; Walser must have been aware he'd found a structuring principle that could be used to best effect in longer works. And in the *Räuber* novel he brings all the advantages of this procedure into play. With a great number of interruptions and announcements of what's to come, at times not entirely without irony, he knots together a broad net of hints and riddles in which the reader gets hopelessly tangled as soon as he's become involved with the text. We wait for much of the promised information in vain, and often it proves (despite earlier claims to the contrary) to be of no account for an understanding of the situation or it adds further riddles to the existing ones rather than clearing them up. Everywhere the reader's deliberately provoked curiosity is channeled into cul-de-sacs or satisfied only after various other irrelevant-seeming matters have been dealt with.

Digressions and insertions complement the techniques of interruption and deferment. This method, too, is systematically employed, even if Walser's introductory sentences, such as "I just want to say quickly," seem at first glance arbitrary and fortuitous. But whereas the ideas are clearly spontaneous, the way they are distributed in the text is carefully planned. In such earlier prose pieces as "A Slap in the Face et-cetera" and "A Lump of Sugar" Walser had demonstrated the combination of unrelated items and continual digression as a principle of construction. Approximately two years after the *Räuber* novel he wrote a prose piece, "Minotaur," in which these techniques were once more played out and defined in paradigmatic fashion; the text's undisguised aim is to lure the reader into a labyrinth.

It isn't difficult to see that similar intentions underlie the *Räuber* novel, particularly in its first sections. Even the narrator admits this after a fashion when in the twelfth section he confesses that he *hopes* that much "in these pages" still seems mysterious to the reader. The justification that follows— that otherwise we would be bored—reveals admittedly only half the truth, since mazes are sometimes more exasperating than entertaining for those trapped in them. A labyrinth in its construction is designed to set up an ambivalent tension between these two feelings and reactions. On one hand, we can be amused at the absurd helplessness of our position and take pleasure in the attempt to extricate ourselves from this tricky predicament with playful acumen. On the other hand, though, the circumstances also put our patience and humor to the test, and we can easily lose them. Then the thorniness of the situation seems personally aimed at the victim—a treachery that can sometimes arouse considerable indignation.

The labyrinth as vexation or pleasure—this is also the choice with which the reader of Walser's *Räuber* novel is faced. If he is susceptible to the charm and refinement with which he has been kept waiting and often has had his leg pulled, he will derive considerable pleasure from the book. That's when he learns to appreciate fully all the "smashing ideas" with which Walser constantly brings everything into disorder. Read in this way, the novel is thoroughly suspenseful and entertaining despite its bitter under-tones, and this is doubtless, as Walser specifically points out in many texts of the Berne period, what he intended. Because of the many traces of a tragic fate that show up throughout the late work, this aspect of his writing is perhaps all too often overlooked. In general, to be sure, laughing and crying are closely connected for Walser, and so even the technical maneuvers in the *Räuber* novel have a more serious meaning behind them. Nevertheless, Walser's humor always displays its characteristically anarchic dynamics and is never merely the superficial side of melancholy. Even when it turns black, it stubbornly retains its pleasurable aspect. This is especially true of the luxuriously subversive mischievousness with which the phenomenon of literary self-importance is parodied, and of the ironically hypocritical manner in which the narrator assumes the role now of the absentminded know-nothing, now of the prudent organizer, or the frolicking roguishness with which tricks are again and again played on the reader. So it seems one has to have as prerequisite a taste for mockery, or being mocked, as well as a confederate's sympathy for the story's "heroes," the robber and the narrator, to enter into the pleasure of this labyrinthine literary delicacy.

It's clear that Walser couldn't count on most of his novel-reading contemporaries meeting these requirements. The middle-class reading public was expecting something else: the discussion of those universally applicable "vital questions" to which Walser had ironically referred in the passage cited above. Valid insights into the nature of time and society, the presentation of mankind's eternal problems, a moral message, self-help tips in whatever form—these characterized the expectations of the majority. Walser, however, points out at the beginning of his book that, to his "enormous regret," he isn't writing for these sorts of "most estimable individuals," or at best is writing for them only in the sense that he intends to make fun of them. It's precisely the culture-hungry reader, who with reverential deference awaits the all-important fruits of the poet's imagination, that Walser prefers to ridicule. He doesn't give him a chance in the labyrinth of his novel. The reader's irritation is guaranteed, particularly as, despite his indignation, he can't deny the suggestiveness of all this apparently meaningless and irrelevant material and therefore assumes that the poet's message to him must be hidden somewhere inside. But wherever he looks, he only stumbles into the numerous traps that have been set for him, containing, in defiance of the seeker, nothing but smiling banalities. As for the message—if there is one—the text obstinately refuses to provide any information. Instead it plays "cops and robbers" with the reader hoping for spiritual guidance.

That the robber evades the grasp of the reader in search of order is perhaps less surprising than the fact that the mysterious role of the narrator is decisive in this. The reciprocal relationship between narrator and robber is yet another of the novel's characteristic traits and like the narrative techniques discussed above, it has several parallels in Walser's short prose of the period. Of particular interest here is the text "Ediths Anbeter" (Edith's Admirer), which also contains a striking number of leitmotifs that recur in the *Räuber* novel. In each of these first-person texts, the narrator knows his protagonists as real fellow citizens and intentionally intervenes in their relationships with one another. Thus narrator and characters stand on the same (fictive) level of reality, even though the former maintains "control" over the latter and they are forced to behave as he sees fit. If the narrator initially seems to want to denounce them altogether, calling one or the other of them a "simpleton" or a "ne'er-do-well" "whose score ought to be settled once and for all," he suggests in both cases that in the end the provisionally disqualified figure might prove to be perfectly acceptable after all. "Let's allow him to hope that with time he'll be found tolerable"—this final sentence from "Ediths Anbeter" differs only slightly from the end of the *Räuber* novel.

Whereas in "Ediths Anbeter" the "hero" could still be given a dressing down from the point of view of a consistent, conventional understanding of normality and in the *Räuber* novel the narrator continues to represent this position, it is undermined in the latter work by contrary tendencies. In the first chapter the narrator uses a clearly audible "us" to identify himself with the other citizens of Berne ("during all the time he [the robber] has been spending among us"). Accordingly he shares the low opinion the robber's neighbors have of him. In the second chapter, however, the narrator suddenly adopts precisely the same behavior that brought the robber his ruinously bad reputation; among other things, he asks a waitress to strike him on the hand with a switch, rather a peculiar contrast to his assurance that he's a "respectable author." It soon becomes evident that the narrator's respectability has been lost only recently: we learn, for example, that a "ladies' café" has been declared off-limits to him, and that in all other respects, too, he's been banished from "elegant circles." Moreover, he's often ignored on the street now and sometimes even treated to "impertinent exclamations on the part of passersby," forcing one to assume that his reputation is no more flattering than the robber's. And the narrator reports increasing difficulty in not confusing himself with the robber. "Where did I see that? Rather, where did the robber see it?"—ostensibly accidental mistakes of this sort frequently occur. Once he even says explicitly: "I have to pay attention constantly so as not to confuse myself with him."

One could make the objection that these occasional superimpositions of robber and narrator are due simply to the hurriedness of the draft and that Walser would have eliminated them had he prepared a fair copy. It's true that the reflections about the identity of narrator and robber occur only in those places where Walser has made a slip of the pen and confused the two. In a few spots, for example, in the robber's conversation with the "Henri Rousseau woman" he meets in the forest, the faulty "I" has even been left uncorrected. Nevertheless, it seems doubtful that Walser would have cleared up these passages in the novel and introduced an unambiguous division between narrator and robber. There are too many similarities between the two for the passages where they are briefly merged to be merely the result of oversight. The affinity between them shows up most clearly in a little remark the narrator makes in which he suddenly presents himself as being even more robberlike than his protagonist. The latter, despite the profession ascribed to him, fails to commit any offenses against private property; the narrator, on the other hand, readily admits to not being all too meticulous in matters of money and personal belongings: he's in the habit of disappointing the trust of his creditors and tends not to pay back loans.

Numerous commentaries to the *Räuber* novel have made the claim that the robber personifies the splitting-off of the antisocial tendencies the narrator is unable to integrate into his own personality. But as the passages mentioned above show, this approach only holds at best for one side of this double strategy. Behind this quasi-official facade, the narrator is the robber's accomplice if not the guiding spirit of the naive "simpleton." Naturally this is always denied outright whenever it's explicitly mentioned; and then the narrator is a decent citizen through and through and indignantly insists he can't possibly have anything in common with such a robber. But as the text progresses, these denials seem more and more at odds with what is being described; their categorical certitude finally proves to be pure irony. This is also true for many of the narrator's statements about himself. When, for example, he claims at the end that he's considered "sober, thank God," for which reason it's to be expected he'll be offered a "manager's post," this is genuinely grotesque. Or when in the last lines of the novel he laconically states, "He's him and I'm me," the next sentence indicates that this is true only in one particular regard: the robber has no money, while the narrator has plenty. In all other respects these two gentlemen, both of whom are writers, seem largely to correspond to one another.

Can the novel be read autobiographically? The setting, easily recognizable as Berne, suggests this, as do the numerous facts and occurrences that have parallels in Walser's own life. Connections can be traced between the robber's places of residence and many of his acquaintances (particularly the female ones) and Walser's own. Still, the claim that character and author are identical is obviously untenable and ignores the novel's massive irreality. The robber's robberhood consists simply in his having stolen a young girl's peace of mind and committed a few petty acts of plagiarism from penny dreadfuls and in his refusal to confront reality as something practical and real, instead exploiting it from an aesthetic standpoint.

To call him a robber for these reasons is perhaps not entirely necessary. In the sentences that tell of the aforementioned deeds, the word *rob* actually seems out of place. But perhaps it is precisely this slight sense of unsuitability in the designation "robber" that makes it possible for Walser to demonstrate that the modern novel is forced to dispense with those characteristics that gave the material of the old-fashioned romantic novel its charm. This word simultaneously invokes the past splendor of a long chain of literary works and demonstrates why it cannot be further continued any longer.

In this connection one should note a portrait of the fifteen-year-old Robert Walser painted by his brother Karl which shows the future writer in the garb of a classic robber, Karl Moor. One can think of this picture as the nucleus around which the novel later crystallized. It shows, and Walser suggests this elsewhere as well, that Schiller's Moor was one of the first figures young Walser identified with in the realm of art. He considered him a paragon of the dramatic hero, and the play itself, *The Robbers,* one of the "golden, ideal lies" of which the stuff of great literature was made.[2] But Walser soon was forced to realize that this kind of art was out of date in the age of modernity; in his Berne period this led him to the conviction that the "decline of all greatness" represented a major characteristic of the age.[3] In the midst of the modern "machinery of civilization,"[4] it was impossible to write fateful, heroic works any longer; with such grandiosity one would fall hopelessly prey to a false romanticism. Nevertheless a collective longing for stories of this sort continued to exist and was shared by Walser; he satisfied it—smiling at himself all the while—by reading penny dreadfuls. "A thriller [robber novel] lay among my military service papers," one reads in "A Slap in the Face et-cetera."[5] What had once been a promising figure for the young Walser to identify with, what had represented for him the paradigm of the poetic hero, had finally, in view of a technical, rational world, entered the realm of anachronistic cliché. It seems as if Walser, by taking on this cliché and transforming it into a grotesquely anomalous but nonetheless appealing hero, meant it as a quirky, ironic song of farewell to his former idol and to the poetry of magnificent lies. So he created a robber who couldn't really be one any longer, a "robber of the sad countenance," so to speak, a descendant of Don Quixote.

Even though the robber, unlike Quixote, doesn't in the least live out his role, both are latecomers to a romantic idea. Instead of becoming a splendid knight, Quixote becomes a fool; instead of being able to represent—if only on paper—a just and rebellious robber, a freedom and folk hero, the robber becomes what rationalism and bourgeois society have made of the fool: a social outsider whose behavior and psyche are under suspicion of pathological derangement.

At this point the designation "robber" proves appropriate in yet another sense; it articulates the judgment of a society based on conformity to a practical mediocrity, to whose order any vivacious originality presents the threatening aspect of criminal anarchy. Several times in his Berne years Walser gave voice to the conviction that despite the wistful admiration the modern era brings to extraordinary, artistically inclined individuals, in practice it refuses to tolerate them. With narrow-minded rigidity it represses everything even a little ingenious; even a harmless crank like the robber runs afoul of their norms. A writer who doesn't partake of the society's self-idealization in exemplary fashion but rather, strolling about the streets, seeks to maintain an unerring sense for the poetic is seen by the petit-bourgeois social order as a *Tagedieb,* a "day thief" or idler. Distrustful eyes *pursue* this individual who alarms his fellow citizens—who after all know perfectly well what is suitable and what's not—with his not precisely calculable difference from the normal code of behavior. The eccentric who lays himself open to attack in this manner can expect two sorts of reactions. First, he will become the target of intensified efforts to "drum some morals into him." Then, when these exertions come to nothing, he will find himself the subject of increasing stigmatization; on the street, the robber (or the narrator) is sometimes ignored, sometimes harrassed; he is turned out of pubs and treated to other exclusionary maneuvers designed to break the victim's resistance and shake his belief in himself.

Nevertheless, the robber is by no means just a victim, as is continually claimed—particularly in light of Walser's own fate. But rather it's the robber (or the narrator) himself who stages many of the incidents that seem to violate "common sense," whereby there is sometimes a great deal of sheerly pleasurable mischievousness involved. For example, he once presents his straw hat with the flourish of a grand seigneur to the waiter of the station restaurant so that the latter might hang it up for him; for example, he suddenly initiates a duel on the street when a gentleman with a lady on his arm blocks his path, or he meets with dubious ladies of the demimonde in public so as to have them recount their life stories for him. All these minor adventures are sought out and often deliberately orchestrated by the robber, apparently for the sole reason that he, like the narrator, is a writer. In the "indecisive time" in which he lives, interesting incidents suitable for use in novels or stories hardly ever occur on their own any longer, but must be artificially induced: in this modern, fully organized world, one can sense only on the outskirts of society something of the vicissitudes of life that once constituted the heartbeat of the poetic, for which reason a writer must also —must above all—be at home in these regions. Only there can one find exceptional modes of existence; only there is the struggle against fate still being fought—admittedly for the most part with a banally materialistic fate, so that the outsider, though potentially the last poetic figure, needs a fantastic disguise to qualify as a romantic hero.

Since the modern world and the romantic poetry of lies diverge so irreconcilably, the hero's almost grotesque state of collapse is just as inevitable as the accompanying disintegration of traditional narrative techniques. They, too, like the roles, are often brought into play only for purposes of parody. Thus the narrator mocks himself when several pages into the book he provides the first chronological reference, with the words: "Finally we're beginning to narrate in an orderly fashion." All other traditional structural elements in the novel are similarly ironized, and so in the end one has to ask whether or not the text can really be called a novel, which hasn't been predetermined since Walser didn't label the manuscript as such. Here, too, as so often with Walser, the answer is double-sided. On one hand, the narrator admits in the second section that the robber is to become the hero of a novel; at the end, on the other hand, he calls the text one "great, enormous gloss, ridiculous and unfathomable." As with all the many other things that are ambivalent in Walser's work, here, too, it is advisable not to insist on an unequivocable resolution, but rather to try to read the book on all its levels: as novel and as gloss on the novel.

Trans. Susan Bernofsky

NOTES

1   In *Selected Stories,* trans. Christopher Middleton and others (New York: Farrar, Straus and Giroux, 1982), 150.
2   *Das Gesamtwerk* (Frankfurt: Suhrkamp, 1978), 3:31.
3   *Aus dem Bleistiftgebiet* (Frankfurt: Suhrkamp, 1985), 1:22.
4   *Gesamtwerk,* 12:433.
5   Trans. Mark Harman, in *Robert Walser Rediscovered,* ed. Mark Harman (Hanover: University Press of New England, 1985), 34.

A Secretive Modernist:
Robert Walser and His Microscripts

Mark Harman

READING THE MICROSCRIPTS is like attending a private rehearsal. The secretive nature and provisional quality of these texts permitted Walser to reveal far more of himself than ever before. He kept prying eyes at bay by resorting to a minuscule handwriting, only one to two millimeters tall, which was long considered indecipherable. Now, thanks to the ingenious efforts of Bernhard Echte and Werner Morlang, the two Zurich editors who decoded the bulk of the microscripts, those secrets are out in the open.

These "new" texts ought to encourage us to modify, or even completely discard, certain old but nonetheless still influential critical notions.[1] First of all, there is Elias Canetti's argument that Walser consistently denies his fear and leaves out "one part of himself" (RWR, 151).[2] Although that thesis is generally persuasive, it fails to account for the microscripts. There Walser allows his anxiety about his exposed predicament to rise repeatedly to the surface of his prose. Whereas Canetti's insight now requires some adjustment, Walter Benjamin's notions about Walser's method of composition need to be put to rest, once and for all. In his brief 1929 essay, Benjamin suggests that Walser is a scribbler of considerable genius who simply writes down whatever comes into his head and never pauses to revise what he has written (RWR, 144). The microscripts show clearly that Walser often subjects his texts to radical, and extremely revealing, revisions.

From the outset, Walser knew that, before submitting the miniature microscripts for publication, he would have to rewrite them in his regular-sized, copperplate handwriting. That awareness made it easier for him to disclose anxieties that he usually hid below a relentless flow of cheerful pitter-patter. Later, when transcribing the microscripts into his copperplate handwriting, he tended to excise revelations that might further undermine his already shaky literary reputation.

The transition from the microscript draft to the copperplate "final product" actually involves three separate Walsers: the sophisticated avant-garde writer of the twenties, who wants to experiment "in the field of language in the hope that there might be in language some unknown liveliness which it would be a joy to awaken" (GW, 12:431-32), the no-holds-barred author of the microscripts, and an anxious censor, who is determined to obliterate traces of personal turmoil from his writing. My observations about this process are based largely on a comparison of the microscript drafts in the Zurich archives with the revised versions that Walser submitted for publication.[3]

While transcribing the microscripts, Walser's avant-garde persona makes liberal use, figuratively speaking, of scissors and paste. He condenses the microscript draft by lifting striking phrases out of the specific context in which they occur and juxtaposing them, either with other phrases from the draft or with new associations that occur to him as he recomposes the text. For good measure, he often throws in new snippets from the popular fiction that he happens to be reading.

Walser admits in one of the microscripts that he is afraid of degenerating into a latter-day "confessional Jean-Jacques Rousseau" (K, 222/1). He makes lavish use of his red pen in an attempt to avert that fate. A comparison of the published version of "Ottilie Wildermuth" and of the original microscript, which is about two-thirds longer, shows Walser, the self-censoring editor, at work.

He complains in the microscript that, after returning to Biel from Berlin, his Swiss compatriots still regarded him as a purveyor of the "cheerfulnesses" characteristic of his earlier Zurich style (K, 229/1). Feeling trapped in the effervescent role that others expect of him, he strips away his literary mask of constant good cheer: "I have every reason to regret having authored in a markedly life-affirming manner." Yet, while rewriting the microscript, Walser imposes on the new text the good cheer rejected so vehemently in the original version.

The revamped persona in the copperplate version of "Wildermuth" congratulates himself on his wonderful "talent for equilibrium" (GW, 11:34). But Walser has achieved that equilibrium by ruthlessly censoring all but the slightest traces of the unsettling biographical predicament described in the microscript. The microscript persona is upset that his fellow countrymen consider him "ridiculous"; his copperplate sibling simply declares that those same countrymen "treasure" his "virtues." The acknowledgment of a painful humiliation gets turned into a rather abstract self-vindication. The tell-tale details of the incident fall by the wayside.

Even oblique references to unpleasant extratextual realities have to go. Walser ends the unpublished microscript version of "Weltstadt" by suggesting that he is only faring well inside the "framework" of the text (K, 91/11/3). That memorable phrase also falls victim to Walser's red pen. It is replaced by a cheerful, if suspiciously vague, assertion: "My capacity for self-sufficiency ensured that things went well for me" (GW, 11:320).

He also eliminates passages that might further alienate the cultural powers-that-be. It was one thing to let off steam about the lack of recognition accorded his work in the microscripts, and quite another to do so in one of his public performances. A lengthy diatribe against the "sentimentality" of the Naturalists culminates in the demand that the playwright Hauptmann be, punningly, "enthauptet," or beheaded (M, 2:489). In the published version (GW, 10:347), this diatribe has, of course, been eliminated. The same holds true for a subtle yet nonetheless transparent reference to Count Tolstoy's "problematic" combination of "eminently artistic and simultaneously unartistic elements" (K, 222/1). Those comments cannot be allowed to remain, since they reflect a crisis in Walser's own artistic self-confidence.

Walser's Bern texts are modern versions of medieval palimpsests. The "ghost" of the original texts, which Walser only half erased, is now showing through again. So we can eavesdrop on a secret dialogue between Walser's copperplate and microscript selves. The most striking instance of this subtle intertextual dialogue occurs in the drastically modified version of "Moonshine Story," in which the copperplate narrator refers to a "less reflective author" who has committed the faux pas of using the phrase "he held her in an embrace" (11:391). The author in question is none other than the creator of the microscript version of "Moonshine Story," in which that very expression occurs (K, 290/5). So, here as elsewhere, the "cool" copperplate persona is having a field day at the expense of his microscript sibling. Needless to say, the latter cannot answer back.

Walser never loses his sovereign sense of humor, even when under considerable duress. He can even poke fun at the censor in himself, and its tendency to ape the mentality of the "Bildungsbürgertum," which he despises. Certain shocking revelations have to be omitted, he says, because they might do in a "Ph.D. in literature" (K, 222/1). But, in the copperplate version, that joke, too, gets eliminated.

The microscripts bring to the surface the yawning human abyss that had always lurked beneath Walser's prose. For much of his career he had skated about cheerfully on a bright, sparkling surface. Darker emotions were banished or, at least, confined to walk-on parts, such as that of the gloomy giant Tomzack in "The Walk" (SS, 54). Those inner Tomzacks multiplied in the course of the twenties, however, and Walser urgently needed to enter into a dialogue with them.

One of the saddest things about Walser's fate is that he wasn't able to indulge in that kind of open, no-holds-barred dialogue with himself during his public performances. He felt, no doubt rightly, that the publication of such agonized soul-searching would have pushed him even further to the margins. So he split his writing self into the freewheeling, uninhibited author of the private microscripts, and the more guarded composer of the public versions. But now we can, and indeed should, read the frequently confessional microscripts side by side with the more impersonal verbal collages of the Bern years. They are complementary expressions of the same brilliant but troubled writer.

Had Walser been able to publish his more deeply self-exploratory microscript writings, such as the *Räuber* novel, it is conceivable that he might have managed to avoid those long years of silence at Herisau. We ought to be skeptical about his implicit claim, in a conversation with his literary executor Carl Seelig, that he was just as content leading the simple life of an inmate as the poet Hölderlin had been during his long years of confinement (S, 49). Instead, we ought to lend credence to the bleaker vision implicit in these haunting lines from a microscript poem: "To know so much and to have seen so much / and to say so little, so little" (RWR, 56).

NOTES

1   The often urgent and personal quality of Walser's writing in the microscripts suggests that his crisis in the mid-twenties is far more intimate than Martin Jürgens has proposed in his cogently argued but excessively theoretical study, *Robert Walser: Die Krise der Darstellbarkeit* (Kronberg/Taunus: Scriptor, 1973).

2   Abbreviations refer to the following editions or archival material: GW = *Gesammelte Werke,* ed. Jochen Greven, 12 vols (Frankfurt: Suhrkamp, 1978); K = manuscripts of unpublished transcriptions from the *Kalendarblätter* in the Robert Walser Archive, Zurich, as numbered by the editors; M = *Aus dem Bleistiftgebiet: Mikrogramme 1924/25,* ed. Bernhard Echte and Werner Morlang, 3 vols (Frankfurt: Suhrkamp, 1985); RWR = *Robert Walser Rediscovered,* ed. Mark Harman (Hanover: University Press of New England, 1985); S = Carl Seelig, *Wanderungen mit Robert Walser* (Frankfurt: Suhrkamp, 1978); SS = Robert Walser, *Selected Stories,* trans. Christopher Middleton et al. (New York: Farrar, Straus and Giroux, 1982).

3   I would like to thank both Dr. Werner Morlang, who generously drew my attention to the archival material, and Bernhard Echte, who kindly shared his expertise. My stay in Zurich was made possible, in part, by a grant from Pro Helvetia, which I would also like to acknowledge here.

Lost Traces: On a Poem by Robert Walser

Adolf Muschg

Schnee (III)

Die Wälder scheinen jetzt zu schlafen,
ähnlich den Lämmern und den Schafen.
Auch ich bin wie mit Schnee bedeckt,
als hätt' ich mich vor mir versteckt.
Schnee liegt vergnügt auf allen Dächern
wie längst vergeßne Brief' in Fächern,
und in Schubladen ist es dunkel,
und im Konzert gibt's ein Gefunkel
von Tönen, und in Sälen blitzen
die Kerzen, und ob guten Witzen
wird dann und wann hell aufgelacht.
Was ist der Schnee für eine Pracht!
Die Landschaft scheint nun wie gemacht,
ein Kind als Bettelein zu dienen,
Dichter dichten fleißig wie Bienen.
In Räumen sausen die Maschinen,
wo nicht getändelt werden kann.
Jünglinge, Mädchen, Fraun und Mann',
welchen Zielen geht ihr entgegen?
Schnee liegt nun auf den vielen Wegen.
Welch eine schöne Zeit ist das!
In feinen Spitzen ragt das Gras
im Acker aus dem Schnee hervor.
Wo er hinfällt, da bleibt er liegen,
bewegt sich nicht, läßt sich nicht biegen.

Snow

The woods seem now to lie in sleep,
just like the little lambs and sheep.
I, too, am as if cloaked in snow,
as though in hiding from myself.
Gaily on rooftops the snow lies
like letters long forgotten in cubbyholes,
and darkness fills up all the drawers,

and the concert hall sparks with an uproar
of notes, and in the ballrooms flash
the candles, and all the witty jokes
make bursts of laughter fly.
How magnificent, this snow!
The landscape now seems expressly made
to serve as bed for a little babe,
poets write poems, hardworking as bees.
Whole rooms hum with loud machines—
this is no place for flirting.
Youths, maidens, women, men,
what destinations are you going toward?
The snow now lies on all the paths.
What a beautiful time this is!
In tiny points the grass pokes up
from beneath the snow in the field.
Wherever it falls, the snow lies spent
and moves no more, and won't be bent.

HOW MANY ASSOCIATIONS can you come up with for snow? Put together a few sentences with snow. Already it sounds like a school essay. The model child, given this assignment, makes the task even more difficult: it writes poetry. The first pair of lines turns out pitifully, but it rhymes! "Ähnlich" (like), which, as the word on which the couplet turns, ought to be inconspicuous, breaks the tone with a screech: at this point I see something like a sudden cramp or tic come over the features of a reciting child. This effect disconcerts the "gentle" listener, sharpens his ear: the innocuously ambiguous "scheinen" (seem) of the first line can in retrospect begin to trouble him. But the poet now strides dutifully along, as he's learned from all the best examples, to the obligatory "I" of the poem. It, too, has to be "wie mit Schnee bedeckt" (as if cloaked in snow). Then what really covers it? The contradiction begins to gnaw at one: a covering of snow can scarcely be separated from the idea of standing in the open, utterly exposed. And this dubious protection, as it turns out, isn't even claimed with regard to the elements, but rather hides the poet from himself. Or to be precise: it's only "as if" the metaphorical snow does this. It's already become disturbing, this puzzle of similes. What seems to be a signifier can't link up with its signified and remains dangling in midair. Whatever it was that triggered this string of metaphors apparently remains mute and incomparable, and what might have put a halt to them eludes comparison.

What is all this? Let's have something safe. "Vergnügt" (gaily) the snow lies on the rooftops, as it should in essays. The next metaphor, though, doesn't have the slightest thing to do with this gaiety. It relegates the cozy rooftops to a horribly narrow, comically distant frame of reference: letters in cubbyholes. Who would think of such a thing? The schema's meaning is carried ad absurdum by the "längst vergessen" (long forgotten)—it almost seems as if the poem, and its author's claim, is speaking only of itself. And now, by way of a dutiful and uncanny reflection on the "Schublade" (drawer), the poem derails into the open field of free association. The things that come up, highlights of so-called society life and its winter season, no longer seem motivated by any purpose, but rather by a hurried compulsion to rhyme, until the language catches its breath in a platitude, too briefly and, so to speak, on the wrong foot. No reader will believe the cry of delight with which the theme pretends to return to itself. In the meantime, too, the author has broken his own rules—a third rhyme on "-acht" has come to him and insists on being added; let's keep stumbling along. But the next obligatory winter image (snow = bed), twice diluted ("scheint . . . wie gemacht"— seems expressly made), transparently reveals its own horror, its child's grave and death by freezing. If an idyllic intent was to have been at work, it turned inside out in the author's mouth.

The characterization of the poet as "bienenfleißig" (hardworking as a bee), coming abruptly as it does, seems at this point almost an unasked-for self-commentary. Then, too, his troubles in love, compared to factory work, are made to look frivolous ("wo nicht getändelt werden kann"—this is no place for flirting) with the ventriloquist's voice of an imaginary supervisor. The paths through life, it seems, are so various that one can only make of them a subject for meditation: admittedly Friederike Kempner would never have allowed herself a plural like "Mann'" [instead of the correct "Männer," men]: it is the individuality of the language speaking here, if unwillingly, from another depth. For what seals the next compulsive exclamation of joy is, strictly speaking, not the love of winter, but a white it's-all-the-same-to-me, which with apparently benevolence has meanwhile covered up the question as to the meaning of all these paths through life. A cold solace amidst all this sincerity.

And then come the "feine Spitzen" (tiny points): the first words in the poem that give the impression of not just being mumbled in a half-dream but actually *seen*. It really does "hervorragen" (poke up), since here and only here a line ends without a rhyme, without an echo. The grass isn't standing here alone pro forma, as its metaphoric relative, the life of man, has always done, though never so inconspicuously forlorn. This place in the poem, though a misfortune in terms of the rhyme, reveals its art; it also suggests the reverse, that art, every art, is a specific form of unhappiness.

The poem then ends, it seems, with a mysterious unwillingness. The absentminded remark that the snow "lässt sich nicht biegen" (cannot be bent), but simply falls, lies there, doesn't move, evokes a subject other than snow. Perhaps the subject the whole poem was about from the beginning, though it couldn't, or wouldn't, speak of it except through precise artistic slips, virtuoso clumsiness and the clowning of white innocence. I don't want to name this subject. The poem stands there on its weak, pitifully cold feet.

Naturally it's tempting to think of Robert Walser's own death in connection with this poem. In 1956, at Christmas, he left the asylum at Herisau to go for a walk and remained in the snow. "The landscape now seems expressly made. . . ." It *was* made for him to find his death in it; in his walking stories, and in this poem as well, he himself had always made it so. Careful readers like Franz Kafka or Walter Benjamin had already noticed early on in Walser's life where these walks of his led. Back to their beginnings, "out of the night, where it is darkest, a Venetian night, one might say, lit by meager lanterns of hope, with some festive cheer in the eyes, but sad to the point of tears." Benjamin speaks further of "figures who have put madness behind them and can thus remain so laceratingly, inhumanly and unfailingly superficial."

Trans. Susan Bernofsky

Ignorance, Analogy, Motion: Robert Walser's "Boat Trip"

Tom Whalen

WE HAVE OBSERVED the scene before: sunlight on a river, trees touching shoulders along the banks, perhaps a cloudless sky, bluer than blue, and beneath it a boat bearing a group of people. How many people Robert Walser never tells us. There is a woman who calls water her "sweetheart," someone who finds it "odd that water is wet and not dry," a storyteller to whom everyone listens attentively, the narrator who wishes he could be "as fascinating a storyteller" as the other, and a "thoughtful girl" who "compare[s] travelling over the water to the imperceptible gliding and progress of growth."[1] Five, then, at least; add others if you wish; the prose here is not autocratic. No one is described. The water, yes, and the banks, the trees, fish—a comparison here and another there. Water is like. Trees are like. Traveling over water is like. Ignorance can be compared to. But no one is described—no hats, smiles, umbrellas, ties, particularities of sex or age. Morning or afternoon, it doesn't matter. It's a boat trip. We ourselves have been on this water, if only in other books. But weren't those scenes more dramatic (Dickens) or more idyllic (Carroll) than this one? And isn't this boat trip both more natural and more strange? What curious details arise here. What strangely apt yet surprising comparisons. And isn't this prose piece more about perception than people; that is, don't the perceptions dominate, aren't they what we find unique? There are no "characters" to speak of, no characterization. And there's no tension, then, created by the characters, no "story." So what is there here to justify William Gass's judgment of "Boat Trip" as "one of the triumphs of Walser's art" (*Masquerade,* xvii)?

It's not enough to point out that now, in 1931, when Walser is a resident at the Waldau Sanitarium, his work has become less anticly ludic, that he is writing a calmer, less "possessed" prose, because throughout his career he would sometimes write in a similar "simpler" manner, as in "Lake Greifen" (1899), "The Gloves" (1905), "Johanna" (1913), "The Boat" (1914), "A Little Ramble" (1914), "Snowdrops" (1919), "The Little Tree" (1925), and even a late work of such intense serenity as "Prose Piece" (1927-28). To Carl Seelig, long after being transferred from Waldau to Herisau and the self-imposed end to his writing, he admonished himself for not writing a prose more accessible to the people, that if he had it to do over again he would keep before him as an example "the terrible beauty of [Keller's] *Der grüne Heinrich* [*Green Henry*]."[2] But such a shifting of perspective, of *weight,* would not have been possible for a writer like Walser, this "child, though a quite clever one to be sure,"[3] who lifted his "hat to the age, but not too high."[4] And of course, within the prose pieces that Walser wrote, no matter how small, lies a vein that glows with a "terrible beauty," one detectable even in the curious and contemplative "Boat Trip." One, however, I would also suggest, that is not imposed from without, but that arises from Walser's ability, in Christopher Middleton's phrase, to "tru[e] language to matter" (Middleton, 101), or, as Hesse said of Walser, to give his works "the magic of an art that has almost become nature again."[5]

How can language, abstracted from nature, become "almost nature again"? Or, more specific to Walser's case, how does the ingenious writer affect ingenuousness? "They laugh at me," he wrote in "Ein ganz klein wenig Watteau" (1925-26), "primarily because I seem in earnest. They think it happens unwittingly, whereas in fact it's by design. But my vocation, my mission, consists mainly in making every effort to keep my audience believing I am truly simple. I give the illusion that unspoiledness and naïveté still exist."[6] This illusion, one can say, is maintained throughout "Boat Trip," but what complexities open up in such "simple" conjectures as "I don't know which is lovelier, boating on a lake or on a river, but this not knowing needn't bother me." This "not knowing" becomes in "Boat Trip" the river we travel down, perceiving what we can by direct observation or analogy. "Not knowing," this "magnificent figure" of "ignorance," as one character calls it, is the condition that dominates experience, that gives the world back to us unmediated.

Not knowing, of course, is an open condition, certitude a closed one. To traverse the abyss between ideas about the thing and the thing itself, we need to dissolve the a priori. Nothing is given, everything can be seen anew. When we enter "Boat Trip" we are immediately put into a condition of uncertainty. The opening sentence is a response to an unheard observation, one we can only imagine, never really know: "Not that the water was crystal clear everywhere." Perhaps it's just been pointed out how clear the water was, how far into its depths one can see. Perhaps we've even been shown, say, a fish, or a school of fish, or the glimmer of light off rocks on the bottom. But we can't say exactly. And note, too, that we enter in medias res, that the boat trip is already in progress, in motion. Not knowing makes for metastasis, and metastasis was Walser's preferred natural standpoint, as exemplified in his frequent walks (in life and prose) and his devotion to contradictions ("I am ready at any moment to admit the contradictoriness here apparent, which, in itself, is of great significance for me" ["The Aviator," 1927; *Selected Stories,* 171]).

Language is always mediation and loss, but it contains the means (or retains enough trace) to turn this loss into something tangential, experiential, tactile. Walser embodies the source by recalling what it consists of. He can do this with characteristic self-consciousness, as at the end of "A Sketch" (1928-29): "The garden somewhat resembled a thought fortunately not thought to a conclusion, and, without having any idea where I get the effrontery to do so, I compare my sketch with a swan singing with unheard of ardor and screechingly giving voice to unmediated things."[7] Or, as in "Boat Trip," by affecting "unspoiledness and naïvité." But in either case, he relies often on the principle of analogy to reveal the truths of the world.

Analogy, initially, fragments the world, but it also ties it together and puts thought (and imagery) in motion. "The garden somewhat resembled a thought fortunately not thought to a conclusion": the "somewhat" is a typically active Walser politeness which, like the comparison, can never be concluded. Walser's "without having any idea" is, again, the natural standpoint (but not a static one) from which and from only which he (or anyone) can give "voice to unmediated things." Ignorance, analogy, motion: "Odd similarities between things at rest and things flowing occurred to me during the trip. . . ."

And besides, it's a pleasure trip we're on, "no reason to overexert" ourselves. We're allowed our ignorance, our curious comparisons. "What cause could there have been" for us to overexert ourselves? "The day is long from early morning to late in the evening. On a pleasure trip the hours don't admonish you to hurry up. It's fine to waste a little time now and then." Walser's casual prose tells us it's all right for us to relax a little, there's no rush, this is just a boat trip after all, a way "to waste a little time," and there's nothing wrong in that. In fact, aren't we more likely to formulate surprising comparisons and yet not be surprised by them on such a languorous voyage?

So we relax, let the boat do what boats do, let our thoughts and the prose ramble a bit. "One member of the party found it odd that water is wet and not dry. It didn't have a grainy, sandy feel to it. When touched, it wriggled supplely about the fingers of one's hand." For this member of the party, like the narrator of Walser's "Snowdrops" (1919), "Everything always reminds one of its opposite" (*Selected Stories,* 127). So why not find it odd that water doesn't exhibit its opposite characteristics? Only man conjectures, only he makes tropes. Nature is what it implacably is. "Not that the water was crystal clear everywhere. Who would want to give orders to Nature? She makes no pretense of being other than she is." So we conjecture and compare. And isn't language itself essentially figuration? "One woman called it her sweetheart, and indeed what caresses more softly and cleanly than that which sustains a gondola but won't let a pebble stay on its surface?"

These two consecutive comparisons are followed by a third, more complicated one: "An elegant border of abundant plants and enchanting, delicate grasses adorned both sides of the river, which displayed numerous branches, like a tree with its trunk and limbs. The wood grows more and more slender, then flows into the leaves which are not unlike the tree's breath, or its thoughts, as it is with man." River to tree to man goes this comparative sequence, but we'd best diagram it specifically if we're to appreciate Walser's careful entwining. The first sentence, after showing us the banks with their "elegant border" and "enchanting, delicate grasses," moves to the river "which displayed numerous branches," and then, by way of a simile, comes back (but on a second level of reality) to the banks; that is, the river and its branches are compared to a tree's trunk and limbs. This comparison is further refined in the next sentence that shows us the trunk and limbs growing "more and more slender" and becoming leaves. Then, again within the sentence, this analogy flows into another—the leaves "are not unlike the tree's breath." Having achieved this third tier, it's easy to traverse to the fourth—"or its thoughts, as it is with man." From the "elegant border" along a river, by means of a riverlike meandering analogy, we have arrived inside our own heads. Man is like a tree which is like a river. Our thoughts are like leaves, and leaves are like breath. Horizontal landscape to vertical object in a landscape (one step removed by means of analogy, but an analogical object that *already resides* within the original) to (vertical) man, atop whose brainstem sway all these fused analogical levels.

One can become lost in the labyrinthine branches of this seemingly quiet, casual comparison, but it's by means of such subtleties that Walser draws the reader into a prose "that has almost become nature." At the end of "Prose Piece," an even shorter and more centrally analogical text, the identification with nature is directly stated. "Waves and branches have snakelike shapes, and there come moments when we know we are no more and no less than waves and snowflakes, or than that which surely feels, now and then, from its so wonderfully charming confinement, the pull of longing: the leaf" (*Masquerade*, 185). But in "Boat Trip" the means to this fusion is simultaneously more casual and complex.

Following the river-tree-man comparison, the narrator (casually) lets us know that he, too, was on this trip. "Odd similarities between things at rest [trees] and things flowing [the river] occurred to me during the trip that I, too, participated in, and I would have been delighted to have been as fascinating a storyteller as one person there, who was asked to invent a tale so that the outing not become boring." But our narrator is no storyteller, only a participant and a perceiver. Everyone listens attentively to the storyteller, even, our narrator notes, the fish: "Here and there fish, driven it seemed by an uncontrollable curiosity, bobbed upward from the depths to visibility, as though wishing to help the listeners be satisfied with the tale." We now expect the narrator to relate at least part of the tale, but his thoughts are elsewhere. Walser, like Hopkins, sees in the everyday what is "counter, original, spare, strange." Rather than relate the told tale, he prefers to reflect on fish: "On fish one finds no arms. Is that why they have such huge eyes and expressive mouths? Is it because they have no legs that they make the best swimmers? Doesn't river, *Fluss,* come from *Flosse,* fins, and aren't the latter an impediment to walking, and isn't it this limitation that forms the foundation of their strength?" Walser's deferential interrogatives keep the text (and the reader, the world) in flux. Does *Fluss* come from *Flosse,* or vice versa? Or don't they both derive from the old meaning of *fliessen,* "to swim"? How apt, in any case, that this boat trip takes us down an etymological river. And how characteristic for Walser to let a seemingly silly observation (fish have no arms) lead him to a metaphysical reflection on the nature of limitation and form.

Only two paragraphs, each one sentence long, remain in the three-paragraph "Boat Trip," and both are dominated by the piece's "main character" and by the ignorance/analogy/motion triad: "A girl sitting with us in the boat compared travelling over the water to the imperceptible gliding and progress of growth, that of fruit for example, which perhaps would have little desire to ripen if it knew to what end." The further analogy the reader can make is to the work he is reading, "Boat Trip," or to the act of reading "Boat Trip," which is, after all, a "travelling over the water," and comparable to "the imperceptible gliding and progress of growth," to life itself whose end will not be unlike that of fruit. A darker journey, then, than we might have thought, if only for the residue of loss and melancholy left in the wake of Walser's whimsy. "The thoughtful girl called ignorance a magnificent figure endowed with unconscious delights, sorrowful and splendid, not like those who learn arithmetic and writing, weep inwardly over their joy, and whose hearts tell them their laughter is a hardness, that they are incapable of enduring anything." Fruit does not know to what end it ripens, but we do, even if, for a moment, while floating on a river, we're allowed to forget, to become one with "the imperceptible gliding and progress of growth," before consciousness again closes the blinds between the idea of the thing and the thing itself. Ignorance indeed is a "magnificent figure endowed with unconscious delights." Like his narrator at the end of *Jakob von Gunten* (1908), Walser wants to give up the life of thought, wants to learn simply to live and be in the world. Ignorance and the unconscious are not for Walser *unconscious* conditions; he proposes instead a being who feels delight and sorrow and does not let consciousness mediate experience.

And yet for all the transparency of Walser's prose, for all his ability to match thought to world, world to word, an opaqueness still obtains. The light strikes the waves in such a way that we suddenly understand what, say, the word *glimmer* means, and know this is the only word to use, so we use it. Then correspondences begin to arise: light off glass, a wave of pain, and beneath the waves a darkness shot through with streaks of light into which fish swim, the light catching a cluster of scales, a not so random eye, a flutter, a fin—until there passes a cloud and the water all over goes dark, becomes simply water again, this substance both transparent and opaque that "wriggle[s] supplely about the fingers of one's hand."

William Gass describes Walser's art as "a response to the moves and meanings of both human life and nature which is purged of every local note and self-interested particularity and which achieves, like the purest poetry, an understanding mix of longing, appreciation, and despair" (*Masquerade*, xviii-xix). I'm not sure, finally, how Walser "purges" his prose of self-interest, how he can be at once one of the most egocentric and selfless of writers. We know, yes, of his devotion to the small, to powerlessness and metastasis, and I've noted above some of the "design" he employs to create the illusion of ingenuousness. And I know that this receptive, open condition cannot be sustained, as Walser himself must have known as he balanced on the tightwire above the abyss.

Or maybe it can, maybe it was only because of external circumstances that Walser was not allowed to continue to write prose like that in "Boat Trip." "[T]he question," Paul Klee wrote at the end of his *Pedagogical Sketchbook*, "is no longer 'to move there' but to be 'everywhere' and consequently also 'There!' "[8] Walser achieved in his prose time and again a fusion of "human life and nature," a oneness with the things of the world, reminding us that consciousness need not separate and sever, but can infuse and enfold.[9]

NOTES

1 Robert Walser, "Boat Trip," trans. Susan Bernofsky and Tom Whalen, in *Masquerade and Other Stories*, trans. Susan Bernofsky, foreword by William H. Gass (Baltimore: Johns Hopkins Univ. Press, 1990), 199-200.

2 Quoted in Paul Nizon, "Robert Walser and the Poet's Life," trans. Christopher Middleton, *Dimension* 9.1-2 (1977): 282.

3 Robert Walser, *Selected Stories*, trans. Christopher Middleton et al. (New York: Farrar, Straus and Giroux, 1982), 165.

4 Quoted in Christopher Middleton, "The Picture of Nobody," *Bolshevism in Art* (Manchester: Carcanet, 1978), 115.

5 Hermann Hesse, "*Der Gehülfe*," *Review of Contemporary Fiction* 12.1 (Spring 1992): 78.

6 Robert Walser, *Das Gesamtwerk*, ed. Jochen Greven (Zurich and Frankfurt: Suhrkamp Verlag, 1978), 10:538.

7 "A Sketch," trans. Mark Harman, *Robert Walser Rediscovered*, ed. Mark Harman (Hanover: University Press of New England, 1985), 51.

8 Paul Klee, *Pedagogical Sketchbook*, ed. and trans. Sibyl Moholy-Nagy (London: Faber and Faber, 1953), 61.

9 This essay was written on a grant from Pro Helvetia (Summer 1990) to do research at the Robert Walser Archives in Zurich.

A Robert Walser Bibliography

Tom Whalen

IN 1978, ROBERT WALSER'S bibliography compiled by Katharina Kerr (in *Über Robert Walser* vol. 2) included over ninety pages of secondary material. Since that time, some thirty books on Walser have been published and numerous more articles. In addition, translations of his books have appeared in English, Dutch, French, Spanish, Italian, Russian, Polish, Swedish, Japanese, Bulgarian, Romanian, Serbo-Croatian, Hebrew, and other languages. In France, Gallimard has purchased the option to publish all of Walser's works and several volumes have already appeared. Though the critical industry surrounding Robert Walser is not that of, say, Kafka (and for many reasons, none having to do with literary quality, will likely never be), all this publishing activity is still remarkable for a writer who at the time of his death in 1956 was so little known.

A complete multilingual bibliography is beyond the scope of this issue. I have limited myself to the latest editions of the primary work, the primary and secondary work available in English, and films based on the work of or relating directly to Walser.

Forthcoming within the next few years are the final two volumes of Walser's known microscript texts, *Aus dem Bleistiftgebiet* vols. 5 and 6, deciphered and edited by Bernhard Echte and Werner Morlang, published by Suhrkamp. (A rumor has it that an anonymous collector possesses additional microscripts.) A monograph by Echte will appear soon from Rowohlt. Morlang is editing a "biographical collage" of memories of Walser, and he and Echte are editing a book of recently discovered letters, prose texts, and poems. A large book of critical essays edited by Klaus-Michael Heinz, *Robert Walser: Materialien,* is forthcoming from Suhrkamp. In addition, a Robert Walser issue of *Sud* (Marseille) will appear soon. Finally, Channel Four, London, now has the rights to *Jakob von Gunten* for a feature-length film to be directed by the Brothers Quay.

The Robert Walser Archives, where the research for this bibliography was completed on a grant from Pro Helvetia, is funded by the Carl Seelig Foundation and housed at Beethovenstrasse 7, CH-8002 Zurich. It opened in 1973 and welcomes visitors and researchers throughout the year.

I. ROBERT WALSER IN GERMAN

Sämtliche Werke in Einzelausgaben. Ed. Jochen Greven. Zurich/Frank-
furt: Suhrkamp, 1985. (Supersedes *Das Gesamtwerk,* 1978.) Contents:
*Fritz Kochers Aufsätze; Geschichten; Aufsätze; Kleine Dichtungen;
Der Spaziergang: Prosastücke und kleine Prosa; Poetenleben; Seeland;
Die Rose; Geschwister Tanner; Der Gehülfe; Jakob von Gunten; Der
Räuber; Die Gedichte; Märchenspiele und szenische Dichtungen;
Bedenkliche Geschichten: Prosa aus der Berliner Zeit; Träumen: Prosa
aus der Bieler Zeit; Wenn Schwache sich für stark halten: Prosa aus
der Berner Zeit I; Zarte Zeilen: Prosa aus der Berner Zeit II;Es war
einmal: Prosa aus der Berner Zeit III; Für die Katz: Prosa aus der
Berner Zeit IV.*
Briefe. Ed. Jörg Schäfer and Robert Mächler. Zurich: Suhrkamp, 1979.
Aus dem Bleistiftgebiet: Mikrogramme 1924/25. Vol. 1. Ed. Bernhard
Echte and Werner Morlang. Frankfurt: Suhrkamp, 1985.
Aus dem Bleistiftgebiet: Mikrogramme 1924/25. Vol. 2. Ed. Bernhard
Echte and Werner Morlang. Frankfurt: Suhrkamp, 1985.
Aus dem Bleistiftgebiet: "Räuber"-Roman / "Felix"-Szenen. Vol. 3. Ed.
Bernhard Echte and Werner Morlang. Frankfurt: Suhrkamp, 1986.
Aus dem Bleistiftgebiet: Mikrogramme 1926/27. Vol. 4. Ed. Bernhard
Echte and Werner Morlang. Frankfurt: Suhrkamp, 1990.

II. WALSER IN ENGLISH

A. Books

The Walk and Other Stories. Trans. and introduction by Christopher
Middleton. London: John Calder, 1957. Incorporated and revised in
Selected Stories, below.
Jakob von Gunten. Trans. and introduction by Christopher Middleton.
Austin: Univ. of Texas Press, 1969; New York: Vintage Books, 1983.
Selected Stories. Trans. by Christopher Middleton and others. Foreword
by Susan Sontag. Postscript by Christopher Middleton. New York:
Farrar Straus Giroux, 1982; New York: Vintage Books, 1983.
*Robert Walser Rediscovered: Stories, Fairy Tale Plays and Critical
Responses.* Ed. with an introduction by Mark Harman. Hanover:
University Press of New England, 1985. Contains Walter Arndt's
translations of the fairy-tale plays *Cinderella* and *Snowwhite,* three
poems translated by Mark Harman, as well as prose pieces translated
by Harman, Arndt, et al. See section III "Secondary Works in English"
for the essays from this work.
Masquerade and Other Stories. Trans. with a preface by Susan Bernofsky.

Introduction by William H. Gass. Baltimore: Johns Hopkins Univ. Press, 1990.

B. Uncollected Stories and Poems

"The Child." Trans. Mark Harman. *Comparative Criticism.* Ed. E. S. Shaffer. Cambridge: Cambridge Univ. Press, 1984, 261-64.
"The Dancer." Trans. E. M. Valk. *Webster Review* 4.2 (Fall 1978): 59-60.
"Green." Trans. Mark Harman. *Georgia Review* 45.2 (Summer 1991): 293-94.
"My Fiftieth Birthday" (poem). Trans. Michael Hamburger. *German Poetry: 1910-1975.* Ed. Michael Hamburger. Manchester: Carcanet, 1977, 26-27.
"The Office" (poem). Trans. Roger Bonner. *Driftwood* (1977): 24.
"Pierrot." Trans. Christopher Middleton. *Texas Quarterly* 8.3 (Fall 1964): 105-12.
"The Seamstress" and "Disaster." Trans. Herbert L. Kaufman. *Lyrik und Prosa* 7 (1974): 4-7.
"Sketch for a Curtainraiser" and "Two Little Fairytales." Trans. James Kirkup. *Atlas Anthology III* (1985): 126-30.

III. SECONDARY WORKS IN ENGLISH

Arndt, Walter. "Forethoughts to Walser's Fairy Plays." In *Robert Walser Rediscovered.* Ed. Mark Harman. Hanover: University Press of New England, 1985, 179-89.
Avery, George C. *Inquiry and Testament: A Study of the Novels and Short Prose of Robert Walser.* Philadelphia: Univ. of Pennsylvania Press, 1968.
―――. "A Poet beyond the Pale: Some Notes on the Shorter Works of Robert Walser." *Modern Language Quarterly* 24.2 (June 1963): 181-90.
―――. "A Writer's Cache: Robert Walser's Prose Microscripts." In *Robert Walser Rediscovered,* 179-89.
Benjamin, Walter. "Robert Walser," trans. Mark Harman. In *Robert Walser Rediscovered,* 144-47.
Birkerts, Sven. "Robert Walser." *An Artificial Wilderness: Essays on 20th Century Literature.* New York: William Morrow, 1987, 41-45.
Canetti, Elias. "Robert Walser," trans. Joachim Neugroschel. In *Robert Walser Rediscovered,* 151-52.
Cardinal, Agnes. *The Figure of Paradox in the Work of Robert Walser.* Stuttgart: Hans Dieter Heinz, 1982.

Evans, Tamara S. " 'A Paul Klee in Prose': Design, Space, and Time in the Work of Robert Walser." *German Quarterly* 57 (1984): 32-34.

———. " 'Am awake and lie yet in deep sleep': Robert Walser and Modern Perception." In *Robert Walser Rediscovered,* 169-78.

Hamburger, Michael. "Explorers: Musil, Walser, Kafka." *A Proliferation of Prophets.* New York: St. Martin's Press, 1984, 255-66.

Harman, Mark. "Stream of Consciousness and the Boundaries of Self-Conscious Fiction: The Works of Robert Walser." *Comparative Criticism.* Ed. E. S. Shaffer. Cambridge: Cambridge Univ. Press, 1984, 119-34.

Keutel, Walter. "In Pursuit of Invisible Tracks: Photographs of a Dead Author." *New German Critique* 50 (1990): 157-72.

Kudszus, Winfried. "Walser's Silence." In *Robert Walser Rediscovered,* 195-201.

Middleton, Christopher. "A Parenthesis to the Discussion of Robert Walser's Schizophrenia." In *Robert Walser Rediscovered,* 190-94.

———. "The Picture of Nobody: Some Remarks on Robert Walser." *Bolshevism in Art.* Manchester: Carcanet, 1978, 95-122.

Musil, Robert. "The *Stories* of Robert Walser," trans. Mark Harman. In *Robert Walser Rediscovered,* 141-43.

Nizon, Paul. "Robert Walser and the Poet's Life," trans. Christopher Middleton. *Dimension* 10.1-2 (1977): 282-87.

Parry, Idris. "The Writer as Servant." *Hand to Mouth and Other Essays.* Manchester: Carcanet, 1981, 19-36.

Pender, Malcolm. "A Writer's Relationship to Society: Robert Walser's '*Räuber*'-Roman." *Modern Language Review* 78 (1983): 103-12.

Unseld, Siegfried. "Robert Walser and His Publishers," trans. Hunter Hannum and Hildegarde Hannum. *The Author and His Publisher.* Chicago: Univ. of Chicago Press, 1980, 191-273.

Waidson, H. M. "Robert Walser." *Swiss Men of Letters.* Ed. Alex Natan. London: Oswald Wolff, 1970, 213-38.

Walser, Martin. "Unrelenting Style," trans. Joseph McClinton. In *Robert Walser Rediscovered,* 153-68.

Whalen, Tom. " 'The Most Enchanting Oblivion': Robert Walser's Self-Effacement." *Crazyquilt* 2.1 (March 1988): 5-11.

———. "Between Heaven and Earth: Robert Walser's 'Die Hochzeits-reise.' " *Studies in Short Fiction* 27.2 (Spring 1990): 191-96.

——— and Susan Bernofsky. "Robert Walser's *Mikrogramme:* Striking Sparks from the Ashes of Language / An Interview with Bernhard Echte and Werner Morlang." *New Orleans Review* 16.3 (Fall 1989): 15-23.

IV. FILMOGRAPHY

Jakob von Gunten. Director: Peter Lilienthal. Script: Ror Wolf and Peter
Lilienthal. Cast: Hanna Schygulla, Alexander May, Reinhard Hauff, et
al. 96 minutes. Color. 1971.

Der Gehülfe. Director: Thomas Koerfer. Script: Dieter Feldhausen and
Thomas Koerfer. Cast: Paul Burian, Ingold Wildenauer, Verena Buss,
Wolfram Berger, et al. 122 minutes. Color. 1975. See also *Film 3:
Kritisches Filmagazin: Der Gehülfe* (August 1976), essays and the
screenplay of *Der Gehülfe;* and Anne Cuneo, *La Machine Fantaisie*
(Vevey: Editions Bertil Galland, 1977), on the film *Der Gehülfe.*

Der Vormund und sein Dichter. Director: Percy Adlon. Script: Percy
Adlon. Cast: Rolf Illig and Horst Raspe. 87 minutes. Color. 1978.

Robert Walser. Director: Hans Helmut Klaus Schoenherr. Script: H.H.K.
Schoenherr. Cast: Peter Yiegel, Niklaus Meienberg, Adolf Muschg, et
al. 90 minutes. Color. 1978.

Waldi. Directors: Reinhard Kahn and Michel Leiner. Based on "Der
Wald" by Robert Walser. 77 minutes. Color. 1980.

Melzer. Director: Heinz Bütler. Script: Heinz Bütler. Cast: Rüdiger
Vogler, Adelheld Arndt, Christel Foertsch, et al. 91 minutes. Color.
1983. Vogler stars as an artist obsessed with Robert Walser.

Der Räuber. Director: Lutz Leonhardt. Script: Lutz Leonhardt. 100
minutes. Black and white. 1983.

Wald. Director: Friedrich Kappeler. Script: Friedrich Kappeler. Text:
"Der Wald" by Robert Walser. Cast: Mathias Gnädinger, Gabriele
Rothmüller, Andreas Stadler. 80 minutes. Color. 1985.

Basta. Director: Anne Cuneo. Text: "Basta" by Robert Walser. Cast:
Jürgen Cziesla, Jane Friedrich, Roger Cuneo, Jacques Roman. 14
minutes. Color. 1986.

*The Comb—From the Museums of Sleep: Fairytale Dramolet to Scenes
and Texts by Robert Walser.* Directors: Brothers Quay. Live action
puppet animation. 18 minutes. Black and white and color. 1990.

An Interview with Diane Williams

John O'Brien

Diane Williams's second collection of stories, *Some Sexual Success Stories Plus Other Stories in Which God Might Choose to Appear,* was published in January by Grove Weidenfeld; her first collection, *This Is about the Body, the Mind, the Soul, the World, Time, and Fate,* appeared in 1990. Her short fiction is among the most interesting being written today—challenging, disturbing, and always compelling. For years Diane and I lived within miles of each other, but had never met—the ongoing problem with the literary scene in Chicago. Rather than meeting in New York sometime, where Diane has now moved, we got together in downtown Chicago in December of 1990, and then conducted this interview the following June.

JOHN O'BRIEN: Why are you moving to New York?

DIANE WILLIAMS: A lot of different reasons.

JOB: Professional?

DW: Well, they're all professional, all my reasons. For scope. And I feel comfortable there.

JOB: Is it Chicago, or is it the North Shore suburbs that don't provide the atmosphere?

DW: Well, I really have never learned Chicago or spent much time in Chicago, although we lived there briefly. In Glencoe I feel somewhat exiled, as if I'm hiding out.

JOB: Why Glencoe?

DW: I don't know, it just happened. We were going to be raising children, and we thought that would be a kind of sweet, safe place to live with children.

JOB: Where did you go to college?

DW: The University of Pennsylvania.

JOB: Why there?

DW: It was something my mother said: go east or go west, don't stay here.

JOB: And you finished at Penn?

DW: Yes.

JOB: What were you studying?

DW: English literature, and sculpture, and drawing and many -ologies, and I did do some creative writing, and I had a course with Philip Roth.

JOB: Was Roth visiting?

DW: He taught there those years, maybe two or three years; he taught fiction writing.

JOB: What was Roth like as a teacher?

DW: He was excellent, very scholarly.

JOB: It was creative writing?

DW: Yes, but we would read—it's so long ago I can't really remember—but we would read texts. I think we read John Cheever stories and *Madame Bovary*. That I recall. And we would talk about literature, and then we would write, and discuss our work in class, and I found it very exciting. He was writing *Portnoy's Complaint* then—it was that period—and he talked about obsession.

JOB: And after college, where to?

DW: I went to New York. I was a dancer but chose not to become a professional. Instead I did dance therapy. I worked at Bellevue Hospital in the acutely psychotic ward doing dance therapy.

JOB: Where did the dancing come from? You weren't doing that in college, were you?

DW: I did that from the time I was eight. I danced in college too. I taught dance. When I was a girl, my teacher wanted me to study every day, to go on full scholarship, but my parents wouldn't allow it. I was a gifted dancer.

JOB: Ballet?

DW: No, modern dance. I loved choreographing and improvising, and pushing myself beyond what I thought I could physically endure.

JOB: So you did dance therapy in New York.

DW: I did that for a while. It didn't last too long; it was very, very depressing—*very* depressing. Most of the people I worked with were so heavily drugged they were zombielike, except in the wards where they were manic—so manic that they couldn't be subdued. We were warned to never say to anyone, "Just relax."

JOB: So you went from the depressives to the manics . . .

DW: Yes, all kinds. And then I went to work at Doubleday, and Doubleday was like heaven. I was a trainee . . .

JOB: Training to be . . . ?

DW: An editor. But in those days, when a young woman wanted to be an editor, there were two tracks—one for men and one for women—and men were immediately assigned editorial assistant positions, but women had to be secretaries. So I was sent to speedwriting school two nights a week. I had to learn speedwriting, and I had to be a secretary—I had to file and I had to take dictation and I had to type and make coffee and sharpen pencils, and I wasn't very good at any of that. My self-esteem sank.

JOB: What year was this?

DW: 1968, '69. So I did that. But there was one moment in time when I realized I would have to turn things around: when I was asked to bring someone coffee—my boss, who was a woman—I put the coffee down so forcefully that it spilled, and then she asked me to sharpen her pencils, and I brought a fistful over to her with their sharpened points very, very close to her face. That was the end of that. No, no, I stayed with her, but that was the turning point, I think—at least I remember it as being *my* turning point.

JOB: So it was just old-fashioned discrimination?

DW: Terrible. But I had training there. I was trained as an editor and we worked on dictionaries and career guidance textbooks, family medical health books.

JOB: What kind of editing did you really want to be doing? Fiction?

DW: I don't know. I don't think I had much of a sense of who I was at that time or what I was supposed to be doing.

JOB: But you were also writing?

DW: I tried, but it didn't really work very well. I mean, I tried and I tried. I had written some successful stories—what I felt were successful and what other people told me were successful—when I was at Penn. But I couldn't reproduce it. Actually it was a heartbreaking period; my ambitious nature was buried. I think I was very depressed and really didn't understand why. When I graduated from college, the fact that I was unmarried was quite a shock to everybody.

JOB: That at the end of college you weren't married?

DW: I was expected to go to college, get married, and that would be it—that would be me, being a mother and a wife would be me. But that didn't happen, so everybody was pretty nonplussed.

JOB: How many years were you with Doubleday?

DW: Three or four years, and I *did* marry. And then we moved to Chicago, and I got a job at Scott Foresman.

JOB: Editing textbooks?

DW: Yes. Doing original writing and editing, putting together basal readers and workbooks at the elementary-school grade level. I really loved that.

JOB: So what was happening with your writing along the way?

DW: Nothing. I had my first child, Jacob. And he was a wonderful, wonderful baby, and he was quite independent and didn't need much attention. I felt quite auxiliary. But I also had this sense of disappearing. The first year was terrific, because I'd been working very hard and when I quit, it was exciting, and felt like a vacation; it was thrilling. And then I felt that I was evaporating, disappearing, and I was frightened for myself. Since I had all this background in writing for children, I thought what I could do was to write children's books. I set for myself a modest goal. I felt very humble then. I wrote three grade-B novels for children about a twelve-year-old detective, Abigail Fox, and I had a New York agent. Everyone agreed that the books were very professional, very well crafted, but that they were naive, and at that time what was wanted was "problem literature." I really did not understand the market. And finally my agent cut out a clipping from the newspaper about a twelve-year-old girl who had hanged herself—and she asked if I could write a novel for twelve-year-olds about this. I said I don't want to do that.

JOB: Is there any similarity between what you wrote for Roth's class and what you write now?

DW: Actually, yes. Very short, and I think it's good. I still admire the work that I did then. But, I couldn't reproduce it, so the fight was to learn how to. That particular piece I had written for Philip Roth, I had sat down and boom! there it was! It was the most exquisite experience. But I couldn't get back to that place to do that. So then it was a long fight. This was 1978, and here I was living out in Glencoe. Friends would tell me to find like-minded people. I tried to find like-minded people where I lived and I did find them, people who wanted to be writers and who were aspiring to something so-called literary.

JOB: So was that *StoryQuarterly?*

DW: Well, I met those people eventually that way. But then it was just working and working; it was a sort of grim determination to see if there was any way I could learn a process or a system. The issue was to learn how to compose and to see if I could repeat the feat. Because I was industrious, I had the energy, I had the will. I succeeded, by which I mean I developed many stories which then were published in good journals, and I was quite proud of myself.

JOB: What happened then?

DW: I met up with Gordon Lish then. I met him at a short-story seminar in Detroit. I heard him read his work there and I participated in one of his workshops. I studied with Gordon for two semesters in New York because I understood what he was offering—the special chance to become hugely conscious of how language can be manipulated to produce maximum effects. So often, in our naturally powerful speech, we only understand dimly how we are doing it, so that we are deprived of the good fortune of being in charge of it, rather than the other way around. We feel merely lucky when a burst of poetical passion occurs, where sound, sense, and purpose are locking together the way that they should. I realized that I should not have to waste so much effort with trial and error.

JOB: In all your stories, there's an on-the-edge intensity.

DW: Well, that's how it feels; that's what my life is like. I really have felt that sense of being close to soul-death that some people experience, and I think there's just a great urgency to survive.

JOB: Do you know when you start one of your odd stories where it's going?

DW: No, no, God no. That's the fun of it. There was a time when I didn't believe there was very much in my own life that was worthy or interesting enough to deal with. One night some writing friends and I went drinking—not too much, because I don't drink much, maybe one drink would do it—

but I started talking about something I had observed—my children—it was the sort of experience where you see it and then say oh God, I didn't see that, no I didn't see that, and you immediately repress it and block it. But having had something to drink, somehow it sputtered out of somewhere, some part of me, and my friend Bill Tester said, Why don't you write about that? I remember repeating, About *that?* First of all, it seemed boring because it was so close to the bone, and it was my life, it was my children, it was my house, it wasn't this kind of something wickedly exciting, exotic, far off, not me, so . . . I decided to write about that, and that was a moment of revelation. Then I thought, now I know how to do it, now I know. It was anything in my life that I wanted to say no to—*that* didn't happen, I didn't see that, that couldn't be. It was the revelation that I could write about what was painful and terrifying.

JOB: Didn't that story become one of the stories in the first collection?

DW: Yes, that's in the book at the beginning. It's called "Dropping the Masters." It's the children playing with the toys while the mother watches. Children, two boys, playing obscenely with dolls—a mother watching her children play obscenely with dolls. That was the beginning. So it really is will and industry. It is an excruciating process, to feel as though I possess a craft, this ability to make fiction.

JOB: Is that still the working principle—to write about what you want to say no to?

DW: The underlying principle is the same in the sense of wanting to get to what would be personally dangerous material, but in order to succeed over and over again I've had to learn how to trick myself into it—some of the time, going backwards toward it to keep myself intrigued. And there are many times in the fiction when I believe I'm writing about someone else, but thinking, oh my God, what if that *were* me? It's assuming a dangerous or perplexing stance whether or not I think it's from my own experience.

JOB: That was one of the things I wanted to ask you. Is that I/she/he always the same kind of consciousness? Sometimes you're talking about "she," or "he," sometimes it's "I." Whether it's you or someone purely fictive, do you think it's always the same kind of "I" that's responding?

DW: Oh, I'm sure that would have to be true. I do believe that, unfortunately, we are bound up in ourselves, and we really can only perceive through our own eyes and our own heart, and what we see is us. We think we're exploring exterior worlds, but we're not, so undoubtedly it's the same consciousness, the same voice. But the intellectual excitement is when you tap into the idiosyncratic, eccentric selfness that you know is time-bound and experience-bound—and I do believe this—that you're tapping into the knowledge of the species. The fact is that you can find your truth, but it's also the truth about human nature.

JOB: And you are able to take advantage of all of your own vices and failings, to use them as material.

DW: Yes, well, pain and screwing up, all that, yes, can be exploited, but also I've always felt that I had no memory to speak of, no really good memory, so if I didn't have a very good memory, how on earth could I be an artist, and I always thought that a writer needed a kind of encyclopedic mind. Now, it's the fragmentary nature of my memory that I exploit, the fact that I remember an aspect of experience that I have no idea why I would remember, you know, somebody's shoelace rather than what they said that I was there to listen to, and the fact that when I think back on any experience, it's so chaotic and so unintelligible that it frightens me as a person who has to perform in the real world, but as an artist it's absolutely liberating because I have less to work with. Artistry is manipulating elements; the fewer there are, the easier the process of composing them. So I am lucky in that respect to be sort of simple, to have a poor memory, to hold experience in a chaotic way, but I used to feel apologetic for that and worry.

JOB: But you're aware that that's the way your mind functions and you take advantage of that fact—which isn't easy to do.

DW: That's what I've learned to do and also I'm not interested at all in any experience that I have previously organized, synthesized and formed an opinion about. All I want is to take experience and rearrange it and come up with something completely new. And so that's the fun of it. That's why doing the work gives me a sense of gaining some personal freedom and relief and healing—that I can take experience that I thought I had certain prescribed attitudes about, and manipulate it and then it's completely different.

JOB: Let's talk about the process. How do you move from line to line? There are sharp leaps. There's one story, "Pornography," whose opening line uses a dash to take the first part of the sentence in a different direction: "I just had a terrible experience—I'm sorry." The second part seems to come from nowhere.

DW: Well, it came from a very real place. And that's another thing that's fun—trusting myself, learning to trust my intuitive judgment rather than my conscious judgment. That story, I could tell you precisely how that whole thing was conceived. It is the scariest story I've ever written. After I had completed it, I was going around to every friend I have saying: Can I put this into the world? Is this right to put this into the world? because this is horrible, I was horrified by this story, it's terrible, terrible, maybe it really is evil.

JOB: How did you get to "I'm sorry"?

DW: OK. I'll tell you. I went to meet a friend for lunch and I was waiting for her to come, she was late. And when she did arrive, she came charging up to the table and said, "I'm sorry I'm late. I just had a terrible experience; I'm sorry." And then she went on to describe what she'd seen—this little old man, a bicycle, a boy on a bicycle being hit by the little old man in his car. So when I sat down to compose, her language was in my head; her agitation, her horror—and I recorded what she said.

JOB: Your explanation of the "real" story is quite different from the story you wrote.

DW: Yes, of course. That people apologize for their terrible experiences, that people feel really guilty about them.

JOB: So what she was saying in real life . . .

DW: She would say that her meaning was different, but it becomes something else. I was really just recording what she said because it was fresh in my mind, but then I let it stay and I'm glad I let it stay, and I see how it has meaning far from the experiences that I took this story from. OK, so the opening was all from her mouth, but that business about that little old man doing more for me than any sex has ever done for me—that's out of my mouth. When she was telling her story, I remember getting chills and feeling the hair stand on my arms for some reason. I had a physical response to her story; in real life, it wasn't sexual, but it was an intense physical response. In writing the story, I just let my mind go, and whatever came in came in, and what came in was another experience I had that was perhaps a month previous, a week previous—driving past a playground near my house, where I saw in the distance an ambulance, and I saw a child being put onto a stretcher. Of course, this is one of a mother's worst fears—I mean, every time I went to a playground I was sure every moment that my boy would be killed; I hate playgrounds. So I saw this, and the sensation I had then was of fear, profound fear, but I can remember feeling that I almost had an obligation to feel this way; that as a moral human being I should respond with anguish to something wretched that had happened to a child, and that as a mother, that was the appropriate response that made me feel good about myself. I tried to hold onto that feeling to console myself that I was moral and had responded correctly in the situation. That was it; trying to hold onto that sensation of horror, for reassurance.

JOB: How did you arrive at the title?

DW: "Pornography"? The title came after the composing, it didn't come before. And then another experience I had just had where I nearly hit two boys who were riding their bikes, I put that in. And then another horrifying experience, that had just occurred recently—my son taking off on his bicycle and I couldn't stop him, and we had had some kind of fight, and he was very young; I had this sense of oh my God, what should I do? what should I do? and feeling completely impotent—there was really nothing to do, because he was gone, and oh my God, he might conceivably just get killed. I remember at that time feeling nothing, nothing, and as a mother, I wanted to experience what I'd felt for someone else's child on the playground—horror—I wanted to feel it, I wanted to feel sensation, but I felt nothing; I felt this calm, I felt this deadness, this numbness, which again, as a mother, made me feel guilty: Why *don't* I feel something? Don't I love my child? What is wrong with me? Do I secretly want his death? It's alarming. And then I put together the chipmunk business because I had just seen that chipmunk running toward me. I didn't know why I put that down, but that chipmunk suddenly running toward me and then away from me, that day I was working on the story, made me think of sexual experience, when you're close to release and it doesn't happen. Did it mean I could have this intense sexual response because someone else's child was in danger, but not for my own boy? So then my own horror, what have I done here? What is this thing I have made? Here is a mother in a rage because she cannot get sexual gratification from the idea that her son might be killed. How did I get to that? This is horrible, this is horrible. Well, then we get pornography. I was really distressed as Diane Williams, the hopefully nice person in the real world. Should this be literature? Is this my business—to produce this? Is this right? Is this really what I want to be doing? And then this certainty that yes, this is exactly what I want to be doing. I am far from the only one who believes that experience teaches us that when you speak a nightmare and speak it to its limit, whatever it is, then that speech has a healing force. And if it's speakable, if the configuration of feeling can be manipulated, can be produced, then it's a true feeling, shared by many, and it's the sort of feeling which should be utterly revealed. But I must say that for me—the respectable version of myself—there's still fear, and a great deal of disgust when I see that story. Then I have to reassert myself as an artist, and say no, this is exactly my business.

JOB: Do you see the stories in the second collection as related?

DW: I think I see a beginning and an end to sort of a personal evolution, a period of time in my life where I had certain goals for myself in terms of my own growth, and certain obstacles to overcome, to get through, to get by, and that was the cycle of time in which these stories were produced. I would appreciate hearing from somebody else, someone else telling me how these stories belong together.

© Bill Hayward

Book Reviews

Diane Williams. *Some Sexual Success Stories Plus Other Stories in Which God Might Choose to Appear.* Grove Weidenfeld, 1992. 132 pp. $16.95.

Diane Williams is a deceptive writer. Although she describes sexual practices, she knows that the body gets only momentary satisfactions. The body is "incomplete."

Thus Williams suggests even more than in her first brilliant collection of stories that she—and her protagonists—long for *something* beyond the limits. They want "perfection"; they long for lasting joy; they hope for destructive "miracles." If we simply look at her titles, we see the truth of these remarks: "The Limits of the World"; "My Highest Mental Achievement"; "A Progress in Spirituality"; "Perfect." I do not mean to imply that Williams is an *earnest* believer, a Midwestern zealot. She is much too ironic to offer usual sermons. Her stories give glimpses of another world, one in which the mind is in charge (only temporarily) of the body. But even these glimpses do not last. They flash; then they die.

Williams is a master of "sudden fiction," momentary lights. She believes that character, plot, and meaning are radically unstable. Therefore she offers darkly comic "summaries"—summaries which are incomplete, oblique, and perverse. Perhaps her "philosophy" and her style are captured in this one long—for her!—summary: "Let us endeavor to sum up. How much repetition does it take? A preservation? Biological investigation is required to explain the impulses and their transformations—the chief traits of a person. It is easy to forget, not that we ever should, that everything in this world is an accident. . . . An accident isn't necessarily ever over." The tone of this "summary" is brutally funny because it suggests that any "summary," any ordered arrangement, any "design" is subject to *transformation,* to *accident.* Life is, if you will, beyond explanation; it is never "closed"; it is subject to other events which destroy whatever order *we* supply in the present.

And I take this interpretation as Williams's "ultimate meaning." (Williams would cut this pompous phrase to shreds.) If life is full of unidentified, mysterious gestures and events, it is finally ambiguous, open, and suspicious. And Williams's stories—or parables, or fragments—are paradoxical. Williams is our sarcastic, biting mistress of secret origins and ends, of occult longings. She maintains that we are "displeased traces" and unhappy truces. [Irving Malin]

*

141

Christine Brooke-Rose. *Stories, Theories & Things.* Cambridge Univ. Press, 1991. 317 pp. $44.50; *Textermination.* Carcanet, 1991. 182 pp. £12.95.

Christine Brooke-Rose's latest collection of essays covers a very broad range of topics mostly connected through the notion of story. Unlike her earlier study *A Rhetoric of the Unreal* (1981) this volume carries a deliberately miscellaneous-sounding title which in effect gives the author priority over any single theoretical topic. This is important because it relates to one of Brooke-Rose's most engaging characteristics as a critic. Although she has taught for twenty years in the very citadel of Gallic theory, Paris VIII, she has avoided many of the pitfalls of continental theorists such as dogmatic generalization and a tendency toward abstraction. The essays gathered here are based on a pair of tacit premises which would run something like this: it is essential to possess an analytical formal awareness of literature, but it is equally essential to test out that aware-ness on specific works. *Stories, Theories & Things* could thus be seen as structured on a series of connections: between general rhetorical principles and specifics, between critic and teacher, between novelist and theorist. A "meta-story" introduces the series by commenting on Brooke-Rose's own fiction from *Between* (1968) onwards and this strategy establishes two themes which recur throughout the book. Firstly literary works are used to test the adequacy of certain theoretical approaches (structuralism, narratology, etc.) which are usually found wanting in some respect. And secondly an impish irony detects a conservatism in supposedly iconoclastic theorists continuing to support a tradi-tional literary canon. The continuing neglect of contemporary experimental writing (of Hélène Cixous's criticism as against her fiction, for instance) becomes a damning indictment of current theorizing.

Every essay bears eloquent testimony to the breadth of Brooke-Rose's reading and her capacity to draw incisive rhetorical distinctions. She insists that a knowledge of rhetoric is essential to critical discussion: "to transgress intelligently one must know the rule." On the other hand she staves off the self-consciousness diagnosed in writers like Barth by converting it into comedy. So she mocks critical labels ("post post? past post?") and converts her own writing into spoofs. Or again she might deflate her own solemnity by inserting tactical colloquialisms; so what she calls "palimpsest histories," i.e., long, quasi-historical novels packed with specialized knowledge, wear that knowledge lightly enough to create a "rattling good story." Again and again Brooke-Rose pauses to comment on her own style or her own metaphors because the ultimate subject of her essays turns out to be some aspect of rhetoric. These topics can vary in generality from the use of the copula and free indirect discourse, to individual works. Particularly rewarding discussions are given of the instability between the two viewpoints (the narrator's and the young protagonist's) of *The Red Badge of Courage;* the structure of opposites in *The Scarlet Letter* which can be represented diagrammatically through the capital A; and the dialectic between hidden and revealed forms of knowledge in *Jude the Obscure.* Even when a specific work is being examined a general issue is extrapolated, whether it is the nature of translation in relation to the *Cantos* or Islamic spiritual narrative in relation to *The Satanic Verses.*

The most controversial area which Brooke-Rose addresses here is that of gender. "A Womb of One's Own?" examines the connections between women's experimental writing and the male avant-garde, then launches into an attack on feminist specificity being based on the unconscious, concluding: "It seems to me that 'specificity' in creation is an individual, not a sexual, racial or class phenomenon." Before too many hackles can rise, however, she directs a different attack at semioticians for possessing a latent nostalgia for stable phallocentric structures; and pursues this tack with a lively meditation on male-centered vocabulary of creativity. Brooke-Rose makes no attempt to duck polemic. On the contrary it gives a leaven to her essays throughout this collection.

In reviewing current discussions of metafiction Brooke-Rose notes an imbalance of attention to the author at the expense of the reader who determines the very existence of characters, and concludes: "the character as created or uncreated by the 'real' reader (who corresponds to the 'real' author and who can be, like the 'real' author, variously surrogated within a fiction), remains to be explored." This statement opens up the possibility of her latest novel, *Textermination,* which is a fantasia on the theme of the reader's activities. Characters from prose narratives ranging from antiquity to the present gather at a "convention" in San Francisco, a deliberate pun which sets up a containing situation and which self-consciously signals to the reader that this novel is meta-fictional in the sense of playing with the processes that constitute narratives. The novel is thus insistently preoccupied with novels and speculates on the sort of attention readers give them. It opens with a series of departures culled from earlier narratives and closes with the characters involved returning to their familiar contexts. The effect resembles that of collage where through lateral shifts characters are placed incongruously together. Out of this incongruity comes the book's humor since rhetorical registers jar (high Victorian against colloquial American) and bizarre combinations form. Emma Woodhouse and Sir Lancelot engage in heavy petting in the back seat of a coach; Goethe registers disapproval of Oedipa Maas's paranoia, and so on. The collage effect is accentuated by Brooke-Rose's many quotations and allusions to earlier works. As in Kathy Acker's novels, this device temporarily appropriates a text just as Brooke-Rose appropriates characters and allows them to articulate their own fates at the hands of readers. Casaubon, for instance, bewails the fact that he is only examined in relation to Dorothea Brooke and never in his own right, a complaint which develops prominent narratorial comments within *Middle-march.*

The title of Brooke-Rose's novel, like its recent predecessors, puns on a sense of process which is here related to the very existence of characters. Emma Woodhouse reflects on the reader; another female figure declares that characters exist out of time; and yet another figure, Mira Enketei (i.e., "in the whale"—a possible allusion to Orwell's essay on writers' commitment) insists on their literary nature. At the end of chapter 10 a slightly Beckettian voice says of Mira: "She can't go on. She doesn't exist." But the voice does. A huge electronic eye has been as it were presiding over the convention hall and this eye here shifts into "I" as the first person takes over the narrative. Whether this voice is unnamed or whether it casts itself as Oedipa Maas, there is not much distinction of idiom between the occurrences, and this composite voice raises many of the issues discussed in *Stories, Essays & Things.* But because the issues are raised within dialogues there is always the possibility of an answering voice. And because they occur within the context of a fiction their status becomes as ambiguous as Stephen Dedalus's theorizing in *A Portrait of the Artist.* A lively and alert spirit of intellectual play informs *Textermination* which should appeal to any reader seriously interested in the range of novelistic expression. [David Seed]

*

Harold Brodkey. *The Runaway Soul.* Farrar, Straus, and Giroux, 1991. 835 pp. $30.00.

It is, of course, impossible to review this remarkable novel in less than five hundred words. I assume, however, that all criticism is mutilated, criminal, "unholy." And I believe that Brodkey continually notes that *his words* can never capture *totalities* of character and history. Thus this review mirrors his epistemological concerns, his obsessive questionings of representation.

Brodkey suggests that there is little stability. Although he writes a novel of family life—narrated by an older Wiley, an "orphan" who looks back at his childhood and adolescence—he refuses to move in a linear way. Does Wiley, the writer-narrator, ever escape from his adopted family, Lila, S. L., and Nonie? Does he ever progress into mature understanding? Do his words explain his various movements? These questions are merely variations on the notion that "time heals all wounds" (or vice versa).

Brodkey, in effect, writes an anti-family novel because he recognizes that any structure—family, country, law—moves in odd, crisscrossing waves. And even his duplicitous design is flawed. *Time* is, perhaps, the underlying "hero" and "structure" of the novel. Thus Brodkey may take fifty pages to describe one event—an event which changes in every presentation, an event which moves in time. At one point Wiley observes: "People really do live like contortionists." Contortion is the clue, possibly, to the text of life—and the "life" of text.

One of the most perverse wonders of the novel is that Wiley (and the other characters?) recognizes that contortion is a "normal" position or structure or force—that disfigurement is temporal *and* spatial. When we look at Brodkey's style, we see that it is an attempt to present contortion. The sentences keep moving in an almost sexual way—language mirrors foreplay, orgasm, post-orgasmic depression. Look, for example, at these sentences: "I imagine revelation as springing from the efforts of certain people. . . . It's like piling up books and stones higher and higher. . . . I can imagine a final, single truth, but not as a knowable frame for here. I think it's cheap and wrong and really dangerous to pull that single-notion stuff down into stuff that goes on with us. It's what you move toward in your mind and in a moment; and you can talk about it; but not seriously—you can't ever use that stuff as a public premise without condoning murder." The narrator cannot stop "talking"; he says one thing, then adds another thing, and then seems to explode his "frame" (pun?) in rage.

Brodkey is a prophet. He rages at the injustices of life *here and now*—and *there and before*—and yet he hopes that after his apocalyptic words destroy (and create) normality, he will come to some revelation, an odd angel (angle) of vision. The book is "a runaway soul"—constantly jerking toward the "final solution" and yet pleading for stillness—if only for a little while. [Irving Malin]

*

Richard Powers. *The Gold Bug Variations.* Morrow, 1991. 639 pp. $25.00.

Early in *The Gold Bug Variations,* in one of many scenes in the novel where characters lose themselves in libraries, the young scientist Stuart Ressler makes "a sadly vindicating tour" of the University of Illinois library that reveals "an 824," the Dewey Decimal designation for literature, "untouched since Henry James died. Humanities have clearly slid into the terminally curatorial, forsaking claim to knowledge." This is 1957, and Ressler is in Illinois to push ahead with the genetic coding research that Watson and Crick initiated in England a few years before. Ressler's task, like Powers's in the telling of this story, is to sort through a mass of discoveries, competing hypotheses, and sheer data for clues to the replicative structure of DNA. I would guess that Powers's scientist hero, like the cryptographer of Poe's "Gold Bug," is to some degree "a coded persona of his inventor," a tireless gatherer of data who seeks to draw life from objective languages, and so make the crucial "jump from information to knowledge."

Powers, knowing that science, no less than literature, is "choked by unrestrained data as a pond is by too luxurious plant growth," attempts through just such analogies to give form to the endlessly proliferating facts of biological science. The book's main structural analogy comes from Bach's Goldberg Variations: four scale-steps, like the four base chemicals of the genetic string, breaking into "combinations, uncountable." Among the multiplying and recurrent set pieces in the novel, those devoted to Glenn Gould's early and late interpretations of the Variations stand out. Indeed, it would not be a bad idea to read this novel with Gould's recordings playing in the background.

An "awful, chromatic awareness" of the genetic code inspires "a curatorial resolve" in Powers's narrator, research librarian Jan O'Deigh, whose own story replicates Ressler's thirty years later. Possibly, O'Deigh is too much in awe of her subject: her inability to get beyond analogy and dutiful encyclopedic reference may have kept Powers from devising a major literary form. Yet *The Gold Bug Variations* is sophisticated in its engagement with science and passionate in its survey of living existence. It merits serious attention from writers and scientists. [Joseph Tabbi]

*

Nick Bantock. *Griffin & Sabine: An Extraordinary Correspondence.* Chronicle Books, 1991. Unnumbered. $16.95.

ZIM
October.
23 1991

GOBBLER BEAD

VIEW OUT MY WINDOW

DEAR NICK BANTOCK,

WHENEVER I RECEIVE A PARCEL FROM MY FRIEND KRISHNA MURTI THE COSMOLOGIST, I OPEN IT EAGERLY. THIS TIME HIS GIFT WENT BEYOND MY WILDEST EXPECTATIONS: HE HAD SENT ME YOUR ENCHANTING GRIFFIN AND SABINE. WHEN I CAME UPON THE FIRST SEALED ENVELOPE, I FELT A SUDDEN RUSH OF EXCITEMENT; THE ACT OF OPENING IT PRODUCED A REAL SHIVER! FOR DAYS NOW I HAVE BEEN LOST IN DELICIOUS CONJECTURE: WHAT IS THE TRUE NATURE OF GRIFFIN'S UNIQUE LOVE, THE MUSE SABINE? IS SHE PRANA? A PHANTOM OF THE MIND? AUTONOMOUS ANIMA? CHIMERA? IS SHE A WHIM? DELIRIUM? IS SHE AN HALLUCINATION? WHATEVER SHE IS, SHE'S ONE OF THE WORLD'S GREAT ANIMATING ELEMENTS.

HERE ON ZIM, I DRAW FOR THE LOCAL MUSEUM. IN KEEPING WITH YOUR EXTRAORDINARY CORRESPONDENCE, I'VE CHOSEN TO ILLUSTRATE MY LETTER WITH ZIMBIC CURIOSITIES. (HOW I WISH I COULD OWN THE ENTIRE COLLECTION OF SABINE'S GORGEOUS STAMPS!) WITH ADMIRATION + AFFECTION, Rikki DUCORNET

PHALLIC AZURITES OF BOG LAKE

A SKIAGRAPHIC SKINK

Seymour Krim. *What's* This *Cat's Story? The Best of Seymour Krim.*
Foreword by James Wolcott. Paragon House, 1991. 194 pp. $21.95.

Beat literature, like Romantic literature, consists largely of poetry; the
movement produced only three novelists of note—Burroughs, Holmes,
Kerouac (four if you consider Chandler Brossard a Beat)—and only one critic:
Seymour Krim. Like Kerouac, Krim was enthralled by Thomas Wolfe, both his
torrential prose style and his heartsick love for a lost America. In his lifetime
(1922-1989) Krim edited one influential anthology (*The Beats,* 1960) and
published three collections of essays: *Views of a Nearsighted Cannoneer*
(1961; expanded 1968), *Shake It for the World, Smartass* (1970), and *You &
Me* (1974). *What's* This *Cat's Story?* consists of the best essays from those
three books (chosen by Krim shortly before his suicide) along with four uncol-
lected essays and an excerpt from his unpublished prose poem "Chaos." The
latter is reminiscent of Kerouac's *Old Angel Midnight:* it's a dense, impres-
sionistic meditation on growing old in America, and I for one hope the complete
text will someday be published. The essays are arranged chronologically: not in
the order they were written, but according to Krim's own chronology, so that the
collection begins with his earliest ambitions to be a writer and ends with a late-
life lament that actors have replaced writers as America's most heroic artists.

Krim's energetic prose and personal involvement will remind some readers of
that other Tom Wolfe, and while Krim's contribution to New Journalism
should not be discounted, he was striving for something more than journalism: a
new form that would unite the novelistic imagination with direct communication. Krim called on the novelist to come out from "behind the mask of fiction"
and to "speak intimately to his readers about these fantastic days we are living
through but declare his credentials by revealing the concrete details and particular sweat of his own inner life." Though there is something self-defensive in
this (Krim was unable to write a novel himself), he splendidly evokes those
"fantastic days" of the late 1940s through the late 1960s when American
literature and culture were turning themselves inside out. If you've never read
Krim, this is the place to start; and even if you have, you'll appreciate the way
his different essays have been brought together here to form the autobiography
of one of our greatest cultural critics. [Steven Moore]

*

Robert Kelly. *Cat Scratch Fever.* McPherson, 1990. 150 pp. $18.00; paper:
$10.00.

Robert Kelly's new collection of short fiction is a beautifully crafted ode to our
contemporary world. If we find our own selves reflected back in any of the
thirty-one pieces here, then we are in good company—for Kelly is a craftsman
who shares our intimate thoughts and knows how to glance along with us at the
chambers of our imagination. In one instance we are with the narrator of the title
piece, "Cat Scratch Fever," climbing up through the trees to gaze at a beautiful

woman who is the object of a first love. In the next instance we are sitting in a café, in the short piece entitled "The New Life," in the company of a man who watches—as he so often does—the body of a woman who walks toward him. This body fires his imagination; he says of himself, "He just wants to watch. . . . He wants the moon to come sailing in his window. He wants her to take her clothes off and come towards him. He wants to watch her left shoulder slide out from her fuzzy sweater like the moon coming out from the clouds. He just wanted to watch." And in another, a comic piece entitled "Murder as Text," we ourselves watch as various professors attempt to puzzle out the murder of a colleague who was deconstructed while in the midst of constructing his own erotic poem.

There is great irony in these fictions. They are fictions caught in the process of being themselves; in fact they seem to be as finely tuned as the art of the Japanese haiku. They are brief more often than not, yet each encapsulates a minute detail that evolves until its significance is as large as the universe of a single day, a single thought. Kelly's lyrical pieces here are profound lessons in the art of knowing how the imagination takes hold of the ordinary world. In his capable hands, this world is as complex as it is now elegantly shaped. [Marilyn Moss]

*

Reinaldo Arenas. *The Doorman*. Trans. Dolores M. Koch. Grove Weidenfeld, 1991. 208 pp. $16.95.

For years now I've been hearing about what great writers the Latin Americans are, how they're the best in the world right now. Despite this, some of the most important of them are not well known. Miguel Asturias, the wonderful Guatamalan author, has been shamefully ignored by a reading public in love with García Márquez, who's very good but not in Asturias's class. The gifted but slick Carlos Fuentes gets a lot of attention, but very few students of fine fiction know about the work of Reinaldo Arenas (1943-1990), a Cuban who fought with Fidel Castro's guerrillas, but later was jailed by Castro for being a homosexual. Arenas came to the U.S. in 1980 as a result of the Mariel boat lift. At the time of his death he lived in poverty in New York's Hell's Kitchen.

Prodigiously talented, Arenas also had a fine sense of humor. He wrote with great passion, purpose, and anger, partly because he had been persecuted by a regime he'd risked his life to install. His long, experimental *Farewell to the Sea* illustrates his lyricism and ranks with the best Spanish-language novels written since 1945.

Having said that, I must admit that *The Doorman* is not one of Arenas's best works, although it's still worth buying and reading. Juan, a young Cuban refugee, is the doorman at a luxury apartment house in Manhattan. Although its inhabitants are far wealthier than he, Juan sees that most are troubled. He empathizes with them, thinks that somewhere there is a "wider door" leading to a place or state in which people experience "true happiness." Juan thinks he has been elected to take the tenants through this door. However, he himself does not know where the door is. Nevertheless, he tries to ingratiate himself with the tenants, doing them favors, listening to their crazy stories, so that when he finds the door, they will be disposed to walk through it with him. The more he tries to help them, however, the more they mistrust him.

The tenants have pets who hate their owners. They want to escape from them and (they all talk English) appeal to Juan for help. He throws in with them and, after being rescued from a mental institution, begins an odyssey that takes them to Baltimore, Cincinnati, across the country to the Pacific, and then south to the tropics, looking for a suitable place to live.

During his description of Juan's escape from the hospital and his cross-country trip with a menagerie including a polar bear (dyed black) and an orangutan, Arenas gets sloppy. I'm willing to suspend belief as quickly as the next guy, but Arenas makes the animal odyssey seem like a cakewalk. Humans don't interfere, all the animals get along harmoniously, some pet fish are transported in their water-filled bowls by birds. . . . Arenas simply doesn't take the trouble to make any of this credible.

The publisher calls *The Doorman* "a bittersweet parable about freedom and community." Maybe so, but it's certainly not apparent what Arenas is trying to do here. Fortunately, most of the book deals with Juan's relations with the human tenants and is consistently amusing and insightful. [Harvey Pekar]

*

Deborah Rebollar Pintonelli. *Ego Monkey.* Another Chicago Press, 1991. 110 pp. Paper: $10.95.

Pintonelli's title points the way to her terrifying, brutal, and painful stories. The ego is a "monkey"; it can never escape from its primitive desires. Thus she gives us stories that are hallucinatory and sadistic. These stories are unusually short because her characters are, in effect, "slices of life"; they are, indeed, fictional shrieks in the darkness.

The typical story describes mutilation. The lovers—whether they are parents, adolescents, or children—are, despite their desperate attempts to find love and normality, secretly longing for wounds. Love is a gaping boil; tenderness is destructive. It doesn't surprise us that even Pintonelli's epigraphs are bleak. Here is one especially painful quotation from Primo Levi: "The world into which one was precipitated was terrible, yes, but also undecipherable; it did not conform to any model; the enemy was all around but also inside."

But we should not dismiss Pintonelli's art. She demonstrates that she can marry pleasure and pain. Her language is so surprising that we remember it more than her sick "monkeys." I offer two passages that capture her dark style: "Years later the Prince's coffin was opened to include a gold necklace that she had loved very much. Upon opening the coffin, it was found that her hairs and nails had grown and grown and grown, filling up the entire box." And here is another "fabulous" example: "John would proceed to use every one of them on her from the smallest paring knife to the shiny never-used butcher knife. With the carver he would slit open Gretchen's chest and extract her heart (sacred heart of Jesus, bleeding heart of Mary). With the chopper he'd chop off all of the small extremities: the garishly painted finger nails and toes, the gold-studded ears, and so on."

Pintonelli is a gifted writer because she *dares to beautify violation,* and, by doing so, hypnotize us. She is a distinctive Gothic artist—and offspring of Poe and Hawkes. [Irving Malin]

*

Harry Mathews. *Immeasurable Distances: The Collected Essays.* Lapis Press (589 N. Venice Blvd., Venice, CA 90291), 1991. 295 pp. $35.00; signed and numbered edition: $75.00.

Over the last twenty years, Mathews's work on his inimitable fiction has been occasionally interrupted by requests from editors for essays. Even though he doesn't consider himself a trained critic, he responded to those requests with essays of great insight and intelligence, all of which are gathered in this sumptuous production. (The high price is justified by the format: it is large [7 x 10], illustrated in color and duotone [a fold-out perforated photo-montage of Mathews that can be used as a jigsaw puzzle], printed in a large point size on heavy cream paper.) Of the fourteen essays here, two concern Mathews's writing methods, six are on the Oulipo and its members (especially Georges Perec), five are on specific books and writers (Lewis Carroll, Raymond Roussel [cowritten with Perec and painstakingly researched], Laura Riding, Kenneth Koch's *Duplications,* and Joseph McElroy's *Women and Men*), and one is on the relation between libretti and music (his college major). Throughout, Mathews demonstrates a novelist's flair for apt metaphors ("Of course it is always reassuring when we extract from a book great bones of conclusion that we can then bury deep in our private gardens, but that is not the way of the best works of modern literature") as well as a novelist's conviction that the reader is a participant in fiction, not a passive receptor. Having written novels that expect much from his readers, Mathews here shows how he participates in the work of others. The results are brilliant, and it is to be hoped that *Immeasurable Distances* will be read not just by Mathews fans but by everyone with an interest in how fiction works. [Steven Moore]

*

Miguel Barnet. *Rachel's Song.* Trans. W. Nick Hill. Curbstone, 1991. 128 pp. Paper: $9.95.

Cuban writer Barnet's portrait of pre-Castro Cuba is an example of political fiction at its finest. The story of Rachel, a famous dance-hall girl and madam (she's known as "The Belle of the Alhambra"), offers a powerful look at three decades of Cuban life, rendered lyrically and subtly, with humor and passion.

Interspersed with Rachel's own musings about her life are a fascinating array of testimonials from people who know Rachel—her friends, enemies, and lovers. Together, these imagined voices bear witness to a bygone era in Cuba, an era filled with excess, frivolity, materialism, racism, and sexism.

"I'm content with what I've had," Rachel says. "As a performer I did whatever struck my fancy. . . . I'm not going to complain for lack of love. I have to recognize that I was despicable too and I made some people suffer a lot with my wickedness and disdain." A former acquaintance says of her, "Rachel is the best example of the prostitution, the vice and the lie wrapped in a red ribbon that reigned in this country." Someone else says, "Rachel is a bitch."

Although Rachel herself is uncomplicated, Barnet succeeds in presenting an extremely complicated world, a world whose complications and contradictions led to a revolution. [Janice Eidus]

*

Ariel Dorfman. *Hard Rain.* Trans. George Shivers with the author. Readers International, 1990. 270 pp. $18.95.

"All you need are a body, a killer, and a detective. Perfect first ingredients. Season well with a few other characteristics (a list of suspects, limited to residents and visitors who had access to the closed space where the crime took place; authorities who feel bewildered and impotent; a criminal who threatens to strike again; a detective who is emotionally involved in the case; an explosive atmosphere) and we've got ourselves a first-rate mystery novel." This is a bewildering opening paragraph to a "novel" about the short, happy presidential life of Salvador Allende of Chile, but it is one way to get the reader's attention. It doesn't take long, however, to realize that we are experiencing a brilliant anti-novel meant to personalize, through the fragments of memory and experience (bits of unfinished literary efforts: newspapers, magazines, books, anthologies, letters, encyclopedia articles, editorials, mostly fictitious), an epoch little understood by most Americans, including Nixon's CIA. Very near the end there is a masterful diatribe, running two full pages (reminiscent of Giancarlo Giannini's bravura outburst at the end of Lina Wertmuller's classic *Seven Beauties*), using hundreds of clichés for rationalizing one's conduct at the crossroads of political decision-making: "They'll tell you you're very young, they'll say you're crazy. . . . They'll say why don't you listen a little, OK, and then you'll know what to do; they'll tell you to get organized first, to think before you act; they'll call you an extremist, a reformist, a bureaucrat, a traitor . . . they'll say you have to read more, they'll say there's no better book than experience . . . they'll tell you to wait until you've had a few kids . . . they'll say Rome wasn't built in a day" and on and on. In between these two excerpts, Ariel Dorfman creates, much like Dos Passos in *U.S.A.,* a personal novellike re-creation of what it was like to live through Allende's last days of glory in Chile. In between we are also given variations on several themes by Dorfman—his revolutionary politics, his views on literature, especially the novel, his philosophy of life, in short, his exploration "of the role of the artist as creator, chronicler, Cassandra and Pygmalion to his continent and people." In the author's "Preface to the English Translation," Dorfman tells us that *Hard Rain* "was written during the last months of 1972, in the middle of one of this century's most fascinating, and tragic, social experiments: the revolution known as the Chilean peaceful road to socialism." *Newsweek* recognizes Dorfman as "one of the six greatest living Latin American novelists," and it is difficult, after reading this first novel, to disagree with them. *Hard Rain* puts Dorfman in the vanguard of contemporary Spanish literature. [Jack Byrne]

*

Jeffrey DeShell. *In Heaven Everything Is Fine.* Fiction Collective Two, 1991. 108 pp. $18.95; paper: $8.95.

If we thought we knew what fiction is, what "art" is, then Jeffrey DeShell, in this "fiction," means to tell us that we've been living a lie—maybe even a false fiction. In his first novel—may I call it a novel?—fiction is poetry, is song, is language where referentiality has been hung out to dry and words are unleashed upon a page that hardly ends. If Barthes ever said that there are texts where works should be, that language is a field of play that travels and unravels from one light year to another—that all we have, ultimately, is textuality itself—then DeShell fleshes out this suggestion. More to the point, having stripped word-meaning that we acknowledge the way we acknowledge punctuation in a text, DeShell is a Derridean bandit, running away with words and going underground to play. We knew that Derridean *écriture* had hit academe where it lives most; now we know it has come to rest in imaginative fiction.

   In Heaven Everything Is Fine introduces us to DeShell's pop mind. It's rock and roll made tragic and cunning, smart and lyrical. There is a protagonist here who suffers an affront to his psychic apparatus. Sweet Jane is his lover but she, along with the other characters who inhabit this text, is constructed only to be deconstructed by the very words that tell the story. Undercutting this love story is its nemesis, art: "ART is: 1) Guerilla warfare; 2) Really good *safe* sex; 3) A rectal thermometer; 4) Ice cream; 5) Genocide; 6) Pornographic books; 7) Setting fire to Burger King; 8) Stealing used clothes; 9) Attempting suicide (and failing); 10) My performance, July 17, La Gallerie Vaché, 1220 21st St. ART is not: 1) Painting of any kind; 2) Posters or prints of any kind; 3) Sculptures of any kind; 4) Writings of any kind except pornography; 5) Architecture of any kind; 6) Food of any kind; 7) Collage of any kind; 8) Film of any kind including video; 9) Anything of any kind; 10) My performance, July 17, La Gallerie Vaché, 1220 21st St."

   This novel is anti-art; it is fun, funny, furious in its energy. DeShell has a linguistic backstroke that makes us howl and wonder where the text went. In the midst of such wondering sits a story that unravels in logic and revs up the excitement of watching words play with themselves to the "beat" of a provocative note. This is aesthetics gone wild and free. [Marilyn Moss]

*

Kathryn Thompson. *Close Your Eyes and Think of Dublin: Portrait of a Girl.*
Fiction Collective Two, 1991. 197 pp. $18.95; paper: $8.95.

Both jarring and intriguing, Kathryn Thompson's first novel (and Fiction
Collective Two's second entry in its women's fiction series, On the Edge)
rethinks what language and the oppressive culture which tries to control it can
and should do. The outcome is an electric just-this-side-of-plotless cacaphony
that's not for the narratologically fainthearted.

Step far enough back from the canvas and a coming-of-gender story arranges
itself through a conglomeration of pla(y)giaristic pyrotechnics and phantas-
magoric monologues. Burroughs's language slam dances with Plath's,
Dostoyevski's with Stein's, the Brontës' with T.S. Eliot's ("I am Pavlov's dog,"
the narrator exclaims. "I am classically conditioned."), but the dead father who
dominates this intertextual nightclub is James Joyce, particularly the Joyce of
Ulysses, more particularly of Oxen of the Sun, Circe, and Penelope, the Joyce
obsessed with music and school, sex and church, birth and death, ultraformalist
experimentation and political commitment. Only here Joyce is a woman
imprisoned in and trying to break free of, not Ireland's parochialism, but a
stultifying "noun-verb-predicate world, the male world."

At the center of this world stands a feminine subjectivity—"protagonist" is
too strong a word. A subverted Molly Bloom, a perverted Stephen Dedalus, she
is in equal parts confused, confusing, masochistic, headstrong, and iconoclastic.
She rants through a pluriverse (often tentatively located in Maine) inhabited by
a bully of a violin teacher, a Humbert Humbert of a lover, a misogynistic
brother and father, a dying mother and dead grandfather. Slowly this feminine
subjectivity gains an education, discovering among the others her own angry
pure female voice that relentlessly uses tradition in order to abuse it, termiting
its way through the foundations of rigid literary and social authority.

Proving the Fiction Collective in its latest incarnation is still crazy after all
these seventeen years, *Close Your Eyes and Think of Dublin* is sometimes
bangingly overstated, sometimes darkly funny, sometimes ear-gratingly shrill,
and always amazing. [Lance Olsen]

*

Denis Belloc. *Neons.* Trans. William Rodarmor. Godine, 1991. 103 pp.
$18.95.

In *Neons,* Denis Belloc paints an unforgettable picture of the Parisian homosexual underworld of the 1960s. Denis, the narrator, recalls the events which
led to his initiation into the world of male prostitution: as a young boy, he
watches his drunk father die in a sideshow boxing match, and he is subsequently

neglected by his mother and beaten by his stepfather. He first engages in prostitution in public restrooms on his way home from school and is apprehended by the police when he is only twelve. By the time he is twenty, he has spent time in prison for stealing a car, has had a series of lovers, works as a hustler, and suffers from syphilis.

Denis notices the neon lights when he spends his first night on the streets, and they come to symbolize the seamy nightlife of Paris. When they light up, the sleazy areas of Clichy and Pigalle come alive, and bizarre characters such as Rumble-Seat, Lunch-bucket, and Iron Maiden take to the streets. Like the harsh neon lights, Belloc's blunt, minimalist style reflects the brutal reality of this world. Although Denis recounts his experiences in a seemingly detached manner, he is unable to hide his intense emotional pain, the self-hatred of a man who describes himself as "just a piece of trash." He turns to hustling to fill the "absence" created by the death of his father, but instead his squalid life increases his self-loathing. Only at the end of the novel does he suggest some hope of escape from his despair when he takes up painting and begins to give artistic expression to his experiences.

At once a coming-of-age novel and a portrait of the artist as a young man, *Neons* makes a powerful social statement. Although some of the episodes contain explicit descriptions of sexual encounters, the stark narrative focuses on the narrator's family life and his emotional state rather than on his sexual exploits. Belloc does not tell a pleasant tale, but it is one which needs to be told, and his disturbing story cannot fail to move the reader. [Susan Ireland]

*

Emmanuel Bove. *Quicksand.* Trans. Dominic Di Bernardi. Marlboro Press, 1991. 187 pp. $18.95.

How is it that a writer praised by Samuel Beckett—"Emmanuel Bove: more than anyone else he has an instinct for the essential detail"—admired by Colette—she used her influence to get his first novel published—Rilke, Gide and John Ashberry, can have been forgotten about so quickly? I looked for his name but could not find it in a number of French literary history books including Henri Peyre's wide-ranging *The Contemporary French Novel* and Sidney Brown's *Dictionary of French Literature.* Dozens of less important writers were cited in these books while Bove (1898-1945) went unmentioned. It's especially strange because Bove wrote a number of novels and was relatively popular in the twenties and thirties.

A blurb on *Quicksand's* jacket pointing out that Bove anticipated the fiction of Camus and Sartre and "introduced the Kafkaesque into French letters" is pretty accurate. It's doubtful that Kafka influenced Bove but they both write about the "little man" who's lost in the crowd. A difference is that Kafka wrote metaphorically while Bove dealt with specific individuals. He claimed to have originated the novel of "impoverished solitude."

Quicksand's protagonist is journalist Joseph Bridet, who wants to escape from France in 1940 to join General de Gaulle's force in England. He unsuccessfully attempts to leave from Vichy and Paris. His anti-German sentiments are too well known; he's kept under surveillance, arrested, then shot as a hostage.

Bove's tense, terse prose, skillfully translated by Di Bernardi, is that of a consummate artist. He does, as Beckett observed, have an instinct for the essential detail. He describes people and their actions economically and even understatedly but makes his characters live. You are swept into Bridet's world, you feel his nervousness, identify with his second guessing of his actions, and are swept into his thoughts as his enemies manipulate him, lie to him and his wife. Beyond his descriptive skill, Bove was interested in moral questions which he frequently raised. He doesn't offer pat answers, however, giving readers plenty of room to draw their own conclusions.

In another novel, *My Friends,* Bove shows that he can write with warmth and humor. Much more of his work should be translated and made available. [Harvey Pekar]

*

Elías Miguel Muñoz. *The Greatest Performance.* Arte Publico Press, 1991. 151 pp. Paper: $8.50.

The title of this novel by Elías Miguel Muñoz asserts a dual message. The greatest performance is at first to live every day while playing a role, but finally means having the courage to be oneself.

Rosa (Rosita) and Mario (Marito) are childhood friends in Cuba who are reunited later in the United States, both émigrés struggling to hold on to their Latino identities in a country often hostile to that. As young adults they are also learning the meaning of their sexual selves (lesbian and gay respectively). They are thus doubly foreigners. In alternating chapters, Rosa and Mario tell of their journey from childhood in a language of poignant revelation. Muñoz is a poet, and his descriptions of places, situations, and states of mind achieve emotional depths that give the reader the same feelings of loneliness that his two characters experience against a barren landscape of modern society. Rosa becomes a teacher, and has an American lover named Joan who speaks Spanish, but otherwise holds only Anglo notions of the culture she imagines she knows. Joan makes television commercials aimed at tapping the buying power of Latin consumers, something Rosa finds superficial. When Rosa listens to the corny pop songs of her youth, Joan suggests Linda Ronstadt as more authentically Spanish. In all of this Rosa must fend off her parents' questions as to why she hasn't married and given them grandchildren. Mario becomes an artist, and overcomes the pain of abuse he suffered as a youth, finding love with a Puerto Rican man during a summer in Harlem. Later, back in California, when he is diagnosed as HIV positive, Rosa offers to care for him. They become the perfectly idealized friends of childhood again, accepting each other without conditions.

The Greatest Performance is absorbing by reason of establishing two true voices which tell of the outsider's struggle to live honestly. [Thomas Filbin]

*

Miguel Torga. *Tales from the Mountains.* Trans. Ivana Carlson. Q.E.D. Press, 1991. 151 pp. Paper: $12.99.

Thomas Hardy has his Sussex, William Faulkner his Yaknapatawpha. In *Tales from the Mountain,* Miguel Torga has his Trás-os-Montes. An economically depressed region in northern Portugal—where the rich are out of place—Trás-os-Montes contains a pastoral setting, a grandiose landscape where shepherds, peasants, and unwed mothers are the heroes, the symbols of struggle and endurance always performed to the rhythm of Mother Earth's heartbeat. From what looks like the cradle of mankind, some perverse Garden of Eden— paradise lost and hell half-defeated—where life is rough but ripe, dreams spring and legends are born.

If the short narratives of *Tales from the Mountain* were as tame and as bucolic as they seem, their second and third editions wouldn't have been smuggled out of Portugal (after having been banned in 1941 by dictator Salazar) to be published in Brazil (in 1955 and 1962), and clandestinely brought back to the edge of the Iberian peninsula, where a Portuguese under-ground intelligentsia read the book. Indeed, Torga embraces the rural masses and their communal living and poverty and grace and occasional cruelty. Not exactly a right-wing point of view here. "To be a writer in Portugal is like being buried alive and scratching the lid of one's own coffin." Torga's words could emanate from his characters.

"The Leper," a symbol of societal corruption; "Alma Grande," ironically named, as the character bearing the name is the killer of struggle—this ancestor of hope; "Fronteira," where survival and smuggling are synonyms; "Christmas," where a beggar dines in company of the Madonna and Child icon, transcends himself to become Joseph for a night, and marries representation to reality; "The Lord," where religion is made flesh through the birth of a child performed by a priest; "Mariana," the proud Mother Earth figure who carries in her belly life planted by different men who erase each other for being inconsequent to her, while her children multiply and bear meaning, forming with their mother a perennial and growing procession—which is an ode to nature and a repudiation of conventions; "Sesame," a tale of a young shepherd searching for the Ali Baba cavern and finding it in the gift of life; and more coffin scratchers' stories, more metaphors for the writer's struggle.

If one wonders why Miguel Torga is the winner of major European literary awards, a Nobel Prize nominee, and "presently the greatest name in Portuguese literature," as Miguel Garcia-Posada calls him, one need only to plunge into *Tales from the Mountain* and discover masterful strokes that remind one of paintings by Millet. [Marie-José Fortis]

Kathrin Perutz. *Writing for Love and Money.* Univ. of Arkansas Press, 1991. 119 pp. Paper: $9.95.

This hilarious, wicked roman à clef inspires the reader to ask such questions as: who *is* Harry/V, the hermaphrodite playwright? and who *is* the homely Richard Gernreich (aka The Frog), the money-hungry book packager and creator of Jacqueline Knightsbridge, best-selling, pseudonymous author of *Vines,* the potboiler saga of the rise of sexy, powerful *Fleur,* queen of the vineyards?

Kate, the charming narrator of this novel/exposé, is Harry/V's best friend, as well as the ghostwriter of *Vines.* Kate, whose very literary first novel (meaning great reviews, few sales) was published back when she was a nubile twenty-one-year-old, has entered a depressed, hard-drinking, unhappily married middle age. Receiving nothing but rejections and kill fees, she's lost both her confidence and her muse, so that when The Frog approaches her to ghostwrite *Vines*— enticing her with dreams of huge money—Kate is more than ready.

Perutz captures so believably the life of a serious writer, especially the rejections, paranoia, and lack of money, that when the literary Kate—*a very, very good writer*—does achieve blockbuster success for *Vines*—*a very, very bad book*—the reader understands *very, very well* that old cliché about "laughing through one's tears." [Janice Eidus]

*

David Shields. *A Handbook for Drowning.* Knopf, 1992. 178 pp. $19.00.

In his third book of fiction and first finely crafted collection of twenty-four short stories, David Shields weaves a crazy quilt of psychologically haunting tales that explore drowning as a metaphor for obsession. Lots of people go under here, figuratively and literally, from the man who while scratching his girl-friend's back imagines penetrating right down to her vertebrae, to the university student who's unable to stop reading *Prometheus Bound* in preparation for a quiz.

Most of these are quiet, domestic, sadly funny pieces set fifteen or twenty years ago in suburban rooms, urban dorms, and sunny beaches in California and Rhode Island. Some, like "Father's Day," a tender account of a father and son attending a Mariners game, and "The Sixties," a whimsical rethinking of Leonard Michaels's "In the Fifties," are almost essayistic. At the center of each stands Walter Jaffe, a geekish young man who carries a bright, innocent belligerence within him, the kind of guy who rummages through his lover's stuff while she sleeps, reads her journal behind her back, and forces her to dance against her will in a sleazy bar.

Throughout, Shields uses up some paint left on his palette from the creation of his excellent first two novels, *Heroes* (1984) and *Dead Languages* (1989). Many ideas and even scenes from those return: a mother dying of cancer, a weak father's sins visited upon a son, failed lovers struggling for power, perils of college life in Providence, Proustian memory's importance, the persistence of basketball as an image of blocked transcendence, political and personal idealists trying to swim in an ocean that is anything but ideal.

While clearly obsessed with these signature situations, Shields seems at least as interested—probably more so—in generating surprising, precise, exquisite sentences, beautifully evident in the Barthelmesque "Gun in the Grass at Your Feet," the emotionally rich "Imaginary Dead Baby Seagull," and thematic pastiches like "Lies" and "War Wounds." In fact, Shields's final obsession is not with death and dying at all, but with a Nabokovian love of language, though perhaps in the end for him these ultimately come down to two sides of the same coin. [Lance Olsen]

*

Nicole Brossard. *Mauve Desert.* Trans. Susanne de Lotbiniére-Harwood. Coach House Press, 1991. 202 pp. Paper: $14.95.

The epigraph to this wonderfully constructed novel is by Calvino: "Reading is going toward something that is about to be, and no one yet knows what it will be." The epigraph suggests that reading is an "adventure"—an approach to some final meaning. But it also implies that this adventure is somehow dangerous—there may not, after all, be a complete disclosure, an ultimate truth. The epigraph hints at uncertainty, misdirection, indirection.

When we first read the novel we don't know how to summarize and interpret it. The novel consists of at least three parts—Melanie travels across the desert to escape her mother and the ordinary life in the motel in which they live. There is a sudden change. We are given part of another novel in which another heroine, Maude Laures, also seeks adventure and knowledge. Maude is a reader of Melanie's life story. In effect, the two women merge, so that we are not completely sure who is *author* and *character.* Does Melanie create Maude or vice versa? And, to complicate matters, we are given an apparent *translation* by Maude of Melanie's journey.

The three sections are, at first, discrete and separate, but then they seem to merge into the very novel we are reading. We note the paradoxes and we recognize that Brossard consciously twists us; she destabilizes our perceptions so that we wonder about the very nature of perception. What is the relationship of words to life? What exactly is the nature of creation? Do we create the novel as we read it? Perhaps the oddest pages of the novel are those which contain shadowy pictures of objects—pictures which are almost out of focus. We are not sure of their relationship to the text. We assume that they also suggest that any representation of matter is uncertain. And then we remember this remarkable passage about "suspected presence": "It can for a second be mistaken for image or mirage, an illusion as can occur when from moment to moment altostratus formations alter the depth of field and the color all around."

Mauve Desert is an interpretation of misinterpretation, a text of countertexts, a brilliant presence of absence. It is suspect, subversive, otherworldly. [Irving Malin]

Yury Tynyanov. *Lieutenant Kijé / Young Vitushishnikov.* Trans. Mirra Ginsburg. Eridanos, 1990. 137 pp. $18.95.

Tynyanov was one of the most versatile artist/intellectuals to emerge in the early Bolshevik years. Noted as a brilliant historian and critic, he also wrote some excellent historical novels and novellas set in the eighteenth and nineteenth centuries. Many historical novels are schlock works written by authors with very trite literary styles. This doesn't always have to be the case, however, as the two satirical novellas in this volume illustrate.

Lieutenant Kijé (1927) deals with two military officers. One doesn't exist; he is created by a clerical error. The other, Lieutenant Sinukhayev, is alive but has wrongly been declared deceased, "of fever." The Russian military creates a whole history, complete with promotions, for the imaginary officer, while the real one is ignored as if he really were dead, and in the end he starts believing it himself. *Young Vitushishnikov* (1933) occurs during the reign of Czar Nicholas I and presents him and his officers as a bunch of vain, corrupt incompetents.

In these almost absurdist novellas Tynyanov was thought to be subtly attacking not only officials of czarist Russia but contemporary Bolshevik leaders as well. Certainly his caricatures seem to have much in common with the officials and bureaucracies of many nations throughout history.

Anticipated by Gogol, Tynyanov also seems to have been influenced by modernists like Andrei Bely. In *Young Vitushishnikov* he does some stream-of-consciousness writing and fragments the text into a number of chapters, some less than a half page in length. He jumps rapidly from character to character, from location to location.

Aside from this book, virtually nothing by Tynyanov has been translated into English. Hopefully it will create more interest in the work of this witty, humane, and original artist, and we will have translations of his highly praised full-length novels in the next few years. [Harvey Pekar]

*

Martin Grzimek. *Shadowlife.* Trans. Breon Mitchell. New Directions, 1991. 224 pp. $22.95; paper: $11.95.

The cover of this fascinating and deceptive novel is appropriate. It is a reproduction of the famous *The Nostalgia of the Infinite* (de Chirico). The printing depicts two shadows (who throw shadows); they stand between two structures. One structure is a building of some sort with few windows; the other structure is half hidden. The entire painting is divided into an interplay of figure and ground—an infinite, undeterminate "series."

The novel itself resembles the painting. We have a letter written by a narrator to his Felicitas (his "beloved"), whom he has not seen in many years. It is filled with uncertainties, evasions, "shadows" of one kind or another. The narrator, who works as a recorder of "lives" for the Central Institute for Biographics, tells Felicitas that he believes his constructions, records, structures are mere mysteries—and tedious ones at that! At one point he exclaims: "Let's face it, Felicitas, what did we know about reality? We grew up in perfect family homes, had pre-programmed careers, uncomplicated lives, and enough money to live on. What more could we want?" His compositions represent his longing for something "special." But these very compositions never fulfill his longings.

And he writes the letter to Felicitas at this time because he wants to reverse his life, to transform it once more. Thus we have several strange images of transformation. He describes pictures on one shoe: "The light-colored leather is covered with small rectangles, little boxes in which a story in pictures has been *inscribed* with colored pens. The story *begins* on the toe of the shoe with the largest picture and ends on the tongue, *hidden* beneath the *overlapping* shoe-strings." One cartoon shows: "The child turns into a butterfly which flutters away; the young girl *turns* into a flower" (my italics).

Felicitas's reply is quite surprising. Although I don't want to reveal its contents, it subverts the narrator's text; it suggests that his *inscription hides* his real feelings, his obsessive memories of their past affair. Thus we have *text* and *counter*-text shadow construction. Which one is true? The novel, therefore, suggests that we can never get to the "final solution," the perfect structure.

It does more: it suggests powerfully and subtly that reading and writing—and rereading and rewriting!—are always open. Criticism is, after all, a "shadow" of the original text. (Or is it the other way?) But we should not rest with these almost-comfortable hesitations and questions. We don't ever know origins and ends, the entire picture. We are indeed back to de Chirico. We long, however, for the finite. [Irving Malin]

*

Antonio Skármeta. *Watch Where the Wolf Is Going: Stories.* Readers International, 1991. 188 pp. Paper: $10.95.

In *Watch Where the Wolf Is Going,* Antonio Skármeta summons a wide geography within which to situate his impassioned mind. Fragmenting himself into disparate personalities, he is a textual traveler who infiltrates Santiago, Chile, no less than New York and California—the days of the conquistadors no less than the cold cityscapes of the modern world. In these real fictive places he disrobes his huge imagination until the intimacies of its disillusionment are displayed. In this collection of stories, most of which were written before 1970, there is the nuance of a traveler who has witnessed atrocities yet whose soul remains alive and tuned to his next adventure.

Skármeta's voices are many. In "The Cigarette" he is a young man in Chile who may or may not have killed a communist rebel during a street battle. Taken away from the brawl by an older woman who means to seduce him, this young man is haunted by his unfortunate deed yet lets sexual seduction wipe out the painful climate of his battered soul. In "Cinderella in San Francisco" Skármeta's protagonist is now the veteran of too many Chilean battles. He's holed up in a deserted building with a young American girl, and this time he is the sexual seducer. Yet seduction in this story amounts to that which takes place in his own psyche. He is haunted by memories of his homeland and the great losses both he and it have suffered. It may be too late to seduce a young woman who knows nothing of his pain, of his embittered mind.

On many of the pages in *Watch Where the Wolf Is Going,* Skármeta links sexual politics to politics of the streets in Chile. Both are dangerous; neither brings clarity nor safety. It is as if Skármeta, in these wonderfully detailed and consistently fresh prose pieces, knows all along that to be the veteran of an apocalyptic modern world is also to be the traveler in a fictive world of the printed page. There is little difference between the two. After all, souls are disparate and geographical places become one and the same textual place. [Marilyn Moss]

*

Julian Green. *Adrienne Mesurat.* Trans. Henry Longan Stuart; revised by Marilyn Gaddis Rose. Holmes & Meier, 1991. 256 pp. $25.95.

Julian Green was born in France in 1900 to American parents, and has lived there most of his life. In 1971 he was the first foreigner elected to the French Academy. The most amazing aspect of reading *Adrienne Mesurat* is reconciling the subtlety of observation embedded in the narrative with the fact that it was written in Green's twenties (when it won the Femina Prize in France and became a Book-of-the-Month Club selection in the United States). His concentrated, mystical, detailed prose has been compared to both Proust and Poe.

Adrienne Mesurat is a young woman cloistered in a French country villa by her suspicious, malicious father, a retired handwriting teacher with an income. Her only companion (whom she detests) is her chronically ill sister Germaine. The stultifying boredom of their lives is well told. Germaine finally runs away to a sanatorium, and her father reacts by threatening to virtually imprison Adrienne in the house. He strikes her several times, and bounds to the unlit staircase. She dashes after him, propelled "as though hurled by some irresistible force into the darkness." She collides with him and he loses his balance, falling forward to his death. It is not premeditated, but not accidental either. The rest of the book tracks her dark descent from an already melancholic state to catatonia, and finally an amnesiac loss of sane connection to the world.

Green writes from invention and inner need, and so the world he gives us, be it as large as all of human consciousness, or as small as a sitting room with every object described, has the stamp of originality. In an author's preface written in 1973 and included in this new edition, he says he felt indifference or even hostility to the theories of psychoanalysis when he wrote the book, but critics praised its insight into the pathology of personality. Green admits psychoanalysis is full of answers, but the purpose of fiction for him is to address all the eternal "whys" that are behind those explanations. [Thomas Filbin]

Frederick Busch. *Closing Arguments.* Ticknor & Fields, 1991. 288 pp. $19.95.

Although many readers of this terrifying, violent novel will view it as a narrative of sexual obsession, of "innocence" and "guilt" (or the ambiguity of each term), they will not notice that Busch is a philosophical writer who is aware of linguistic uncertainty, epistemological difficulty. The novel, we can say, moves on two levels. The narrator, a Vietnam survivor, is a lawyer asked to defend Estella, a "forceful" woman accused of murdering her lover in bed. The violence of the war is subtly married to the violence of sexuality. And we are never allowed to forget the violence. The narration is jagged, broken, dislocated; the sections of the novel are abruptly short. There is a sense of mutilation as the sections—and the language of each section—start and end suddenly. Busch understands that no story—in court or out of court—can have closure, finality, absolute truth. Busch believes that our identities are unsure, mixed, fragile. We refuse, for the most part, to accept our notions of "self," of continuous existence. For such reasons the trial is a fiction that remains incomplete—despite summations and closing arguments, justice loses. The truth is never revealed completely.

Once we accept Busch's premises, we see that he distrusts language; he recognizes that it is a violent instrument. Consider, for example, this passage: "The father's word: 'bonding.' Like ducks with ducks and dogs with dogs and children with parents: bond. They didn't like their progress as a family. They thought they'd try divorcing their child." The narrator calls into question the silliness of the word *bonding;* he recognizes that such words are useless. What exactly is *bonding?* Isn't it merely an example of pop psychology? And, to continue, isn't any word open to creative ambiguity?

The narrator constantly makes lists. They suggest that there is sequence, order, direction. But his lists are crazy: "Responsibility. Defense of freedom. To achieve independence for South Vietnam. To do only what is necessary. To increase response to increased attack. To therefore make attacks by air." The repetitions create a sense of certainty, but they also remain odd. What is "necessary"? What is "attack"? What is "increase"? The more we explore his lists, the less we understand their rationale.

One final irony: Busch puts the novel on trial. Can it be true to life? Isn't it true in a *deceptive* manner? Isn't it an open, not a shut case? [Irving Malin]

*

M. Mark, ed. *Disorderly Conduct: The "VLS" Reader.* Serpent's Tail, 1991. 272 pp. Paper: $12.95.

Along with erratic, eclectic, but always entertaining coverage of new books, the *Voice Literary Supplement* regularly publishes pieces of fiction, twenty-five of which have been gathered into this eclectic and entertaining anthology. The clear stand-outs are the trans-historical ventriloquism of Kathy Acker's "First

Season in Hell: Medea," Angela Carter's meta-fairy tale "Ashputtle," the curt lyricism of Michelle Cliff's "Election Day 1984," Susan Daitch's erudite, Robbe-Grillean "The Restorer," Janice Eidus's doo-wop fairy tale "Vito Loves Geraldine," the child's world of Suzanne Gardiner's " △," Karen Karbo's broken-English tragicomedy "The Palace of Marriage," and Harry Mathews's outlandish "Country Cooking from Central France." The rest are slightly unconventional stories told in fairly conventional ways, though with enough twists and tropes to separate this from other anthologies. There is some light reading here (the fiction contributions by gossip columnists Michael Musto and Max Phillips) as well as more homosexual stories than in your average anthology, making *Disorderly Conduct,* all in all, one of the liveliest collections to appear in some time and deserving of a wide readership. [Steven Moore]

*

John O'Brien. *Leaving Las Vegas.* Watermark Press, 1990. 189 pp. $19.50.

Sera is a hooker with a heart of gold (some of which she is happy to risk at the blackjack table) working for a pimp from Oman who ingratiatingly calls himself Al. Ben is an alcoholic who sees his impending death by drowning (in booze, that is) as a creative act of self-expression. Eventually, the two meet when Ben rents Sera for some drunken sex. They find in each other the glimmerings of mutual affection and understanding, and we wonder if Sera will be able (or care to try) to save Ben from himself. And whether Ben will free Sera from Al and a life she perhaps only thinks is satisfactory.

I won't spoil the novel by revealing how things turn out, but I will say that John O'Brien (who, should you care to know, is not the John O'Brien of this journal) is not intent on delivering in his first novel the stuff of clichéd romance, however much my barebones plot summary might suggest otherwise. What he offers, rather, is a clear-eyed look at the lives of two people who followed the sound of a different drummer—a far different drummer than Thoreau ever imagined—and marched straight into purgatory anyway. My sheltered life has not prepared me to assess the accuracy of O'Brien's portraits of either the prostitute Sera or the gonzo alcoholic Ben, but both portraits have the ring of truth, as does O'Brien's evocation of Las Vegas. Never preachy, O'Brien is strongest when evoking Ben's addled logic and rationalizations: "He knows that he won't fuck up by driving sloppily and getting busted; he'll just fail to react quickly to a situation one day and either kill himself or someone else. He finds the latter possibility, murder, intolerable, so he tries not to think about it." But Sera, too, is presented with a calm horror that has nothing in it of the prurient or the sensational; thus, after having been beaten, sodomized, and urinated upon by three frightened college boys, Sera, finally regaining consciousness, simply "wipes the blood and makeup from her swollen face, realizing that she won't be able to work for at least a week," and "hopes that she can do well at the [blackjack] tables today, for a change."

O'Brien's is, in short, a serious novel however filled it may be with stock characters and devices. Its prose is clean and hard (although occasionally given to rhetorical portentousness, usually when Al is on stage) and conjures two characters not soon to be forgotten. If I've any complaint, it is that Al, who vies with Sera and Ben for an equal role in this novel, fails to become quite real, his story eventually set aside as though his creator had, along with everyone else in the novel, lost interest in him. [Brooke Horvath]

*

Henry Miller. *Crazy Cock.* Foreword by Erica Jong. Introduction by Mary V. Dearborn. Grove Weidenfeld, 1991. 202 pp. $18.95.

Henry Miller, in his masterful autobiographical novels, thought of *Tropic of Cancer* as Cancer the Crab, the North, Paris as Gomorrah; *Tropic of Capricorn* as Capricorn the Goat, the South, New York as Sodom; *Black Spring* came somewhere in between. Now we learn that before *Cancer* there was *Crazy Cock,* begun by Miller in 1927 and finished just before he left for Paris in 1930. Published for the first time, it is an important addition to his work. The original title was to have been *Lovely Lesbians,* because at the heart of this third attempt at a publishable novel was his torment over his second wife's affair with Jean Kronski, an affair that ended when June and Jean ran way to Europe. The title might better have been *Scenes from a Crazy Ménage à Trois,* because there is little that is lovely in this "world swirling with violence, sex, and passion, the three [struggling] with their desires, inching ever nearer to insanity, each unable to break away from this dangerous and consuming love triangle." The world described is, of course, the "sordid world of Greenwich Village in the 1920s." According to Erica Jong, "He had been struggling for years to find his voice as a writer, and *Crazy Cock* is interesting principally for the way it recounts that struggle. Put beside *Tropic of Cancer* it is almost a textbook study of a writer looking for a voice." True, but put beside *Cancer,* it is also a brave attempt to create a persona strong enough in character to develop into the "Henry" of Miller's masterpieces. Unfortunately, Tony Bring is quite unlike the Henry of *Capricorn* who, at fifteen, seduces his piano teacher and takes it from there. Tony is not yet the Miller who, according to Jong, "invented first person, present tense exuberance for the twentieth century." He reminds one more of the members of the *Saturday Night Live* skit where men of the "P-Whipped" Self-Help Group discuss their relationships with their women, always checking with them by phone for verification of their opinions. But the final chapter does presage the Henry who will write in *Capricorn:* "My people were entirely Nordic, which is to say *idiots.* Every wrong idea which has ever been expounded was theirs. Among them was the doctrine of cleanliness, to say nothing of righteousness. They were painfully clean. But inwardly they stank." This is the voice Miller was searching for in *Crazy Cock,* the pure voice of Miller's rebellious Henry. In the final chapter, Tony Bring rants and raves against a world he never made, "not doubting God but denying Him, flaying

Him, spitting on Him," drops out of the "P-Whipped" club and rises from his bed of pain (hemorrhoids) to write as never before, after which he leaves for Paris where he will become the Henry of *Tropic of Cancer.* [Jack Byrne]

*

Paul Bowles. *Days: Tangier Journal, 1987-1989.* Ecco, 1991. 128 pp. $15.95.

It is interesting to read this journal. We assume that it will be a complete record of the days in the life of Bowles. But we are immediately alerted in the forward that he is *suspicious:* he doubts the veracity of the *form,* the relation of life and "art." He tells us: "I suppose the point of publishing such a document is to demonstrate the way in which the hours of a day can as satisfactorily be filled with trivia as with important events." This remark is especially suggestive. Although Bowles distinguishes between the "trivial" and "important" event, he never really defines the difference. It seems that he wants his reader to question the value of days—of life itself. And this is itself filled with "absence"—we are not given *all* of the days, not *all* of any recorded day. Thus we have a strangely ordered, incomplete text. And to complicate matters, Bowles uses such words as *suppose* and *doubtless* to reinforce the intentional ambiguity of *Days.* The journal becomes an odd anti-journal; it resembles that odd anti-autobiography, *Without Stopping.*

   Almost every entry is elusive. We are never sure that the entry is complete and real. I take it that this is Bowles's intention. He mixes comic and terrifying meanings to reinforce his epistemological certainties or uncertainties. I plan to duplicate Bowles's apparent procedure. I will look at a few days and comment on them. But I'm not sure why I choose these passages—or why *they choose me.* In an entry for one day, Bowles writes: "The most ridiculous gadget of the year in the show window of an Indian shop on the Boulevard Pasteur: a deodorant stick with a built-in compass." Surely other events occurred on this day. Why is Bowles drawn to this "ridiculous" object? Is it the *juxtaposition* of two objects which should not be together? Is it the compass (possibly a reminder of his obsessions with space, direction, precision)? In another entry Bowles writes: "I shan't go. I'm too old to put up with being stared at." Doesn't he realize that we are staring at his days? Does he prefer to be stared at as a written character? Is writing more "private" than public? And this question leads to a more fascinating one. Is "Paul Bowles" a written character, created *role?* The text, then, is ultimately a philosophical one. It compels us to question what we mean by "days," "words," "person(a)." And in a perverse way, it asks us to interpret mysteries—mysteries which, I assume, can never be solved. But do these mysteries *exist?* [Irving Malin]

*

Richard Wright. *Early Works; Later Works.* Library of America, 1991. 936, 887 pp. $35.00 each.

The magisterial Library of America includes only two post-World War II writers: Flannery O'Connor and now Richard Wright. There are probably several reasons why there aren't more—unavailability of rights, certainly, but perhaps a reluctance to identify which contemporary writers are likely to prove of historical importance—but one looks forward to the day when today's best writers are treated as handsomely as Wright is here. With the exception of *Uncle Tom's Cabin* in the *Early Works* volume, the texts are new: *Lawd Today!* and *The Outsider* from Wright's typescripts, *Native Son* from bound page proofs, and *Black Boy* and *American Hunger* together (and unexpurgated) as Wright intended. Typos have been corrected, censored passages restored, fulsome annotations (by Arnold Rampersad) appended—almost everything one could desire.

Except the format: the two volumes run only 936 and 887 pages respectively, but are priced at $35.00 each, making them shorter and yet more expensive than most of the other volumes in the series. The contents of these two should have been combined into one volume at that price (there are a few other Library of America volumes nearly as long), or the two volumes expanded to include Wright's other works (especially the novel *The Long Dream* and the stories of *Eight Men*) to form a two-volume complete Wright. As it is, these splendid volumes won't find the large readership they deserve. [Steven Moore]

*

Arthur M. Saltzman. *Designs of Darkness in Contemporary American Fiction.* Univ. of Pennsylvania, 1990. 168 pp. $21.95.

Arthur M. Saltzman's *Designs of Darkness* boasts a solid base of scholarship, incisive analysis of a host of novels, and a generally engaging narrative style. After a short introduction, the next two chapters contrast ideologies. There Saltzman explores postmodern fiction's rejection of either an irreducible, single truth that flames out dazzling and irrefutable or a truthful, coherent narrative that provides both a complete and consistent explanation of events. To the former, "anti-epiphanic" fiction allows ambiguities to "blossom everywhere"; to the latter, it is honest only in the paradoxical Heraclitean way: unlike history, it admits to being an elegant lie. The next two chapters reiterate the structural subversions of such fiction: its insistent debunking of conventional theme (particularly the quest), plot, character, and language. In the final chapter, an epilogue, Saltzman merely states that these novels "exhibit a drive for renewal."

Designs abounds in rich, lively discussion of specific works by numerous writers: both the more established, such as Sorrentino, Abish, Barthelme, Doctorow, and the lesser knowns, such as Kenneth Gangemi (and here Saltzman's analysis is enticing enough to encourage reading Gangemi). Yet the time has passed for explaining postmodernism or recounting the ways writers are indeed postmodern; the time has come for close scrutiny of the ways their unique responses not only set them apart from each other but illuminate their means of coping with so much hollowness, so much loss. While *Designs* does mention coping and even renewal, it generally serves up a standard postmodern stew of disruption, despair, and kitsch. More fruitful would be the articulation of fine distinctions within postmodern fiction that illuminate if and how these writers fashion renewal, forge a nonprescriptive, pluralistic ethics, or fund a postmodern hope—or reject it. Some contemporary American postmodern writers do invoke value, not a transcendental truth but a value nonetheless: action in the world. "Meganovelists" Pynchon and Gaddis, for instance, do abhor "revelation," but their novels do not become "one more 'motionless object' for us to pass through or move around." Rather these writers are more reminiscent of Walter Benjamin's "destructive character" who exposes loss for the purposes of "leading a way through it."

For all that, Saltzman's study is among the better analyses of the treacherous and conspiratorial ways that American contemporary fiction employs ambiguity, opacity, and indecipherability to subvert the assumed irrefragable absolutes of order, stability, and coherence. [Judith Chambers]

*

Joseph Dewey. *In a Dark Time: The Apocalyptic Temper in the American Novel of the Nuclear Age.* Purdue Univ. Press, 1990. 255 pp. $27.50.

For me the highlight of Joseph Dewey's excellent study of contemporary American apocalyptic fiction is his brilliant chapter on William Gaddis's *Carpenter's Gothic,* which has received minimal critical attention since its publication in 1985. Dewey displays a fine grasp of the novel's mazy complications and cleverly teases out the many metaphoric implications of Gaddis's structure, allusions, and details. This chapter alone makes *In a Dark Time* invaluable, but the reader is also treated to an informative overview of American literature's long apocalyptic tradition and to extended readings of several contemporary novels that have grappled with the ways the potential of nuclear war has threatened to literalize the religious metaphor of apocalypse. These include Vonnegut's two best novels (*Cat's Cradle* and *Slaughterhouse-Five*), Coover's *Origin of the Brunists* (another underappreciated novel), two by Percy (*Love in the Ruins* and *The Thanatos Syndrome*), Pynchon's *Gravity's Rainbow,* and DeLillo's *White Noise.* Dewey's prose is colorful and refreshingly free of critical jargon; his research is thorough but unobtrusive. In a dark time when many younger critics are producing unreadable books overburdened by critical theory, Dewey has written an accessible, illuminating book that should prove of permanent value. [Steven Moore]

*

Lawrence S. Friedman. *Understanding Cynthia Ozick.* Univ. of South Carolina Press, 1991. 192 pp. $24.95.

That there will be thick scholarly-critical books devoted to Cynthia Ozick's fiction and essays is a certainty, but until they appear Friedman's book can be counted among the stronger efforts at introduction. Ozick, of course, presents special difficulties to anybody trying to make her work available to a wider audience: she not only draws from a variety of Jewish sources likely to be unfamiliar to most readers, but she also spends considerable effort—in her essays—explaining why she writes fiction as she does. Not surprisingly, the result is the sinking feeling, among her critics, that they have already been scooped.

Friedman handles both of these problems admirably. His introductory chapter lays out the preoccupations, themes, and techniques that characterize her vision generally; and he follows this with chapters that take up Ozick's work from *Trust* (1966) to *The Messiah of Stockholm* (1987). The result is a study that "instructs," one that balances Friedman's clear prose and patient explications with representative samples taken from Ozick's fiction and her essays. In an age when most academic critics write with their feet, Friedman is a refreshing exception. His book makes good on the promises of the University of South Carolina's "Understanding" series—namely, to address the special demands of much contemporary literature in ways that will be simultaneously helpful and accessible. [Sanford Pinsker]

*

Books Received

Akins, Ellen. *World Like a Knife.* Johns Hopkins Univ. Press, 1991. $30.00; paper: $11.95. (F)

Andrews, Raymond. *Jessie and Jesus and Cousin Claire.* Peachtree Publishers, 1991. $16.95. (F)

Assouline, Pierre. *An Artful Life: A Biography of D. H. Kahnweiler.* Trans. Charles Ruas. Fromm International, 1991. Paper: $14.95. (NF)

Bacho, Peter. *Cebu.* Univ. of Washington Press, 1991. $25.00; paper: $12.95. (F)

Bellow, Saul. *Something to Remember Me By.* Viking/Signet, 1991. $21.95; paper: $5.99. (F)

Boyd, Brendan. *Blue Ruin: A Novel of the 1919 World Series.* Norton, 1991. $19.95. (F)

Brown, Wesley, and Amy Ling, eds. *Imagining America: Stories from the Promised Land.* Persea Books, 1992. $24.95; paper: $11.95. (F)

Burgin, Richard. *Private Fame.* Univ. of Illinois Press, 1991. $16.95. (F)

Busch, Frederick. *Absent Friends.* New Directions, 1991. Paper: $11.95. (F)

Byatt, A. S. *Possession.* Vintage International, 1991. Paper: $12.00. (F)

———. *Still Life.* Collier Books, 1991. Paper: $8.95. (F)

Callahan, Bob, ed. *The New Comics Anthology.* Collier/Macmillan, 1991. Paper: $19.95. (F)

Cela, Camilo José. *San Camilo, 1936.* Trans. John H. R. Polt. Duke Univ. Press, 1991. $45.95; paper: $14.95. (F)

Chernoff, Maxine. *Plain Grief.* Summit, 1991. $19.00. (F)

Colchie, Thomas, ed. *A Hammock Beneath the Mangoes: Stories from Latin America.* Dutton, 1991. $22.95. (F)

Corngold, Stanley, and Irene Giersing. *Borrowed Lives.* State Univ. of New York, 1991. $44.50; paper: $14.95. (F)

Costello, Bonnie. *Elizabeth Bishop: Questions of Mastery.* Harvard Univ. Press, 1991. $29.95. (NF)

Daneshvar, Simin. *A Persian Requiem.* Trans. Roxane Zand. Braziller, 1992. $22.50; paper: $12.50. (F)

Davis, Thulani. *1959.* Grove Weidenfeld, 1992. $18.95. (F)

Davison, Peter. *Half Remembered.* Story Line Press, 1991. Paper: $16.95. (NF)

Delbanco, Nicholas, and Laurence Goldstein, eds. *Writers and Their Craft.* Wayne State Univ. Press, 1991. $24.95. (F/NF)

Desani, G. V. *"Hali" and Collected Stories.* McPherson, 1991. $20.00. (F)

Dworkin, Andrea. *Mercy.* Four Walls Eight Windows, 1991. $22.00. (F)

Epstein, Joseph. *The Goldin Boys.* Norton, 1991. $19.95. (F)

Fichte, Hubert. *The Orphanage.* Trans. Martin Chalmers. Serpent's Tail, 1990. Paper: $10.95. (F)

Fitzgerald, Penelope. *The Gate of Angels.* Doubleday, 1992. $19.00. (F)

Fletcher, Angus. *Colors of the Mind: Conjectures on Thinking in Literature.* Harvard Univ. Press, 1991. $37.50. (NF)

Foster, Edward Halsey. *William Saroyan: A Study of the Short Fiction.* Twayne, 1991. $21.95. (NF)

Freeman, Judith. *Set for Life.* Norton, 1991. $19.95. (F)

Fuks, Ladislav. *Mr. Theodore Mundstock.* Four Walls Eight Windows, 1991. Paper: $10.95. (F)

Garrett, George. *Death of the Fox.* Harvest/HBJ, 1991. Paper: $14.95. (F)

———. *Entered from the Sun.* Harvest/HBJ, 1991. Paper: $10.95. (F)

———. *The Succession.* Harvest/HBJ, 1991. Paper: $12.95. (F)

Gerhardie, William. *Futility.* Intro. Edith Wharton. New Directions, 1991. Paper: $10.95. (F)

Ghose, Zulfikar. *The Art of Creating Fiction.* Macmillan, 1991. No price given. (NF)

Glantz, Margo. *The Family Tree.* Trans. Susan Bassnett. Serpent's Tail, 1991. Paper: $14.95. (F)

González, Genaro. *Only Sons.* Arte Publico, 1991. Paper: $8.50. (F)

Gordon, Giles, and David Hughes, eds. *Best English Short Stories.* Norton, 1991. $21.95. (F)

Hall, James B. *Bereavements.* Story Line Press, 1991. $19.95; paper: $14.95. (Poetry)

Herrin, Lamar. *The Lies Boys Tell.* Norton, 1991. $19.95. (F)

Iossel, Mikhail. *Every Hunter Wants to Know.* Norton, 1991. $21.95. (F)

Jelinek, Elfriede. *The Piano Teacher.* Trans. Joachim Neugroschel. Serpent's Tail, 1989. Paper: £7.95. (F)

Jönsson, Reidar. *My Father, His Son.* Trans. Marianne Ruuth. Arcade, 1991. $19.95. (F)

Judson, Jerome. *Nude: A Novel.* Applezaba, 1991. $24.95; paper: $12.95. (F)

Jungk, Peter Stephan. *Franz Werfel: A Life in Prague, Vienna, and Hollywood.* Trans. Anselm Hollo. Fromm International, 1991. Paper: $12.95. (NF)

Kendrick, Walter. *The Thrill of Fear: 250 Years of Scary Entertainment.* Grove Weidenfeld, 1991. $21.95. (NF)

Kolm, Ron. *Rank Cologne.* P.O.N. Press, 1991. Paper: $3.00. (Poetry)

Kristof, Agota. *The Proof.* Trans. David Watson. Grove Weidenfeld, 1991. $17.95. (F)

Lang, Berel. *Writing and the Moral Self.* Routledge, 1991. $42.50; paper: $13.95. (NF)

Levine, Suzanne Jill. *The Subversive Scribe: Translating Latin American Fiction.* Graywolf, 1991. Paper: $12.00. (NF)

Malone, Michael. *Foolscap.* Little, Brown, 1991. $19.95. (F)

Mangala, Christine. *The Firewalkers.* Aquila Books (Australia), 1991. $27.95; paper: $9.95 (Australian). (F)

Marshall, Paule. *Daughters.* Atheneum, 1991. $19.95. (F)

Masters, Olga. *The Rose Fancier.* Norton, 1991. $18.95. (F)

McLaurin, Tim. *Keeper of the Moon: A Southern Boyhood.* Norton, 1991. $19.95. (NF)

Metcalf, Paul, ed. *Enter Isabel: The Herman Melville Correspondence of Clare Spark and Paul Metcalf.* Univ. of New Mexico Press, 1991. $17.95. (NF)

———. *Genoa.* Univ. of New Mexico Press, 1991. Paper: $14.95. (F)

Miller, Jane. *Seductions: Studies in Reading and Culture.* Harvard Univ. Press, 1991. $22.95. (NF)

Miller, Henry. *Aller Retour New York.* New Directions, 1991. $15.95. (NF)

Mitgutsch, Anna. *Jakob.* Trans. Deborah Schneider. Harcourt Brace Jovanovich, 1991. $22.95. (F)

Miyoshi, Masao. *Off Center: Power and Culture Relations between Japan and The U.S.* Harvard Univ. Press, 1991. $27.95. (NF)

Montero, Rosa. *Absent Love.* Trans. Cristina de la Torre and Diana Glad. Univ. of Nebraska Press, 1991. $25.00; paper: $9.95. (F)

Moore, Richard. *The Investigator.* Story Line Press, 1991. $18.95. (F)

Morales, Alejandro. *The Rag Doll Plagues.* Arte Publico, 1992. $17.95. (F)

Neihardt, John G. *Life's Lure.* Univ. of Nebraska Press, 1991. $45.00. (F)

———. *Man-Song.* Univ. of Nebraska Press, 1991. $35.00. (F)

Ordóñez, Elizabeth J. *Voices of Their Own: Contemporary Spanish Narrative by Women.* Bucknell Univ. Press, 1991. No price given. (NF)

Packer, George. *The Half Man.* Random House, 1991. $20.00. (F)

Parks, Tim. *Goodness.* Grove Weidenfeld, 1991. $18.95. (F)

Pavić, Milorad. *Landscape Painted with Tea.* Trans. Christina Pribićević-Zorić. Vintage, 1991. Paper: $12.00. (F)

Pekar, Harvey. *The New American Splendor Anthology.* Four Walls Eight Windows, 1991. $18.95. (Graphic fiction)

Pinsker, Sanford. *Bearing the Bad News: Contemporary American Literature and Culture.* Univ. of Iowa Press, 1990. $22.95. (NF)

Pitt-Kethley, Fiona. *The Misfortunes of Nigel.* Dufour/Peter Owen, 1992. $29.00. (F)

Purdy, James. *63: Dream Palace: Selected Stories 1956-1987.* Black Sparrow, 1991. $25.00; paper: $15.00. (F)

Ramos. *Blue Burns the Night, True Is the Light.* Xanthyros, 1991. Paper: $17.95. (F)

Reilly, Edward C. *Understanding John Irving.* Univ. of South Carolina Press, 1991. $24.95. (NF)

Robinson, Lou. *Napoleon's Mare.* Fiction Collective Two, 1991. $18.95; paper: $8.95. (F)

Rollyson, Carl. *The Lives of Norman Mailer: A Biography.* Paragon, 1991. $26.95. (NF)

Rowe, Marsha, ed. *So Very English.* Serpent's Tail, 1991. Paper: $14.95. (F)

Saer, Juan José. *The Witness.* Trans. Margaret Jull Costa. Serpent's Tail, 1990. Paper: $13.95. (F)

Sapia, Yvonne Veronica. *Valentino's Hair.* Fiction Collective Two, 1991. $18.95; paper: $8.95. (F)

Shaham, Nathan. *The Rosendorf Quartet.* Trans. Dalya Bilu. Grove Weidenfeld, 1991. $19.95. (F)

Slavitt, David R. *Short Stories Are Not Real Life.* Louisiana State Univ. Press, 1991. $18.95. (F)

Smyth, Edmund, ed. *Postmodernism and Contemporary Fiction.* B. T. Batsford, 1991. £9.95. (NF)

Taylor, Erika. *The Sun Maiden.* Atheneum, 1991. $19.95. (F)

Thomas, Audrey. *The Wild Blue Yonder.* Viking, 1990. $19.95. (F)

Torres, Omar. *Fallen Angels Sing.* Arte Publico, 1991. Paper: $8.50. (F)

Tremblay, Michel. *The Fat Woman Next Door Is Pregnant.* Trans. Sheila Fischman. Serpent's Tail, 1991. Paper: $14.95. (F)

Walsh, John Evangelist. *This Brief Tragedy: Unraveling the Todd-Dickinson Affair.* Grove Weidenfeld, 1991. $19.95. (NF)

Walter, Otto F. *Time of the Pheasant.* Trans. Leila Vennewitz. Fromm International, 1991. $21.95. (F)

Weiss, Jason. *Writing at Risk: Interviews in Paris with Uncommon Writers.* Univ. of Iowa Press, 1991. $35.00; paper: $12.95. (NF)

Willson, Harry. *A World for the Meek: A Fantasy Novel.* Amador, 1991. Paper: $9.00. (F)

Wilson, Edmund. *Axel's Castle: A Study of Imaginative Literature of 1870-1930.* Collier, 1991. Paper: $12.95. (NF)

Young-Bruehl, Elisabeth. *Creative Characters.* Routledge, 1991. $25.00. (NF)

Contributors

SUSAN BERNOFSKY is the translator of *Masquerade and Other Stories* by Robert Walser. She currently is teaching at the University of Stuttgart and recently was awarded an NEA grant to translate more of Walser's work.

PETER BICHSEL lives in Solothurn, Switzerland, and is the author of numerous short prose collections, including two translated into English, *Stories for Children* and *And Really Frau Blum Would Very Much Like to Meet the Milkman.*

JOHN BIGUENET is a professor of English at Loyola University (New Orleans) and the editor of *Foreign Fictions* and co-editor of *The Craft of Translation.*

BERNHARD ECHTE is the co-transcriber of Robert Walser's microscripts, and has edited work by Friedrich Glauser and Ferdinand Hardekopf. He is the co-editor of *Karl und Robert Walser: Maler und Dichter.*

TAMARA S. EVANS is a professor of German at Queens College and the author of *Robert Walsers Moderne.*

MARK HARMAN edited *Robert Walser Rediscovered* and is the translator of a volume of Hermann Hesse's letters.

HERMANN HESSE (1877-1962) wrote four essays on Walser in addition to his many well-known novels.

PHILLIP LOPATE is the author of numerous books including *Against Joie de Vivre* and *The Rug Merchant.*

CHRISTOPHER MIDDLETON's most recent book is *Selected Writings: A Reader.* He is a professor of German at the University of Texas, Austin, and the translator of *Jakob von Gunten* and *Selected Stories* by Robert Walser.

WERNER MORLANG, the director of the Robert Walser Archives in Zurich, is co-transcriber and co-editor (with Bernhard Echte) of Walser's microscripts in the four volumes of microscript texts, *Aus dem Bleistiftgebiet.*

ADOLF MUSCHG is a professor at the Eidgenössische Technische Universität in Zurich, as well as a critic, novelist, and short-story writer. His works in English include *The Blue Man and Other Stories.*

THE BROTHERS QUAY have made such films as *The Street of Crocodiles,* based on the work of Bruno Schulz, *Rehearsals for Extinct Anatomies,* and *The Cabinet of Jan Svankmajer.*

LYNNE SHARON SCHWARTZ is the author of *The Melting Pot, Rough Strife, Disturbances in the Field, Leaving Brooklyn,* and other works of fiction.

MARTIN WALSER is a German novelist and critic whose numerous novels translated into English include *Letter to Lord Liszt, The Swan Villa,* and *No Man's Land.*

TOM WHALEN teaches creative writing at Loyola University and the New Orleans Center for Creative Arts. His stories and essays have appeared in numerous journals, and his collaborative translations of stories by Walser are in *Selected Stories* and *Masquerade.*

From the Winner of the 1989 Nobel Prize for Literature

San Camilo, 1936

Camilo José Cela

Translated by John H. R. Polt

"A 20-year-old, skein-like novel by the 1989 Nobel winner—a tour-de-force that proceeds in chapter-length sentences, on-rushing with asides and tiny glimpses into the life of a neighborhood and its people during the first few weeks of the Spanish Civil War. . . . This may be Cela's bitterly flowing masterpiece."—*Kirkus*

327 pages, paper $14.95, library cloth edition $45.95

Storming the Reality Studio: A Casebook of Cyberpunk and Postmodern Science Fiction

Larry McCaffery, editor

"The intent is to explore the phenomenon of cyberpunk sf,

its relationship to postmodern fiction, and its influence on the literary mainstream. . . . Splendid, stirring stuff."—*Kirkus*

344 pages, 8 illustrations, paper $17.95, library cloth edition $49.95

Donald Barthelme: An Exhibition

Jerome Klinkowitz

"[This] is a compelling piece of work, written by a critic who admires and understands Donald Barthelme's work. A genuine pleasure to read." —Melvin J. Friedman, University of Wisconsin, Milwaukee

158 pages, cloth $29.95

Narratology Revisited

Special issues of *Poetics Today*

Brian McHale and Ruth Ronen, guest editors

In "Narratology Revisited," parts I, II, and III, narratologists and other scholars of narrative and fiction reflect on the progress (or lack of progress) in narrative theory over the past decade and on the current state of the art.

Single issues, $11.00

Special offer: *Poetics Today*, volumes 11 & 12, 8 issues including "Narratology Revisited," $24.00.

Duke University Press

6697 College Station Durham, NC 27708

THE LATEST FROM

Nicholas Mosley. *Hopeful Monsters.* Cloth, $21.95. "The most ambitious English novel written in the past 50 years. . . . *Hopeful Monsters* is an amazing achievement—and a hopeful one." —*Washington Post Book World.* "Nicholas Mosley's *Hopeful Monsters* is a . . . heroic masterpiece." —Sven Birkerts. "Quite simply, the best English novel to have been written since the Second World War." —A. N. Wilson. "A vast novel of ideas that's brainy but not pretentious, grand but not grandiose. . . . The short, urgent sentences, rapid-fire dialogue, and frequent location changes (West Africa, Berlin, Paris, Seville), all set off by Eleanor and Max's remembrances of each other, make this one of the grandest epistolary novels of ideas of our time." —*Voice Literary Supplement.* "*Hopeful Monsters* is an extraordinary novel." —*Boston Globe*

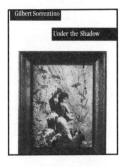

Gilbert Sorrentino. *Under the Shadow.* Cloth, $19.95. Sorrentino's newest novel takes the form of fifty-nine brief sketches with simple nouns as titles. These exquisite vignettes take place on a plane at once surreal, abstract, and ominous, describing a set of people and incidents derived largely from fragments of conversation and gossip gathered here and there. They remind us of Raymond Roussel's characters amid his inimitable ersatz pastorals, with tableaux both innocent and grotesque.

Gilbert Sorrentino. *Imaginative Qualities of Actual Things.* Paper, $9.95. This by-now legendary novel, first published by Pantheon in 1971 and never before available in paperback, is about the New York artistic and literary world of the 1950s and '60s. Told in the weary voice of a cynical and sardonic narrator, the novel is crammed with fantastic characters, incidents, and episodes, and moves from wit and satire, through elegiac brooding, to bitter invective. It is a superb re-creation of a real time and place.

Esther Tusquets. *Stranded.* Trans. with an afterword by Susan E. Clark. Cloth, $19.95. A novel about love and betrayal among friends and lovers in post-Franco Spain. Using a stream-of-consciousness technique reminiscent of Dorothy Richardson and Virginia Woolf, Tusquets explores the idea "that the loss of love is always hard bitter sad that its end is always painful for everyone and surely much more so for women." Novelist Carmen Martin Gaite calls *Stranded* Tusquets's "best work."

Available from Dalkey Archive Press, 236 S. Washington, Naperville,

DALKEY ARCHIVE

Thomas McGonigle. *Going to Patchogue.* Cloth, $19.95. "[A] novel of memory with a narrator contemplating suicide. Tracing a journey to Patchogue from "the City," a stay there and a return, the narrator (whose name is Tom McGonigle) tells an episodic and disjointed tale in earthy and demented prose, echoing that of Céline. . . . While many may find this literate and haunting novel difficult, others will treasure it as an exploration of those recesses of the mind where we can be most honestly ourselves. For McGonigle that territory is called Patchogue." —*Publishers Weekly*

Djuna Barnes. *Ladies Almanack.* Paper, $9.95. This affectionate lampoon of the expatriate lesbian community in Paris was privately printed in 1928 and hard to come by ever since. Arranged by month, it records the life and loves of Dame Evangeline Musset (modeled after salon hostess Natalie Barney) in a robust style taken from Shakespeare and Burton's *Anatomy,* and is illustrated throughout with Barnes's own drawings. This new edition also carries an afterword providing details on the book's original publication and a key to its real-life models.

June Akers Seese. *Is This What Other Women Feel Too?* Cloth, $19.95. Seese's second novel (following *What Waiting Really Means*) is about books and the people who read them: it's about a rare-book dealer and his mistress, set in that era when words like *mistress* were still used, and recalling the years when Lenny Bruce and Freud might occupy the same paragraph in an after-hours night spot. Seese writes movingly, tightly, without recourse to adjectives, from the gut and to the gut.

Claude Simon. *The Invitation.* Trans. Jim Cross with an afterword by Lois Oppenheim. This 1987 novel by the Nobel Prize-winner is a sardonic look at glasnost Russia, where recent reforms and improvements carry all the conviction of rouge on a corpse. In long, convoluted sentences that have become Simon's trademark style, a traveler records his impressions of a society whose recent renovations ill disguise a bloody and repressive past. *The Invitation* is a compact masterpiece of political satire in which Simon "shows himself to be France's greatest living author" (*Le Matin*).

IL 60540. One book, 10% off; two or more, 20% off; add $3 postage.

STUDIES IN 20th CENTURY LITERATURE

A JOURNAL DEVOTED TO LITERARY THEORY AND
PRACTICAL CRITICISM OF LITERATURE OF THE
TWENTIETH CENTURY

A Special Issue on
CONTEMPORARY SPANISH POETRY: 1939-1990
Guest Editor: Andrew Debicki
University of Kansas

Andrew Debicki: Critical Perspectives
José Olivio Jiménez: Spanish Poetry, 1939-1989
Judith Nantell: Epistemology and the Generation of 1956
John Wilcox: Angela Figuera and Francisca Aguirre
Guillermo Carnero: Culturalism and the "New" Poetry
Margaret Persin: Pere Gimferrer's "Los espejos"
Ignacio Javier López: The Poetry of the "Novísmos"
Biruté Ciplijauskaité: Recent Poetry and the Essential Word
Sharon Keefe Ugalde: Spanish Women's Poetry of the 1980s

Also from STCL: Contemporary Latin American fin de Siècle
    Guest Editor: Jean Franco

Special Issue Africa: Literature & Politics
    Guest Editor: Claire L. Dehon

Essays in European Literature
    Vol. 1, STCL Monographs (Order Separately)

Subscriptions: Institutions--$20 for one year ($35 for two years); Individuals--$15 for one year ($28 for two years). Add $5 for air mail.

Michael Ossar, Editor
Eisenhower 104
Kansas State University
Manhattan, KS 66506-1003
Submissions in:
  German and Russian

Marshall Olds, Editor
1111 Oldfather Hall
University of Nebraska
Lincoln, NE 68588-0318
Submissions in:
  French and Spanish

The master of the hit-and-run aesthetic

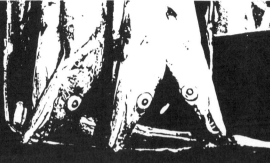

Peter Wortsman

A Modern Way to Die

SMALL STORIES AND MICROTALES

From the title story, a surreal parable on death as a spectator sport, to *The House of Phantasy,* a voyeuristic glimpse at the psycho-sexual underpinnings of the Third Reich, Peter Wortsman's first collection of short fiction incorporates outrageous reportage and strict imagination, extreme realism and wild fantasy, nightmare parable and black humor—while challenging our preconception of the genre.

"It is about time that others discover that very special Wortsman phenomenon: those 'insolite' stories where humor and humanity are edged with a surrealist and hallucinatory chaos that one is bound to recognize; it finally pays us all a visit at one time or another in our lives."—James Gill, publisher, *2Plus2: A Collection of International Writing*

AT ALL BOOKSTORES

 FROMM INTERNATIONAL PUBLISHING CORPORATION
Distributed by National Book Network, Lanham, Maryland

boundary 2

an international journal of literature and culture

Paul A. Bové, editor

Future special issues include

Japan in the World
edited by Masao Miyoshi and H.D. Harootunian
Postmodern Feminisms
edited by Margaret Ferguson and Jennifer Wicke
Postmodern America and the New Americanists
edited by Donald E. Pease

Recent and forthcoming essays

Correcting Kant: Bakhtin and Intercultural Interactions / *Wlad Godzich*

"Through All Things Modern": Second Thoughts on Testimonio / *John Beverley*

"The Most Suffering Class": Gender, Class, and Consciousness in Pre-Marxist France / *Margaret Cohen*

Eurocentric Reflections: On the Modernism of Soseki / *Fredric Jameson*

Subscription prices for 1991: $36 institutions, $20 individuals. Add $6 for postage outside the U.S.

Duke University Press Journals Division
6697 College Station, Durham NC 27708

THE NEW
GOTHIC

EDITED BY
BRADFORD MORROW AND PATRICK McGRATH

**A dazzling collection of
contemporary Gothic fiction by the
premier writers of our time**

Anne Rice, Robert Coover,
Jamaica Kincaid, Joyce Carol Oates,
Ruth Rendell, Martin Amis, Peter Straub,
John Edgar Wideman, Scott Bradfield,
John Hawkes, Jeanette Winterson,
Angela Carter, Paul West,
William T. Vollmann, Emma Tennant,
Janice Galloway, Lynne Tillman,
Kathy Acker, Yannick Murphy,
Bradford Morrow, and Patrick McGrath

**21 works of
present-day
evil, madness,
and perversion—
most never
before published**

At bookstores now

RANDOM 🏠 HOUSE

CRITICAL STUDIES
A Journal of Critical Theory, Literature & Culture
Editor Myriam Díaz-Diocaretz

Critical Studies will present innovative articles dealing with literature among discourses, literary criticism as institution, discourse theories, and areas of scholarship which seek to effect change and which challenge received ideas throughout the range of cross-disciplinary inquiry.

"This is an impressive scholarly publication ...recommended"

Library Journal

Recent and Forthcoming Issues:

Volume 1, **The Bakhtin Circle Today**
Nr. 2: Edited by Myriam Díaz-Diocaretz Hfl. 75,—/US-$ 37.50

Volume 2, **M. Bakhtin and the Epistomology** Paper Hfl. 30,—/US-$ 15.—
Nrs. 1-2: **of Discourse** Bound Hfl. 90,—/US-$ 45.—
  Guest Editor Clive Thomson

Volume 3, **Cultural Studies:**
  Crossing Boundaries Paper ca. Hfl. 30,—/US-$ 15.—
Nr. 1: Guest Editor Roberta Salper Bound ca. Hfl. 90,—/US-$ 45.—

USA/Canada: Editions Rodopi, 233 Peachtree Street, N.E., Suite 404, Atlanta, Ga. 30303-1504, Telephone (404) 523-1964, only USA 1-800-225-3998, Fax (404) —522-7116
And Others: Editions Rodopi B.V., Keizersgracht 302-304, 1016 EX Amsterdam, Telephone (020) —622.75.07, Fax (020) — 638.09.48

Innovative
writings and translations
from around the world

William S.
Burroughs

Michael
Palmer

Lydia
Davis

Leslie
Scalapino

Contemporary French Writing
The Russian Avant Garde

Single Issue $7.50
Subscriptions: 2 Issues $12.00

avec P.O. Box 1059 • Penngrove • CA • 94951

EPOCH

SINCE 1947   FICTION, POETRY, ESSAYS

Published
three times
per year.

Sample
copy
$4.00

One year
subscription
$11.00

Painting (detail) by Richard Estell. Courtesy of Ruth Siegel Gallery, New York

Available from 251 Goldwin Smith Hall, Cornell University, Ithaca, NY 14853

"... One legal journal that should be in every humanities collection. Highly recommended."

Library Journal

Cardozo Studies in Law and Literature

a publication of
Benjamin N. Cardozo School of Law/Yeshiva University
General Editor, Richard H. Weisberg

VOL. III, #1 (Spring-Summer, 1991): A diverse group of essays that will take our readers from 10th century Iceland to a 20th century Algerian courtroom. C.R.B. Dunlop offers a comprehensive survey and analysis of Law and Literature theory and pedagogy. Henry Ordower and Jeffrey L. Slusher discuss one of the earliest and greatest of Law and Literature stories, *Njal's Saga.* Ernest Simon insightfully furthers the debate on Camus' *L'Etranger.* John Denvir explores recent theories of "Constitutional Dialogue" by reference, among other texts, to James Joyce's "The Dead." Also included are excerpts from Edward de Grazia's forthcoming book *Girls Lean Back Everywhere: The Law of Obscenity and the Assault on Genius* (Random House: March, 1992).

VOL. III, #2 (Fall, 1991): This issue will focus on "Testimony" in Law and Literature. It will include the first English-language publication of the "Lamentations of the Widows of Civitella" - an Italian town whose men where slaughtered by the Nazis in 1944. Essays by Victoria de Grazia, Shoshana Felman, and Lea Hamaoui will appear, exploring the historical and theoretical possibilities of testimonial narrative. This issue will also feature testimony from the recent lawsuit by E.L. Doctorow, William Styron, and others against the government relating to information control during the Gulf War.

Cardozo Studies in Law and Literature
Benjamin N. Cardozo School of Law/Yeshiva University
Brookdale Center/55 Fifth Ave., Rm 520/NY, NY 10003

Name _____

Title _____

Affiliation _____

Address _____

City _____ State _____ Zip _____

Please enter my subscription, my check is enclosed.
(Foreign funds must be in international money orders.)
One-year (two numbers per year): $50 for institutions, $20 for individuals, $18 for students.

Please make check payable to:
Cardozo Studies in Law & Literature

Subscriptions make great gifts!

Lost Creek Letters

is read for
Best American Short Stories
and nominates poetry,
fiction and essays
for the Pushcart Prize.

Mail orders &
submissions to:

Lost Creek Publications
Pamela Montgomery
RR 2, Box 373A
Rushville, MO   64484

Submissions Guidelines

- Manuscripts typed, double spaced
- No restrictions on subject, style, or genre, but bear in mind our literary audience
- Fiction, Poetry, Essays, Cover Art
- Send SASE with plenty of postage for return or disposable manuscript with reply SASE

Deadlines

Spring	February 1
Summer	May 1
Autumn	August 1
Winter	November 1

We strongly recommend that before you submit your work, you send for a sample copy. Reviewing an issue is the best method of discerning the editor's tastes and your best strategy for getting published. A sample copy is $4.75 postpaid.

Subscription/Order Coupon

Name _____

Address _____

City _____ State _____ Zip _____

Total enclosed: _____
Make checks payable to Lost Creek Publications

☐ One Year, 4 Issues $16
Subscriptions will start with the most current issue unless otherwise specified.

☐ One Issue, $4.75 postpd.
Send me the following issue (circle one or more):

Spring 1990	Summer 1990
Autumn 1990	Winter 1990
Spring 1991	Summer 1991
Autumn 1991	Winter 1991

For writers and readers, a welcome bridge between literary quarterlies and commercial magazines.

 High Plains Literary Review

WHO WRITES FOR *HIGH PLAINS?*

Julia Alvarez — Tony Ardizzone — Richard Currey
John Domini — Rita Dove — Malcolm Glass — Lowell Jaeger
Marilyn Krysl — Nancy Lord — Cris Mazza — Michael Martone
Askold Melnyczuk — Njabulo S. Ndebele — Naomi Shihab Nye
Joyce Carol Oates — William Pitt Root — Darrell Spencer
Pamela Stewart — Floyd C. Stuart — Denise Thomas

"Every issue of the independent
High Plains Literary Review is a
fascinating blend of poetry,
fiction, essays and reviews."
—*Small Press*

"Contributions from all parts of the world
and the result is a general magazine more
along the lines of *Atlantic* and *Harpers'*
than the esoteric literary quarterlies."
—*Bill Katz* — *Library Journal*

"A quality product, attractively
designed, edited and smartly informed."
— *George Myers, Jr., Columbus Dispatch*

"A rich blend of
intelligent voices."
— *Choice*

Subscription Rate: $20.00 for three issues per year (outside U.S.
add $3.00/year) — $7.00 for a single issue.

High Plains Literary Review
180 Adams Street, #250, Denver, Colorado 80206

COLUMBIA
A Magazine of Poetry & Prose

Poetry · Fiction · Essays · Interviews

"Invigorating, informative
and important."
          —George Plimpton

Editors' Awards

Fiction & Poetry

First Prize $350
Second Prize $150

COLUMBIA

13

Manuscripts must be postmarked by April 1 to be considered
for Editors' Awards. The contest fee is $6 (includes the
upcoming issue of COLUMBIA). Please send a SASE for
contest guidelines.

Past Contributors:
Jorge Luis Borges, Harold Brodkey, Italo Calvino, Raymond
Carver, Alfred Corn, Robert Creeley, Amy Gerstler, Allen
Ginsberg, Amy Hempel, Carolyn Kizer, Phillip Lopate,
Thomas Lux, William Matthews, Czeslaw Milosz, Lorrie
Moore, Sharon Olds, Grace Paley, Marge Piercy, Gilbert
Sorrentino, Derek Walcott and others.

- -

COLUMBIA
is published semiannually. Subscription rates are:

☐ $6 one issue.   ☐ $11 two issues.
☐ $15 three issues.

Name _____

Address _____

_____

Make checks payable to: *Columbia: A Magazine of Poetry & Prose* and
send to: 404 Dodge Hall, Columbia University, New York, NY 10027

Review

Mississippi ● A Magazine of New Literature

MR47/48: CYBERPUNK. Guest edited by Larry McCaffery; fiction by William Gibson, Bruce Sterling, John Shirley; interview with William Gibson; symposium; essays by Timothy Leary, George Slusser. 288 pp, $5.50.

MR49/50: PANIC SEX. Guest edited by Ken Watson & Robert Mielke; essays by Marc Shell, Jean-Joseph Goux, Michael Speaks, Arthur Kroker, James Hans. 241 pp, $5.50.

MR51: BLAST/LENIN ISSUE. Fiction by Sara Lewis, David Lipsky, Alice Mattison, Katharine Haake; poems by Marc Doty, Rich Ives, Jean Tardieu, and James Gill. 120 pp, $5.50

MR52: THE REDHEAD. Fiction by Elizabeth Tallent, John Holman, Paul Lisicky, Larry French; poems by Bin Ramke, Roger Weingarten, Christopher Merrill, and Paul Hoover; Cynthia Kadohata on Breece D'J Pancake. 127 pp, $7.50.

MR53/54: BEGINNINGS. One hundred forty seven paragraph-length openings from one hundred forty seven stories by working writers. 154 pp, $8.00

MR55/56: THE WORKSHOP ISSUE. Stories and poems from 80 US writing programs; also, a mini-symposium on teaching creative writing. 358 pp, $12.00

MR57: NEW POETRY. Guest edited by Angela Ball and David Berry; a survey of and symposium on contemporary American poetry. Spring 1991, 175 pp, $8.00.

MR58/59: INTERVIEWS. Interviews with new writers (Ishiguro, Acker, others), and with Larry McCaffery on the art of the interview. Fall 1991, 200 pp, $8.00.

Mississippi Review publishes twice yearly (a single and a double issue). Subscriptions are $15 one year, $28 two years. Write Mississippi Review, Southern Station Box 5144, Hattiesburg, MS 39406-5144.

college
Literature

A triannual journal addressing topics in the college literature classroom from Plato to poststructuralism.

Recent and forthcoming special issues:
The Politics of Teaching Literature (June/October 1990)
Literary Theory in the Classroom (June 1991)
Teaching Minority Literatures (October 1991)
Special section on Cultural Studies (February 1992)
Teaching Commonwealth or Postcolonial Literatures (June 1992)
The Waste Land and Ulysses (October 1992)

Recent contributors include Houston A. Baker, Jr., Patrick Brantlinger, Robert Con Davis, Elizabeth A. Flynn, Barbara Foley, Henry A. Giroux, Adele King, Cary Nelson, Hershel Parker, Michael Payne, Paul Smith, Mas'ud Zavarzadeh and Donald Morton

Subscription prices: Individuals $15/year, $27/2 years
Institutions $18/year, $33/2 years
Outside U.S. and Canada, add $5/year surface or $10/year air mail
Prepaid orders to *College Literature* Fund, 544 Main Hall, West Chester University, West Chester, PA 19383, USA. 215-436-2901. Payment in U.S. funds only.

DENVER
QUARTERLY

●●● Is Pleased To Publish ●●●

PROSE POETRY

A special issue for

SPRING 1991

Featuring new work, translations, and commentaries by

Stephen Berg ● Russell Edson ● Clayton Eshleman
Michael Palmer ● Marjorie Perloff
Susan Stewart ● James Tate
and many others

● ● ● ● ●

Please send me ____ copies of the Prose Poetry issue at
$5 each. Payment enclosed.

Name

Address

City

State   Zip

OR

Please begin my subscription to the Denver Quarterly
($15 per year) with the Prose Poetry issue.

UNIVERSITY of DENVER
University Park, Denver, Colorado 80208
●
DENVER QUARTERLY
Department of English

Prize Winning
Illustrated Texts

Harry Mathews
Immeasurable Distances
The Collected Essays

Collected for the first time. Color hardcover edition,
Japanese endpapers, with a cut-out photo sheet for
creating your own illustrations. 7"x 10", 296 pages.

$35.00
$75.00 *signed limited edition, 100 copies*

Julien Gracq
The Castle of Argol
Translated by Louise Varèse

The ultimate Gothic novel; a literary masterpiece. With a
forest panorama printed in color on the cloth binding, and
numerous interior plates; two elaborate fold-out plates on
translucent papers, and Gothic vignettes throughout. An
extraordinary edition, suffused with the landscape of
Argol. 7"x 10", 175 pages.

$45.00

August Strindberg
A Witch

The first English translation of this novella—
a demonized *Bovary*. Color hardcover, many color plates
and a glassine image. Illustrated with photos of
Strindberg, his daughter Karin, and his rare landscape
paintings-- all embroiled with images of fire. Text
printed on gray paper. A first for any text in this format.
7"x 10", 140 pages.

$45.00

The
Lapis
Press

All prices include sales tax and UPS shipment.

589 No. Venice Blvd., Venice, California 90291